RENEWING
THE
COVENANT

RENEWING THE COVENANT

A Kabbalistic
Guide to Jewish
Spirituality

LEONORA LEET

Inner Traditions
Rochester, Vermont

To my dear daughters
Tamar Brodwin Goodman and
Susannah Rachel Brodwin

Inner Traditions International
One Park Street
Rochester, Vermont 05767
www.InnerTraditions.com

Library of Congress Cataloging-in-Publication Data
Leet, Leonora.
Renewing the covenant : a kabbalistic guide to
Jewish spirituality / Leonora Leet.
p.   cm.
Includes bibliographical references and index.
ISBN 0-89281-713-5 (alk. paper)
1. Spiritual life—Judaism.   2. Cabala.   3. Meditation—Judaism.
4. Prayer—Judaism.   I. Title.
BM723.L39   1999
296.1′6—dc21   98-47553
CIP

Printed and bound in the United States

10 9 8 7 6 5 4 3 2 1

This book was typeset in Goudy

Contents

Preface

The covenant, that instrument of divine grace through which God bound Himself to Abraham in a special relationship of obligation and empowerment, was renewed by God with the two succeeding Patriarchs and with Israel at Sinai and Moab. Each of these specifically Jewish covenants can be associated with a particular spiritual practice: the Patriarchal Covenant with Father Isaac's practice of meditation; the Sinai Covenant, centered in the Ten Commandments, with the Sabbath observance that is its "sign"; and the Moab Covenant, comprising the whole of the Torah, with the form of prayer derived from the declaration of faith, called the "Sh'ma," that appears directly after the Moabite repetition of the Ten Commandments. These covenant-related practices form a ladder of increasing potency, and this work will show how these rungs of the covenant can each become available for personal renewal.

This is the first of a four-book project on the Kabbalah begun in 1978. The second will be published in the spring of 1999 by Inner Traditions and will be entitled *The Secret Doctrine of the Kabbalah: Recovering the Key to Hebraic Sacred Science*. This larger work will develop the new interpretation of the Jewish mystical tradition that is more briefly touched on here, providing the theoretical foundation and larger cosmological context for much of the treatment of the Jewish spiritual practices with which we will be concerned in this book. The present book may be said to complete the more theoretical formulations to follow by developing from authentic sources practices that can fulfill the goal of that conjoined human and cosmic evolution my books will show to have always been projected by this mystical tradition.

The forthcoming book will give full acknowledgment to the many individuals who have helped me in various ways through the years with this ever expanding project. But I would like to give special mention here to St. John's University for the generous support it has given to this project through research leaves, teaching reductions, and in the final preparation of the manuscript, with particular appreciation to former Vice President Paul T. Medici and the Faculty Support Center. Finally, I wish to express my deepest gratitude for the support and various forms of help given to me by five remarkable individuals most knowledgeable about the mystical heart of Judaism: Zalman Schachter-Shalomi, Aryeh Kaplan, Michael Lerner, Gerald Epstein, and especially my dearest friend Esse Chasin.

CHAPTER 1

Covenantal Judaism

Spiritual Practice and the Covenants

A revitalization of Jewish spirituality is what the present moment especially calls for, and this book attempts to contribute to such a revitalization by providing a new approach to Jewish ritual practice appropriate to the new era of the world and of Judaism on whose threshold we now are standing. To that end, the following three chapters are concerned with ascending levels of spiritual practice, each of which can be correlated with one of the three specifically Jewish biblical covenants, those with the Patriarchs and with Israel at Sinai and Moab. The subjects of these chapters will range from the rediscovery of forgotten meditative practices, in the second chapter, to reformulations of the most basic of Jewish practices—Sabbath observance and ritual prayer—in the third and fourth chapters. In each case the Bible will be reexamined to determine the essential nature of those practices that claim to convey sanctification or empowerment. The remainder of this section will be devoted to introducing the later chapters that detail these covenant-related spiritual practices, the next section to exploring the larger historical context for this new approach to the Torah, and the final two sections to offering more radical suggestions for integrating such practices into a new mode of Jewish covenantal commitment that can tap into its original power while renewing its nature.

It may well be asked whether such a new interpretation of Scriptural Law is necessary when a complete and coherent interpretation of the Law—the Oral Torah of the talmudic tradition—is already in place. Indeed, the tradition that derives from the talmudic sages and contains the accumulated strength of millennia of communal devotion has developed its own spiritual power to sanctify its adherents, and there is clearly no reason for anyone who experiences the empowerment transmitted through this tradition to wish, or need, to alter his or her practices. But the spirit conveyed through the rabbinic tradition is not the same as that which can be tapped directly through observance of the Mosaic Torah, and for many the tradition of the rabbis no longer enhances but impedes their spiritual progress toward communion with God. It may be time, therefore, to try once more to provide new paths either to enter or reenter the treasurehouse of Jewish spirituality. These paths to religious experience and power may become a satisfying end in themselves or the beginning of a further journey both back to more traditional modes of observance and forward to endowing such traditions with new Kavanot,[1] new spiritual enhancements. The Mosaic Torah details three levels of specifically Jewish covenant, and this new approach to the ladder of increasingly demanding and potent covenantal practices may aid many to ascend to ever higher levels of mystical Judaism.

The first practice with which we shall be concerned is also one that extends beyond the specific lineage of Abraham, namely directed meditation. Since the only biblical figure to be specifically associated with the practice of meditation is the Patriarch Isaac, it seems appropriate to correlate meditation with the Patriarchal Covenant. We are told that coming "from the way of the well Lahai-roi" (Gen. 24:62),[2] the well mystically revealed to Hagar by an angel, "Isaac went out to meditate [suach] in the field at the eventide" (Gen. 24:63). Aryeh Kaplan has analyzed this and other biblical references to meditation in terms of both classical commentaries and his own philological investigations to show that there was a rich tradition of biblical meditation, one whose later associations are primarily with the prophets and the psalms. He shows that there were two forms of biblical meditation—the floating, tranquil state of suach experienced by Isaac and the more directed form of *hagah*, as in "the meditation of my heart shall be of understanding" (Ps. 49:3).[3]

Chapter 2 concerns kabbalistic meditation. It begins with a brief summary of kabbalistic concepts in the first section and proceeds to an extended study of classic kabbalistic texts on meditative practice in the next section. A later section considers the *Sefer Yetzirah*, the first extant text of the Kabbalah, dated as early as the third century C.E., and shows that this seminal kabbalistic text contains encoded directions for a particular meditative technique. Its method of verbal repetition is the focus of this later section, which contains a full-scale treatment of the process of meditative attunement and techniques to lift one into the meditative state specified by classic Jewish texts. This is followed by a guided Master Meditation, a form of directing the will while in the meditative state to achieve both transformation and knowledge. This form of directed or *hagah* meditation is the standard mode of meditation detailed in the kabbalistic texts on meditation discussed earlier in the second section.

For those whose practice has not yet been extended to include the traditional ritual prayers, there is a section prior to the full instructions for meditation that develops a mode of performing the essential "Sh'ma" of Deuteronomy 6:4–5 as a prelude to a meditation, and that may be regarded as bringing the practice of meditation within the sanctity of Torah. The section on the Sh'ma is further introduced by one that provides evidence from early Jewish sources for such a combination of meditation and prayer. In the form of the Sh'ma developed in this context, as in the following guided meditation, use is made of the biblical word *vehayah*, which the King James Version translates as "and it shall come to pass." Here I suggest that this was actually a biblical power word for directing the manifesting power of God, but comprehensive support for this claim is reserved for the appendix. The central credal affirmation of the Sh'ma, normally translated as "Hear, O Israel, the Lord our God is one Lord," will be further considered in the extended treatment of liturgical prayer in the culminating fourth chapter. Thus, though the Sh'ma is properly the mark of the new covenant enacted at Moab just prior to Israel's entrance into the Promised Land, the subject of chapter 4, it seems worthwhile to introduce a form of its performance into the logically prior practice of kabbalistic meditation both to bring the power of Torah into the meditative act and to ensure this connection to Torah for those who might make the full meditative process presented in chapter 2 their primary form of spiritual practice.

Meditation is the best place to begin the journey to authentic spiritual experience because it is almost guaranteed to produce two results, a verifiable enlargement of consciousness and a sensitizing of the consciousness to still more subtle spiritual energies. The two main forms of Jewish practice that are considered next, Sabbath observance and liturgical prayer, are more profound in their effects than even the kabbalistic meditation that will here be developed, but their power is more subtle and apt to be missed by those whose spiritual sensitivities have not been developed by some form of meditative experience. Though there are certainly many religious Jews whose souls have been uplifted to the highest levels just through scrupulous observance of all the laws of Torah, there are perhaps even more who go through all the motions of Davening (ritual prayer) and Sabbath observance without ever feeling their real power. This is even truer for those who attempt to begin Jewish observance without the prior experience of growing up in an observant community or the spiritual growth that in our day is most often developed through some form of Eastern meditation. For any form of meditation can so enhance the religious sensibilities that one will be better able to experience and respond to the powerful energies conveyed through traditional ritual observances. If this is true of any long continued religious tradition, it is particularly true of Jewish observance, which is part of the oldest continuous religious tradition in the world and so has accumulated the greatest reservoir of "spiritual voltage." The practice most closely associated with the Jews as a people, defining them as "a kingdom of priests, and an holy nation" (Ex. 19:6), is observance of the Sabbath. And experiencing its enormous power to sanctify is something quite different from the experience of meditation; it is a religious experience. It may be characterized that way because it provides what seems to be clear evidence of a spiritual dimension beyond one's conjuring. However powerful the effects of meditation, there is always the sense that they are self-induced, a product of the skillful manipulation of brain chemistry. But for anyone who has experienced the power of the Sabbath, the sensation is quite different, the sense that one is being filled with a power from beyond the self, that one has become a vessel for the divine influx or Shefa.

Unlike the somewhat artificial correlation of meditative practice with the Patriarchal Covenant, there is no doubt that Sabbath observance is the "sign" (Ex. 31:13) of the Sinai Covenant. The essential covenant of God with Israel is the one written on the tablets: "And he wrote upon the tables the words of the covenant, the ten commandments" (Ex. 34:28). Of these Ten Commandments, the only one that involves ritual is the fourth, which commands Sabbath observance, and of this we are told that "the Lord blessed the sabbath day, and hallowed it" (Ex. 29:11). Thus ritual observance of the Sabbath is the means prescribed to achieve that national holiness promised in the Sinai Covenant. For this reason the whole of this Covenant of Holiness may be regarded as contained solely in the observance of the Sabbath: "Wherefore the children of Israel shall keep the sabbath, to observe the sabbath throughout their generations, for a perpetual covenant" (Ex. 31:16). So also has the rabbinical tradition long held that those who observe the Sabbath have fulfilled the whole Torah. Because of the supreme importance of Sabbath observance in establishing one's covenantal relationship with God, it is necessary to understand those Mosaic laws of the Sabbath that can transform this period of immaterial time into a unique conveyer of the sanctifying divine holiness. The new look at the Sabbath undertaken in chapter 3 begins with a study of the three Mosaic laws whose skillful observance can tap a reservoir of holy power going back at least to the institution of this practice by Moses and beyond this to the very beginning of the world: "For in six days the Lord made heaven and earth . . . and rested the seventh day: wherefore the Lord blessed the sabbath day" (Ex. 20:11). The return to the Sinai Sabbath through observance of its Mosaic laws can reactivate the original channel of its sanctification with undiminished power and begin the distinctively Jewish stage of the covenantal relationship with God.

Study of the Mosaic Sabbath laws is followed by consideration of the four stages of the Sabbath as the divine Presence lifts the soul of the participant up through the main soul levels recognized in the Kabbalah, from his normal Nefesh state through the spiritual Ruach dimension to the Neshamah state that can fully embody the Neshamah Yeterah (additional soul) traditionally understood to enter a person at the beginning of the Sabbath and leave at its close, at that sunset hour whose unique holiness is given special attention. Among the various practices suggested as appropriate to these four stages is the incorporation of the kabbalistic meditation developed in the previous chapter during the Sabbath morning. The chapter closes with a consideration of the remaining Mosaic holidays, distinguishing the Sabbath's intrinsic holiness from their Temple-dependent holiness but showing how they can be meaningfully observed in this post-Temple period.

Just as meditation can render the spirit more receptive to the subtle energy of the Sabbath, so weekly experience of the Sabbath's holiness can expand it still further until it finally becomes capable of the highest of religious practices—the mystical prayer that marks the culminating level of divine covenant. When Moses gathered Israel together in Moab to renew the covenant before entering the Promised Land, his rehearsal of the Law was marked by a most important new addition. Right after the repetition of the Ten Commandments, he added the proclamation of the divine unity, the Sh'ma, followed by the new commandment to love God and to repeat the words of the Sh'ma twice daily. The twice-daily service of the heart in repeating a special verbal formula was associated with the love of God from the very beginning, and it is from this liturgical core that a new channel of love between man and God was opened that has continued to inform the enlarged prayer services built around it. Just as Sabbath observance is the sign of the Covenant of Holiness enacted at Sinai, so may the twice-daily saying of the Sh'ma with its surrounding prayers be considered the sign of the Covenant of Love, the covenant enacted at Moab that marks the highest biblical development of Jewish spirituality.

Once one has experienced the communion of liturgical prayer, the services become an ever ready conduit to the highest and most effortless of religious experience, and its grace becomes the instrument for that final perfection of the soul in which the purpose of creation finds its realization. All prior spiritual practices are but a preparation for this ultimate chariot of mystical experience that has always held the central place in traditional observance, though its mystical core has more often been played down than appreciated. For it was in the prayer services that the mystical core of Judaism, which finally surfaced in the Kabbalah, was transmitted to the populace through the years. This core seems to be ultimately derived from the ancient Hebraic priesthood. From the time of the priest Ezra, and of his followers in the Great Assembly, the prayer services were carefully crafted to enshrine and fulfill the priestly understanding of salvation and to transfer to it the holiness attending the sacrificial services. This transfer enabled ritual Judaism to survive the destruction of the Second Temple and keep its observances undiminished in their power to convey holiness.

Though the prayer services became the heart of exoteric Judaism, their further elaborations seem to have always been the work of those inspired by the esoteric mystical tradition, from the various hymns derived from early Merkabah texts to those rabbis who the Talmud tells us were engaged in mystical studies and practices. Those embued with kabbalistic knowledge were also the ones who tried to explain the mystical content and purpose of the prayer services and to enhance their effectiveness through special Kavanot, through the saying of the prayers with special attention to their mystical meaning. The final chapter on the spiritual practice of liturgical prayer attempts to uncover this mystical heart of the services once more and to explain how performing them can fulfill the purpose of creation as developed in kabbalistic cosmology. For at all times in the history of Jewish mysticism, spiritual practice has been closely linked to cosmology, seen as the way through which the purpose of creation is to be fulfilled. This cosmology has also influenced the form of such practice so that it might become an ever more perfect reflection and facilitator of this purpose.

Chapter 4 begins with an attempt to understand the meaning of the commandment to love God and how it can be related to prayer and the atonement experience. Following this explanation of the power of true prayer to open the heart to the love of God, the central section is concerned with the order of the prayer service, with those portions whose structure encodes the hidden purpose of mystical prayer, and with suggestions as to how they might be performed to increase their spiritual effectiveness. The miracle of the effectiveness of prayer is explored in the third section, which not only completes this study of Jewish spiritual practices but also the new interpretation advanced in my works of the origin and meaning of kabbalistic cosmology. Drawing upon the writings of Franz Rosenzweig, Martin Buber, and Abraham

Isaac Kook, as well as those of the long line of Lurianic and hasidic thinkers, this section establishes the nature of the divine unification accomplished by prayer. The chapter closes with a discussion of the Kingdom of God and how it may be realized on Earth by those souls that have been perfected through the culminating practice of mystical prayer.

The approach to ascending levels of Jewish spiritual practice just summarized may well be given the name of Covenantal Judaism. This approach acknowledges the superior power of sanctification provided by the final and most complete of the biblical covenants, while recognizing that many who are not yet ready and able to release its spiritual power can still begin the covenantal relationship at the lesser degree of spiritual practice correlated with an earlier covenant. Proceeding at their own rate of development through the sequence of the historical covenants, which still retain their power and are available for personal commitment, their progress will be aided at each stage by the covenantal power present in its associated spiritual practice. From meditation, to Sabbath observance, and finally to liturgical prayer, the soul can thus be progressively expanded until it reaches the Neshamah level through the divine unification of prayer in which it shares. Because true prayer is far more fulfilling than meditation, it will normally replace meditation in one's spiritual practice, particularly on the Sabbath. The inclusion of meditation in the discussion of Sabbath observance must be understood, therefore, as a temporary measure before its final replacement by the prayer services. But the following chapters recognize all these Jewish spiritual practices as unique conveyers of spiritual energy and that they are performed not simply because they have been commanded, but also because of their effectiveness in filling the human spirit with the ever greater bliss that can both spur and reward development into higher consciousness.

In addition to defining the concept of covenantal stages, which may be considered a major principle of Covenantal Judaism, the following chapters also demonstrate Covenantal Judaism's other main principle, a new methodology of interpreting the Law. And though the ramifications of these principles may be far-reaching, the analyses of the biblical sources of Jewish spiritual practices and suggestions for their more effective performance are such that they can still be largely incorporated into any of the current modes of Jewish religious understanding and observance. Nonetheless, it seems advisable to spell out these ramifications more fully, not for those committed to one or another mode of observance, but for those who have not yet made a covenantal commitment or who have not been fulfilled by their previous forms of observance. Indeed, my argument is less with the Orthodox, who do have a coherent method of interpreting and observing the whole of the Torah, than with the more popular denominations that show no coherence either of belief or practice. In the final sections, then, the more radical argument for a new mode of Torah observance will be presented for those who may have need of it. This argument is based upon a consideration of the historical context and its still larger cosmic frame.

For we are now at the threshold of a new era and a new millennium. In the precession of the equinoxes this period marks our entry into the new Age of Aquarius, an age that in a later phase may well show characteristics corresponding to the Messianic Age, which traditional chronology places just two hundred and fifty years in the future. To gain a better understanding of the direction the restructuring of Torah should take to make it suitable to express the changed orientation of this new astrological age, the foundation of Judaism should first be considered in this astrological context. This consideration will be aided by the extended discussion of the biblical Shofar, the ram's horn, in the next section, which will support a significant association of biblical Judaism with the astrological Age of Aries, whose symbol is also the ram's horns. It is within this larger framework of astrological-historical time that we may perhaps also recognize the significance both of the intervening epoch and of the trends in recent Jewish cultural history that have forever altered the shape of Judaism and may be preparing it to accept just such a restructuring.

Of course, belief in the actual influence on human cultural history of solar positions through the precession of the equinoxes is not a prerequisite for benefiting from the use of these temporal periods to order the divisions of cultural history. Perhaps their approximately two-thousand-year span is, for whatever reason, a better marker of major historical periods than that of single millennia. But since the possibility of such influence has long been believed, especially by Kabbalists, and since it provides a suggestive perspective from which to view the main cultural forms taken during the successive periods of Jewish history, it might be useful to adopt a principle from Coleridge regarding similar truth-resembling works of the imagination, "that willing suspension of disbelief for the moment, which constitutes poetic faith."[4] We will thus be accepting the notion of astrological ages as though it were true for the simple reason that it provides the best way of relating the newness always felt to accompany the dawning of a new millennium to the two previous ages of Jewish history. It relates most importantly to biblical religion, which we will see arose during the Age of Aries and which is particularly relevant to the restructuring of the concept of covenant that will soon be outlined. It is, then, to the understanding of biblical Judaism conveyed through the unique symbol of its astrological age that we should now turn and not only because it will support the relevance of this temporal context; even more important is the light it can cast on the essence of Judaism that we are now especially called upon both to conserve and transform.

The Shofar and Biblical Judaism

The extensive and coherently symbolic use of the horn in biblical literature and Jewish ritual is a subject that has not previously interested most interpreters of the Judaic tradition,[5] but this section will show the Shofar to be a unique conveyor of what can justly be called the "Arian Revelation," a term relating biblical Judaism to the most celebrated use of the ram's horn in history, as the zodiacal sign for Aries. This connection may not seem so far-fetched once one understands the astrological concept of the precession of the equinoxes. This involves the fact that in its yearly circuit through the band of the zodiac, the sun comes somewhat short of making an exact circle; it loses about one degree in every seventy-two years. Since each sign or its constellation contains thirty degrees, this means that the sun regresses through an entire sign in approximately 2,160 years. More specifically, the sun crosses the equator at the vernal equinox in one particular sign for 2,160 years and then passes for the next 2,160 years into the previous sign. As has been much heralded, we are now passing into the zodiacal "Age of Aquarius," after spending slightly more than the last two thousand years in the Piscean Age, whose symbol is the twin fishes. The approximately two thousand years before that were the Arian Age, symbolized by the ram's horns. And that age was preceded by the Taurian Age, which takes us back four thousand years B.C.E. The symbol of that age was the bull, in particular its horned head. Students of the subject believe that each of these zodiacal ages had a dominant form of religious worship whose symbolism highlighted the animal that functionally represented the "personality" of the age. Thus Christianity, which has dominated the Piscean Age, equated Jesus with the symbol of the fish. Similarly, in the Taurian Age the dominant religion was that of Egypt, and it was the bull Apis that figured prominently in Egyptian religion, particularly when sanctified to the sun god as Apis-Aten. The Minoan culture of Crete, which also developed during this period, made similar religious use of the bull, specifically the minotaur, which was half man and half bull. Between these two lies the Age of Aries, stretching back two thousand years B.C.E., a period that exactly parallels the period of biblical Judaism, the religion whose primary animal symbol, as I now hope to show, was and is the ram's horn. It seems more than coincidental that the high point of Abraham's career, now dated somewhere between 2000 and 1700 B.C.E., should have involved the ram's horns and, in particular, the appointment of the ram in place of a child as a sacrifice fitting to God. Though the symbolic significance of the ram's horn to the Jewish religion seems to have escaped the notice of astrologers almost as completely as it has the serious attention of historians of religion, I suggest that there was an important such connection. The following analysis will go far toward validating the astrological notion of the Age of Aries as the period in which the religion of biblical Judaism was of utmost spiritual significance and for which the ram's horns were the most exact of symbols.

The first biblical reference occurs in the significant context known as the Akedah ("The Binding of Isaac") when Abraham is about to sacrifice Isaac:

> And Abraham lifted up his eyes, and looked, and behold behind him a ram caught in a thicket by his horns and Abraham went and took the ram, and offered him up for a burnt offering in the stead of his son. (Gen. 22:13)

Here we see that it is by virtue of its horns that the ram becomes a substitute that redeems not only Isaac but all the Earth: "And in thy seed shall all the nations of the earth be blessed; because thou hast obeyed my voice" (Gen. 22:18). In the Temple ritual later established on Sinai, the sacrificial ram was especially designated for the consecration of Aaron (Ex. 29 and Lev. 8) and as "the ram of the atonement" (Num. 5:8). It remains, as in the Akedah, a symbol of atonement and an offering acceptable to God whereby the material is transformed into a more ethereal element and the Community of Israel can join with God in the communion of the sacrificial feast on one of the three pilgrimage festivals (Deut. 16:16).

But the ram's horn's most significant role in Jewish literature and ritual is as a musical instrument—the Shofar. As an essential element of the Rosh Hashanah service, it retains its ritual symbolism to this day: "In the seventh month, in the first day of the month, shall ye have a sabbath, a memorial of blowing of trumpets" (Lev. 23:24). It is the Shofar that has been traditionally blown on Rosh Hashanah, though the text contains only the words for *memorial* and *blowing*, and does not mention the Shofar. As instituted, the Jewish New Year of Rosh Hashanah is a sacred holiday devoted to "memorial blowing" of the ram's horn. The later ritual of this holiday makes clear that the major event so commemorated is God's revelation of Himself to the people of Israel on Mount Sinai amid the sound of the divinely blown Shofar: "There were thunders and lightnings, and a thick cloud upon the mount, and the voice of the trumpet [Shofar] exceeding loud" (Ex. 19:16).[6] The ram's horn blown on Mount Sinai can be taken to be that spiral instrumentality of historical process—of time repeating and yet progressing—through which the spirit of God makes itself known as an inspiring breath, the *Ruach Elohim Chayyim* (Breath of the Living God), a term that we will meet again in the next chapter. The purpose of this divine blasting of the ram's horn is to provide the awesome proof of God's power that will forever confirm the people of Israel in the covenant they have just made. But this covenant is also importantly placed in the context of redemption, particularly from Egyptian slavery: "Ye have seen what I did unto the Egyptians, and how I bare you on eagles' wings, and brought you unto myself" (Ex. 19:4). It was to make this covenant of freedom that Israel was redeemed from slavery and brought to the revelation of God that was accompanied by the sounding of the Shofar.

A similar association of the sound of the Shofar with freedom from slavery is made in the commandment concerning the Jubilee:

> Then shalt thou cause the trumpet [Shofar] of the Jubilee to sound on the tenth day of the seventh month, in the day of atonement. . . . And ye shall hallow the fiftieth year and proclaim liberty throughout all the land. (Lev. 25: 9–10)

The association of liberty, particularly the emancipation of slaves, with the sounding of the ram's horn on the Jubilee leads to the broader association of the Jubilee with the ultimate concept of redemption in the Messianic future. This association leads to the further elaboration of the Jubilee cycle into a structure of cosmic time in the concept of the Shemittot, a concept to be discussed later in this chapter. Thus the covenant on Mount Sinai, its ritual commemoration on Rosh Hashanah, and the establishment of the Jubilee can all be considered as both preparations for and a foreshadowing of the final Messianic redemption.

Fully conscious of the singular symbolic role of the ram's horn in the Torah, the Prophets attest to a renewed sounding of the "great Shofar" heard on Sinai to herald the coming of the Messianic Age:

> And it shall come to pass in that day, that the great trumpet [Shofar] shall be blown, and they shall come which were ready to perish in the land of Assyria, and the outcasts in the land of Egypt, and shall worship the Lord in the holy mount at Jerusalem. (Isa. 27:13)

> And the Lord shall be seen over them, and his arrow shall go forth as the lightning: and the Lord God shall blow the trumpet [shofar], and shall go with whirlwinds of the south. (Zech. 9:14)

In the second quotation, the divinely blown Shofar becomes one with the whirlwinds and recalls the triple identification of wind, breath, and spirit signified by the word *ruach*. Both of these references bring us back to the original Sinai experience of the Shofar with the expectation that this new redemption from Egypt will finally accomplish what the Exodus failed to do, elevate Israel into "a kingdom of priests, and an holy nation" (Ex. 19:6).

For Jeremiah, the human blowing of the Shofar becomes a way of answering God's call to a new covenant:

> Circumcise yourselves to the Lord, and take away the foreskins of your heart. . . . Declare ye in Judah, and publish in Jerusalem; and say, Blow ye the trumpet [Shofar] in the land. . . . Behold, the days come, saith the Lord, that I will make a new covenant with the house of Israel. . . . I will put the law in their inward parts, and write it in their hearts; and . . . they shall all know me, from the least of them unto the greatest. (Jer. 4:4, 5; 31:31, 33, 34)

A nation of people filled with such inward knowledge of God, *da'at*, with the law written in their hearts, would truly be a holy nation, each individual a sanctified Priest. So also David, from whose house the Messiah was prophesied to come, thought it fitting to bring the ark into Jerusalem, accompanied by the Shofar: "So David and all the house of Israel brought up the ark of the Lord with shouting, and with the sound of the trumpet [Shofar]" (II Sam. 6:15). But whether blown by God or by His people, the Shofar attests to the power of God and of His Presence. Perhaps the most famous example of this power is at the walls of Jericho:

> And the Lord said unto Joshua, See I have given into thine hand Jericho. . . . And seven priests shall bear before the ark seven trumpets of ram's horns: and the seventh day ye shall compass the city seven times, and the priests shall blow with the trumpets [Shofarot] . . . and the wall of the city shall fall down flat. (Jos. 6:2, 4, 5)

In this procession of power, only the priests are authorized to blow the ram's horns, and they do so to herald the approach of the divine Presence residing above the ark. So, too, the blowing of the great Shofar will herald the day when the holy Presence will animate the whole of a holy nation, each of whose members will be an ark containing the Torah written in their hearts, with the figure of the Messiah among them and personifying the collective holiness of this redeemed nation.

As indicated in connection with the Jubilee, the sounding of the Shofar to proclaim the emancipation of the Jubilee will be made on

Yom Kippur, the Day of Atonement. This reinforces the original reference to the ram's horns as providing a substitute for the intended sacrifice of Isaac. And in the later priestly rituals of the Temple, animal sacrifice was a means by which the Holy Spirit, with which the High Priest had communed in the holy sanctuary of the ark, could be further communicated to the congregation of worshipers.[7] The divinely established rituals of salvific communion practiced in the desert Sanctuary and Solomon's Temple were continued throughout the period of the Second Temple, but with the rebuilding of the Temple there was also a restructuring of the covenant.

In the restructured covenant established by the priest Ezra, it seems that the divine Presence was also to be communicated through both the physical showing of the Torah scrolls and the ritual reading of its contents, to be followed by private observance of its laws:

> And Ezra opened the book in the sight of all the people; (for he was above all the people;) and when he opened it, all the people stood up . . . and they bowed their heads, and worshipped the Lord . . . and the children of Israel were assembled with fasting, and with sackclothes . . . and confessed their sins. . . . And because of all this we make a sure covenant, and write it . . . to walk in God's law, which was given by Moses the servant of God. (Neh. 8:5, 6; 9:1, 2, 38; 10:29)

So was established the modern structure of synagogue observance in whose Torah scrolls resides the divine power around which all the ritual of congregational worship revolves. This power seems to have been transferred from the original Temple services involving animal sacrifice to this new vehicle of divine communion through the authority of the priesthood, whose sanctified function as curators of the holy was their capacity to endow ritual with divine power. But this new covenant of worship established by the priests of the Second Temple under the charismatic leadership of Ezra was significantly prefaced by a period of ritual atonement made by the people for their sins.

The yet newer covenant to be established in the rebuilt Temple of the Messianic period will also be prefaced by a period of atonement and will be accompanied by wars and devastation, whether physical or spiritual. This complex of events is associated with prophecies of the coming Day of the Lord that always include the sounding of the Shofar, as in the following:

> Blow ye the trumpet [Shofar] in Zion, and sound an alarm in my holy mountain: let all the inhabitants of the land tremble: for the day of the Lord cometh, for it is nigh at hand; A day of darkness and of gloominess. (Joel. 2:1–2)

The later Kabbalah of Isaac Luria, the sixteenth-century Kabbalist of Palestinian Safed who has had the greatest influence on the subsequent development of this tradition, tells us that we are trapped in the "shells" (kelipot) of materiality. Thus any such Messianic emancipation must be from an enslavement that has a strong hold over us and from which we can only be freed through sacrifice and pain. Thus is it also that the New Year, begun with the Rosh Hashanah ritual of sounding the Shofar, a sounding that not only reminds us of the divine revelation on Mount Sinai but also looks forward to the coming age of Messianic fulfillment, must close with a preparatory ritual of atonement on Yom Kippur. As the movement of the Israelites from Egyptian slavery through the Sinai revelation to the Promised Land can be considered a symbolic paradigm for the whole of Jewish history, still centered at Sinai but living in expectation of a Messianic Promised Land, so the High Holidays can be considered a miniature model of this prophetically structured history that every year makes the Messianic future a present spiritual reality.

In this survey of biblical references to the Shofar, we have seen that it is consistently viewed as an instrument whereby God reveals his power and trumpets the approach of a Messianic redemption in which knowledge of God will fill all of Israel. The question we have now to ask is what further meaning may be implied by the sounding of the Shofar and its cognates in other traditions. The best known analogue would be the Muslim call to prayer, issued from the minaret tower by the blowing of a horn. And Buddhists, too, make impressive use of their extremely elongated metallic horns in processions and in major ceremonies. In all cases, the function of these horns seems to be the higher attunement of those who hear them as a necessary preparation for the next level of their spiritual development. The tone of the horn may be said to function ideally as a kind of tuning fork whereby lower and various vibrational levels can be raised into harmony with this one pure tone. What is more, the priests and other functionaries empowered to blow these ceremonial horns are acting as divine surrogates, and so this tone may be said to convey the breath of God, that breath which first quite literally inspired Adam and whose vibrational level can redeem those descendants whom it spiritually inspires to rise to its level. Thus the breath that causes the horn to sound is always a means of bringing the spirit of God into communion with man. It reveals the power of God and calls man to prepare his vessel for the transmission of power that constitutes true communion.

The preceding discussion should indicate how the horn was ideally suited to become the vehicle for the complex of symbolic meanings that may fittingly be called the Arian Revelation, in view of the illuminating association that can be made between the ritual employment of the horns of the ram in the Jewish tradition and its most celebrated use in history as the zodiacal sign for Aries. But if the Jewish revelation is not to be consigned to the Arian Age and can be granted a continuing power, then we shall have to explore more deeply the universal meaning of this Arian Revelation. More particularly, we shall have to understand what archetypal function could be attributed to the ram's horn to make it symbolic of the special truth of this age.

One aspect of this period well recognized by classical historians is that it was an age of direct oral revelation. As "the Lord talked with Moses" (Ex. 33:11) and through the prophets, so too, according to the ancient Greeks, did Apollo speak through the Delphic oracle. With the coming of the Piscean Age the historical period of the prophets also comes to an end, and Plutarch reports a similar cessation of the oracles. Greek literature has many accounts of oracular messages. Agamemnon is told by an oracle that if he wishes the winds to return so that he can leave Aulis and go on to conquer Troy, he must sacrifice his daughter Iphigenia as reparation for a deer, sacred to Apollo, which had been killed by his men. Again at Troy, when Apollo is raining arrows down on the Greeks, the oracle explains that this is in punishment for Agamemnon's capture of a daughter of a priest of Apollo, and that it will stop only with her return.[8] In both instances we see not only the involvement of a divine force in human history but also an involvement whose purpose it is to remind man of a sacred realm on which his success is dependent and to which he should show reverence.

So is it also with the sacred writings of the Jews. Biblical literature not only provides a context for the giving of the codified law on Sinai, it is also an extended record of history as a revelation of the Way of God, *Derekh ha-Shem*. In the Book of Judges we can see most clearly the divine guidance of history and that, while it is the spirit of God working through chosen leaders that achieves victory, that victory will be fulfilling for those leaders like Gideon whose only concern is to serve the will of God and it will prove self-defeating for those like Jephthah whose primary concern is personal power. The historical books are one with the prophets in presenting historical events as a transparent garment for the will of God as it works itself out through a temporal process involving communities and nations that is just as revealing as the timeless theophanies granted to the few. In this shaping of history to reflect an inner truth, temporal process, itself, becomes a theophany. The difference is only that in history the revelation of God is largely indirect while in a theophany it is direct. Both modes of vision are essential, however, to what may be called the Arian Revelation.

What is distinctive about this vision of ultimate truth is that it proclaims the existence of a divine realm through the twin mediums of direct transmission and temporal process. And it is in its power to combine these different modes of revelation that the ram's horn becomes the perfect symbol. Blown as the Shofar it transmits the vibratory power of God directly; it is an immediate revelation of God. But its form is a spiral, which may be said to characterize the dimension of time appearing in the world of material reality, that of cyclic progression—with each birthday we are a year older. The spiral form of the ram's horn is, then, symbolic of the historical process of this world, and it suggests that this is a process vitalized by the breath of God blowing through it. A final characteristic of the Arian Revelation is that its direct revelations are also prophetic in the sense of foretelling the future. Indeed, they show that history is divinely guided for a purpose, and that it is this future purpose that influences and inspires the present. The Jewish record of revelation—with the traditions it inspired—is perhaps unique in positing a golden age in the future as well as in the past, and all the other uses of the Shofar may be considered as foreshadowings of its primary revelation as a herald of the Messianic future. Thus the vision of divine truth that took shape during the astrological Age of Aries found its most fitting symbol in the ram's horn, and though it retains the characteristics that define its specific vision of truth, as a true vision it remains universal. Ernst Cassirer has shown that ultimate truth can only be made visible through the particular definitions of symbolic forms:

> Special symbolic forms are not imitations, but *organs* of reality, since it is solely by their agency that anything real becomes an object for intellectual apprehension, and as such is made visible to us.[9]

If any symbolic form may truly be called an "organ of reality," it is surely the ram's horn, which reveals the God of Israel.

In conclusion we might well look to *The Odyssey* and the two gates it tells us of through which dreams must pass from the Underworld to man; through the Gate of Ivory pass false dreams and through the Gate of Horn dreams that are true visions. For it does seem that, as the Age of Aries passed into that of Pisces, so did the Gate of Horn give way to that of Ivory, the impenetrable bone of the tusk that is unlike that of the horn in transmitting no sound, no voice of true revelation. The sacred writings of the Piscean Age show no record of a hidden God who speaks directly to man "face to face, as a man speaketh unto his friend" (Ex. 33:11). But if the prophecies hold true, the new era now before us will be again informed by such direct knowledge of the divine as has ever been symbolized by the Shofar and that will call for a new approach to Torah observance that can revitalize the essence of the original revelation. The next section will show that this revitalization has already begun and requires precisely such a deeper vision of biblical Judaism as that made possible through the special perspective of the Gate of Horn.

Prospectus for a New Mode of Covenantal Judaism

Whether or not the Age of Aquarius now beginning is to be equated with the Messianic Age, it does seem to be heralding the truth of a new age of Judaism. The first rumblings of this new age began in the 1820s with the founding of the Reform Movement, followed in 1845 by the founding of Conservative Judaism, and in 1896 by Herzl's formulation of Zionism. In our own time the two main effects of these various nineteenth-century movements have been the religious fragmentation of the Jewish people and the restoration of its national homeland in *Eretz Yisrael*. These two facts of Jewish history have unalterably changed the character of Judaism at a time that seems more than coincidental to the dawning of the Aquarian Age and that may be fitting Judaism to play a unique role in defining the spirituality of this new astrological age. Some further historical background will help to frame the pertinence and nature of the new mode of Torah observance that will be offered here under the title of Covenantal Judaism.

The association of Jewish history with the precession of the equinoxes is suggestive not only for the biblical age of Judaism, which we have just seen to conform exactly to the time of the Age of Aries, as well as for the present transitional period, but also for the intervening Piscean Age. Though this was dominated by Christianity, the Piscean Age also marked a new age for Judaism. The preceeding Arian Age had been characterized by the biblical covenants with their provisions for Temple observance through an ordained priesthood in the Promised Land of Israel. The Piscean Age may truly be said to begin for Judaism in the year 70 C.E. with the destruction of the Second Temple and the dispersion of the Jewish people from Israel. Its foundations had earlier been laid by the developing rabbinical institutions of sacred teachers, synagogues, and the steadily enlarging body of Oral Law that was to grow into the compendium of the Talmud. These rabbinical traditions were uniquely suited to the needs of Jewish survival during the Diaspora. The Oral Torah welded the dispersed Jewish people into a homogeneous religious community wherever they were situated. Though there were differences in observance between the major divisions of Ashkenazim and Sefardim—the Yiddish- and Ladino- (Spanish) speaking communities of Jews, respectively—within either of these communities the halakhic traditions of rabbinical Judaism had the binding authority of law. The final form of the Oral Torah appeared in the *Shulchan Arukh*, Joseph Karo's seventeenth-century codification of talmudic law that was gradually accepted as the ultimate authority for Jewish ritual. Although the homogeneity of

Judaism was disrupted by the nineteenth-century movements earlier noted, Karo's work is still the basis of the halakhic observance of contemporary Orthodoxy. It is, then, the great edifice of rabbinical law that characterizes Piscean Judaism.

If Piscean Judaism begins with the exile of the Jewish people from Israel in 70 C.E., Aquarian Judaism may similarly be dated from the reestablishment of the Jewish homeland in 1948. And as the foundations for Piscean Judaism had been laid a few centuries earlier with the development of the Pharisaic movement, so Aquarian Judaism may be said to have begun during the Jewish Enlightenment—the Haskalah—of the eighteenth century and to have ripened through the Reform and Zionist movements of the nineteenth and twentieth centuries. Both movements may have been necessary to prepare Judaism to play a creative spiritual role in the Aquarian Age. The success of Zionism with the establishment of a Jewish state meant that the survival of the Jewish people would now be assured without the necessity for individual Jews to externally differentiate themselves from their non-Jewish neighbors by rabbinically prescribed ritual behavior. The "success" of the Reform movement in fragmenting the Jewish Diaspora communities has deprived the remaining Orthodox Jews of the power of sanctions they once enjoyed to enforce the Halakhah monolithically on all who would call themselves Jews. Thus much of the purpose and power of halakhic observance has been broken in our time. Whether for good or ill, we are now in a new age of Judaism, and in these changed circumstances it behooves us to seek the new forms of Jewish observance that will enable a transformed Judaism to survive and flourish in the remaining two thousand years of the Aquarian Age.

While it is certainly premature to speculate on the final shape of Aquarian spirituality and to decide whether or not it will approximate the Messianic prophecies, it seems possible to associate the astrological ages with the concept of the Shemittot, or cosmic eras, developed in a fourteenth-century kabbalistic work, the *Sefer ha-Temunah*.[10] Because the concept of the Shemittot involves the Tree of Life Diagram, an illustration and a review of the pertinent meanings of this central kabbalistic diagram will be useful. It is shown here in the form that is associated with the Lurianic Kabbalah: developed in sixteenth-century Safed, Palestine. This form of the diagram

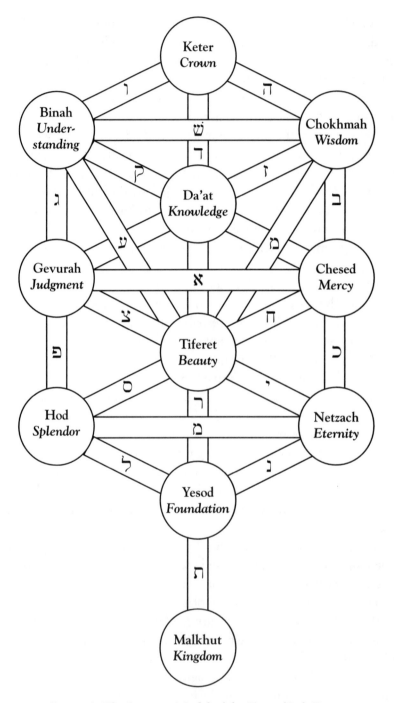

Figure 1. The Lurianic Model of the Tree of Life Diagram

features Isaac Luria's distinctive assignments of Hebrew letters to the twenty-two paths and includes the non-Sefirah Da'at (knowledge).

As the covenantal mode of Judaism developed here will be shown in the next section to connect its new approach to Torah with the principles of kabbalistic cosmology, this is an appropriate point to introduce some relevant background material on this subject pertaining to the Tree of Life Diagram. As can be seen in figure 1, this is a model composed essentially of ten circles or spheres and the twenty-two paths connecting them. In the *Sefer Yetzirah*, that earliest of strictly kabbalistic works, the ten spheres (called Sefirot, the plural of Sefirah) originally indicated the ten abstract numerals and the paths indicated the twenty-two letters of the Hebrew alphabet. But by the time of the *Bahir*, the next important kabbalistic text, which appeared in twelfth-century Provence, the Sefirot had become identified with the divine attributes. Some references in this text suggest a single, anthropomorphically described divine body, later identified as Adam Kadmon, the original cosmic man. Most important for our purposes are the Sefirot of the middle triad associated with the attributes of the divine heart in this understanding: Chesed (Mercy) representing the essential quality of the expansive right pillar; Gevurah (Judgment), or Din as it is sometimes known, the opposing quality of the constrictive left pillar; and Tiferet (Beauty), the harmonizing and balancing of these complementary opposites associated with the middle pillar. Although a fuller summary of the various identifications of the Sefirot and of their associations with kabbalistic cosmology has been deferred to the beginning of the next chapter, there is one further concept in the *Bahir* that must be introduced here. This involves a significant way of viewing the Sefirot that divides them into a supernal three and a lower seven, the latter identified with the days and works of creation. These lower seven become synthesized in the *Sefer ha-Temunah* with the concept of the Shemittot going back to the Talmud.

The *Sefer ha-Temunah* identified the Shemittah or age in which it was written with the Sefirah of Gevurah (Judgment) on the kabbalistic Tree of Life Diagram. It also identified the previous Shemittah with the Sefirah of Chesed (Mercy), and it affirmed that each Shemittah would experience a new revelation of the Torah. As Gershom Scholem summarizes the *Sefer ha-Temunah's* doctrine of the changing Torah:

"In the previous *shemittah* the Torah was read completely differently and did not contain the prohibitions which are the product of the power of judgment; similarly, it will be read differently in the *shemittot* to come."[11] In the Kabbalah the previous Shemittah of Chesed was associated with the Edenic past, and the coming Shemittah, presumably of Tiferet, the Sefirah following Gevurah on the Tree, was linked with the Messianic future. But in light of the present discussion, it also seems possible to associate these three central Shemittot with the three ages of historical Judaism with which we have been concerned: the Shemittah of Chesed with the Arian Age of biblical Judaism, the Shemittah of Gevurah with the Piscean Age of rabbinical Judaism, and the Shemittah of Tiferet with the Aquarian Age and the new Judaism it will spawn. Now if each of these ages is to be defined by its mode of reading the Torah, we have only to identify the Arian Age of the Shemittah Chesed with the Written Torah and the Piscean Age of the Shemittah Gevurah with the Oral Torah. What then of the Aquarian Age whose Torah is to be defined by the Sefirah of balance and harmony, Tiferet?

The one thing that we can say is that if the Aquarian Age of Judaism is to be marked by the Torah of Tiferet, then it is to be marked by Torah; the Law, rather than being abrogated, will be given a complete and coherent reinterpretation by which the covenantal relationship of Israel to its source will be renewed and sustained. Where Reform Judaism went wrong was first in abrogating the complete ritual Torah and then in readmitting it only in bits and pieces. Where Conservative Judaism went wrong was in attempting at first only to modernize the *Shulchan Arukh* and then gradually abandoning its insistence on total observance of even its modernized Halakhah. Where Neo-Orthodoxy went wrong was in clinging rigidly to rituals that had earlier been adapted to the historical conditions of the seventeenth and eighteenth centuries and so became anomalies in our time.

The way to the future was, nonetheless, shown by an early stance of the Reform movement. As Robert Gordis points out with regard to the Reform position developed at the Rochester meeting of 1895:

[The report] merely denied the authority of the rabbinical codes, saying nothing about the abrogation of Biblical law as well. . . . Reform was a type of Karaism. . . . Reform began in an anti-talmudic spirit,

and declared itself to be "Mosaic," but it quickly surrendered the binding authority of Biblical law as well.[12]

Though the time was not propitious for the partial Karaism of some
segments of the early Reform movement, it may now be ripe for a new
attempt to formulate a Neo-Karaism suitable for the Covenantal Judaism of the Aquarian Age, and it is such a program that I shall now
suggest.

A brief review of the Karaite strand in Judaism will help to define
the alternative approach to Torah observance that, in one form or
another, has been present in Jewish history since at least the Second
Temple period. The actual movement called Karaism has had a twelve-
hundred-year history since its founding by the Babylonian Anan ben
David in 760 C.E. Its principal position is a literal observance of the
Written Torah and opposition to the whole Oral tradition including
the Talmud. The Karaites were brilliant biblical scholars, applying
what we would now view as modern critical methods to Scripture as
early as the eleventh and twelfth centuries, their most creative period. But they were then as opposed to contemporary kabbalistic mysticism as they were to the extrabiblical laws and regulations of those
they called "Rabbanites." They claimed to be direct descendants of
the Sadducees, the priestly class during the Second Temple period;
and though there is no historical evidence to back this claim, they
did, in fact, observe the priestly Code of Purity. Their asceticism even
extended to abstention from meat and wine for those who lived in the
Holy Land, and their most dramatic practice was the total darkness of
their homes on the Sabbath eve in literal conformity to the law given
in Exodus 35:3 against Sabbath kindling. Whether or not there was
any direct link between the Karaites and the Sadducees, the Karaites
were right in claiming to be the spiritual heirs of the Sadducees at
least in their approach to religious practice; for, in the Second Temple
period, the Sadducees were the great champions of the Mosaic Law
and opponents of the Pharisaic elaborations of the laws.

The nature of the Torah the Karaites attempted to reinstitute dif-
fered importantly, however, from that of the Sadducees, for fully half
of its commandments—those relating to Temple practices—had been
necessarily abrogated through the historical destruction of the Temple.
But to make the Mosaic Torah function in the Diaspora and without

the atonement provisions provided through Temple sacrifice, the Karaites were forced to develop their own body of binding interpreted practices. As Gordis has pointed out: "Karaism had begun by challenging the authority of the Talmud, and cleaving to the text of Scripture, but soon found it necessary, in order to make biblical law function, to create its own Oral Law."[13]

Since a legal constitution like the Covenantal Torah must always be subject to interpretation if it is to be applied successfully to changing times and circumstances, we may well ask again: What is the point of calling for a radical reinterpretation of Scriptural Law when the complete and coherent Oral Torah of the talmudic tradition is already in place? The answer is that this tradition no longer works for most contemporary Jews. Its spirit is no longer attuned to the temper of the times and so for many it hinders rather than enhances their attempts to reconnect with their own pure channel of religious communion. It may be time, therefore, to attempt once more to return to the mode of sanctification given at Sinai, a return that can no longer be strictly to the Torah of Chesed but must rather be to a Torah whose interpretation is guided by the harmonizing spirit of Tiferet.

But in what sense can the Torah as originally given at Sinai be characterized as a Torah of Chesed (Mercy)? The answer seems to lie not simply in the beneficent presence of God throughout the Sinai experience but in the easy mode of atonement provided through animal sacrifice for such conditions as ritual uncleanliness. With this mechanism of atonement no longer operative, the understanding of uncleanliness and the nature of purification must also be restructured. From a largely physical and external process, though one that we may be sure did communicate an efficacious holiness, the method of purification must become internalized and spiritual. It is in this spiritualized mode of Torah practice that the element of Tiferet comes in. Although Isaac Luria had attempted to internalize the practice of the Oral Torah through such Kavanot, mystical intentions, the effect of his innovations was not to simplify but to further elaborate and compound the number of ritual observances the devout were expected to perform. The Tiferet Torah, on the other hand, should combine both an increased spiritualization and a simplification of ritual practice, a return to the Sinai experience of covenant with a meditative consciousness informed as well by the mystical principles and techniques of the Kabbalah and availing itself, where appropriate, of some of the more potent forms of ritual poetry developed through the intervening millennia. This should, indeed, be a *new* Karaism, one that can release the new spiritual energies of the Aquarian Age rather than following the old Karaite path of resisting the more powerful flow of Piscean energies through the channels of talmudic law.

The new form of Torah observance that I am proposing here under the name of Covenantal Judaism is based on an acceptance of the Mosaic Torah as sacramental, as transmitting a spiritual power to the observant. As shown earlier, however, there are two Mosaic Covenants, each providing a different form of this power. The first covenant made at Sinai promises holiness and priestly empowerment to the observer:

> Ye have seen what I did unto the Egyptians, and how I bare you on eagles' wings, and brought you unto myself. Now therefore, if ye will obey my voice indeed, and keep my covenant, then ye shall be a peculiar treasure unto me above all people: for all the earth is mine: And ye shall be unto me a kingdom of priests, and an holy nation. (Ex. 19:4–6)

This Covenant of Holiness involves only the observance of the Ten Commandments. Though additional commandments are given between the divine proclamation of the Ten Commandments "from heaven" (Ex. 20:22) and the communal ratification (Ex. 24:3), it is clear from God's further actions after the shattering of the original tablets that the Sinai Covenant is based exclusively on the Ten Commandments:

> And the Lord said unto Moses, Hew thee two tables of stone like unto the first: and I will write upon these tables the words that were in the first tables, which thou brakest . . . for after the tenor of these words I have made a covenant with thee and with Israel. . . . And he wrote upon the tables the words of the covenant, the ten commandments. (Ex. 34:1, 27–28)

It seems to be God's understanding that the original covenant ratified at Sinai involved a promise of holy empowerment *through* (a better translation of *alti* than "after the tenor of") the practice of observing just the Ten Commandments, whose holiness is concentrated in the one ritual observance they demand—the Sabbath. It should be noted again in this context that the observance of the Sabbath signifies the covenantal relationship in and of itself:

> Verily my sabbaths ye shall keep: for it is a sign between me and you throughout your generations; that ye may know that I am the Lord that doth sanctify you. . . . Wherefore the children of Israel shall keep the sabbath, to observe the sabbath throughout their generations, for a perpetual covenant. (Ex. 31:13, 16)

The Fourth Commandment not only represents the Torah in epitome but is the means by which the Sinai Covenant remains available to the children of Israel throughout their generations, perpetually serving to transmit its holy power of sanctification.

In contrast to the Ten Commandments covenanted at Sinai or, as it is otherwise called, Horeb, the final Mosaic Covenant made at Moab includes the whole of the Written Torah and promises the observer the additional blessing of prosperity:

> These are the words of the covenant, which the Lord commanded Moses to make with the children of Israel in the land of Moab, beside the covenant which he made with them in Horeb. . . . Keep therefore the words of this covenant, and do them, that ye may prosper in all that ye do. . . . Neither with you only do I make this covenant and this oath; But with him that standeth here with us this day before the Lord our God, and also with him that is not here with us this day. (Deut. 29:1, 9, 14–15)

Where the Sinai Covenant requires the ritual observance only of the Sabbath, the complete Mosaic Covenant involves that total sacramentalizing of existence that may well be considered the Promised Land. And as the first covenant is epitomized in the holiness of the Sabbath, so this final covenant is epitomized in the ritual saying of the Sh'ma that defines it as a Covenant of Love. Though the later Covenant of Love may be said to contain the earlier covenant, the opposite is also true since both are informed by the same infinite power; and the Sinai Covenant, both in its Fifth Commandment promise "that thy days may be long upon the land which the Lord thy God giveth thee" (Ex. 20:12) and in the terms that accompany its ratification (Ex. 23:20–33), not only promises long life in the Promised Land but a continuing divine presence: "Behold, I send an Angel before thee, to keep thee in the way, and to bring thee into the place which I have prepared . . . for my name is in him" (Ex. 23:20–21).

Covenantal Judaism recognizes both the essential and extended forms of the Torah that define the two Mosaic Covenants as representing the same Way of God, *Derekh ha-Shem*, divine paths to the prepared place. For some the Covenant of Holiness may be viewed as a first step to the fuller commitment of the Covenant of Love; for others it may be as far as they can or need go. For though the greater covenant is finally the more rewarding, the two Mosaic Covenants represent but a single Covenant of Power between God and Israel, the Ten Commandments containing the whole of the later Law implicit within it, the Written Torah explicating that distilled Law with greater particularity.

Covenantal Judaism offers the individual the opportunity to make a personal covenant based upon either set of graded requirements and rewards, a covenant to be guided by two principles from the Torah:

> Ye shall not add unto the work which I command you, neither shall ye diminish ought from it, that ye may keep the commandments of the Lord your God which I command you. (Deut. 4:2)

> For this commandment which I command thee this day, it is not hidden from thee, neither is it far off. It is not in heaven, that thou shouldest say, Who shall go up for us to heaven, and bring it unto us, that we may hear it, and do it? Neither is it beyond the sea. . . . But the word is very nigh unto thee, in thy mouth, and in thy heart, that thou mayest do it. (Deut. 30:11–14)

The first principle stresses that the interpreter is not to pick and choose which of the commandments he will obey and which ignore but that he must come to terms with each and every one of the commandments and develop a coherent interpretation that can contain all that are not subject to abrogation on the basis of consistent historical principles. The second principle states that the task of developing such a coherent interpretation of the commandments is within the capabilities of every individual covenantor. Everyone can interpret how he or she is to perform the commandments without the help of exalted and distanced experts because it is the nature of the commandments to instruct the practitioner directly through the heart how best to perform them.

While Covenantal Judaism can accept Jewish Orthodoxy as one coherent mode of interpreting the Torah, its spirit is radically different. For where traditional observance has been concerned to build ever wider fences around the Mosaic Torah in the attempt to preserve its sanctity, Covenantal Judaism would tear down most of these fences of extrabiblical laws to get back to the pure current of Mosaic spirituality. Its interest is not in increasing the requirements for observance but in reducing them to the minimum that cannot be abrogated through any conscientious mode of interpretation, one based not on convenience but on a careful study of the biblical laws. It would accept the force of historical change upon such laws by being ready to abrogate all laws that can be shown to be dependent either on the no longer operative regulations pertaining to the Temple sacrifices or those pertaining to the land of a Torah-governed Israel. But a law not so subject to abrogation it will abide by, concerned only to interpret it through comparative biblical study in such a way that one "mayest do it." For it is the conviction of Covenantal Judaism that observance of the laws of the covenant is sanctifying, conveying a power to redeem life from the toils of meaninglessness and fit it for the highest purposes of the cosmos. It also believes that the higher one's covenantal commitment the more one will receive the holy empowerment that is its greatest gift. How the Torah may be further interpreted in light of the principles of Covenantal Judaism will be suggested in the final section.

Interpreting the Tiferet Torah

As originally given, the Torah was made available for individual interpretation. It was not meant to be fixed monolithically in interpreted codes to which all members of the community were to conform. That this has thus far been the history of Torah interpretation, whether rabbinical or Karaite, need not spell failure for a similar attempt in our time. What is desirable is not that one person should define a new mode of Torah observance for all but that each person who wishes to develop holiness through the Sinai Covenant, or further to rectify his or her life by that observance of the whole Written Torah through which all he or she does will prosper, should make an individual covenant based upon his or her own complete and coherent interpretation of the commandments involved.

For the Covenant of Holiness this means an individual interpretation of how the minimum ritual of the Sabbath is to be observed. The third chapter of this book develops one such interpretation of Sabbath observance that provides a model of how this crowning *mitzvah* (sanctifying commandment) may be restructured in accordance with Mosaic law "that thou mayest do it." Such weekly sanctification combined with daily attention to the remaining commandments, particularly the first and tenth—the commandments to have no other gods before God and to free one's soul of coveting—will surely lead to the development of holiness. It may be argued that this is not only the highest of spiritual disciplines but the only form of the Mosaic Covenant ordained for the Diaspora, since the Moabite Covenant was specifically restricted to practice within the Promised Land and should therefore now be practiced only within the state of Israel:

> Behold, I have taught you statutes and judgments, even as the Lord my God commanded me, that ye should do so in the land whither ye go to possess it. . . . And the Lord spake unto you out of the midst of the fire. . . . And he declared unto you his covenant, which he commanded you to perform, even ten commandments; and he wrote them upon two tables of stone. And the Lord commanded me at that time to teach you statutes and judgments, that ye might do them in the land whither ye go over to possess it. (Deut. 4:5, 12–14)

If, however, the Promised Land be interpreted less literally as meaning that realm of Torah observance in which "ye may prosper in all that ye do," then it is important to understand the nature of the additional laws whose proper observance can so regulate and enhance one's vital powers that all one's endeavors flow in accordance with the direction of Providence, with the Way of God, to manifest one's highest desires.

Most important is the commandment that immediately follows the restatement of the Ten Commandments in the Moabite Covenant, the requirement for a twice-daily repetition of the Sh'ma (Deut. 6:4–7). As the only form of ritual prayer commanded in the Torah, the Sh'ma is the designated instrument for the daily enhancement of spirituality, and its proper performance can best focus the sanctifying power of Torah into the fabric of one's daily life. In the last words of Moses, observance of the whole Torah is defined as "not a vain thing for you; because it is your life" (Deut. 32:47), the determiner of your effectiveness and continuity, and such daily spiritual practice has been recognized by all traditions as the surest means of lifting the consciousness into that harmony with cosmic purpose that can accomplish all things. In addition to this extension of ritual practice from the once-weekly observance of the Sabbath to the twice-daily practice of a form of meditative prayer, a practice that can be observed in at least the minimal form given in the next chapter, the complete Torah connects one's life in another manner with sacred time, taking us now from the weekly to the yearly round. Its seven additional Mosaic holidays connect one's life with the cosmic flow of time through the seasons, each year increasing the early and late fruits that their redemptive practices can still harvest. As indicated earlier, these Mosaic holidays are discussed in the concluding section of the third chapter.

There are, of course, a multitude of other laws that the covenantor will either have to accept in their traditional understanding or reinterpret for him- or herself. At this point only two such categories can be considered, the first perhaps the most important after these considerations of sacred time, the category of diet. Next to setting aside certain regular times for ritual sanctification, the Torah deems the regulation of diet to be the most important means of lifting the consciousness. It bids us pay attention not only to the purification of the corporeal through direct spiritual techniques but through what we take into our bodies. There are three dietary areas that need to be considered. Of the first there can be no disputing. Certain foods such as pork and seafood are simply and strictly forbidden. Of the second and third there can be some disputing.

The second, the prohibition of eating meat with blood, which is the basis of Kosher slaughtering (shechitah), appears in three different contexts. The first is that of the Noahide Covenant in which the following commandment appears: "But flesh with the life thereof, which is the blood thereof, shall ye not eat" (Gen. 9:4). The rabbinical interpretation of this law, however, has been that it only prohibits "eating flesh cut from a living animal."[14] The second involves forbidden ritual practices. In Lev. 17:3–14, it is in terms of "sacrifices, which they offer in the open field" (Lev. 17:5) rather than presenting "as an offering unto the Lord before the tabernacle of the Lord" (Lev. 17:4): "For the life of the flesh is in the blood; and I have given it to you upon the altar to make atonement for your souls" (Lev. 17:11). And in Lev. 19:26— "Ye shall not eat anything with the blood; neither shall ye use enchantment, nor observe times"—it is in the context of the occult. As Aryeh Kaplan observes of this verse: "This refers to occult practices (Rambam), or perhaps a meal accompanying human sacrifice (Rashbam) or eaten on a murderer's grave (Chizzkuni)."[15] Though the commandment in these contexts may be abrogated because it is related to animal sacrifice and hence Temple-dependent or discounted because it refers only to occult practices, it seems clear from other references that the law involving the noneating of blood was made Temple-independent and so is not subject to absolute abrogation.

In Deut. 12:13–25, we are twice told:

> If the place which the Lord thy God hath chosen to put his name there be too far from thee, then thou shalt kill of thy herd and of thy flock, which the Lord hath given thee, as I have commanded thee, and thou shalt eat in thy gates, whatsoever thy soul lusteth after. . . . Only be sure thou eat not the blood: for the blood is the life. (Deut. 12:21–23)

As in the earlier such qualification—"Notwithstanding thou mayest kill and eat flesh in all thy gates. . . . Only ye shall not eat the blood" (Deut. 12:15–16)—the restriction on eating blood seems to be strictly applicable only to activity within "thy gates." So also in the earlier more general statements of this commandment:

> It shall be a perpetual statute for your generations throughout all your dwellings, that ye eat neither fat nor blood. (Lev. 3:17)

> Moreover ye shall eat no manner of blood, whether it be of fowl or

of beef, in any of your dwellings. Whatsoever soul it be that eateth
any manner of blood, even that soul shall be cut off from his people.
(Lev. 7:26–27)

Though the punishment of *karet*, being cut off from the Jewish people,
could be viewed as applying to use of non-Kosher meat, in all the
Temple-independent references it is significantly limited to domestic
behavior within one's gate *(sha'ar)* or dwelling *(moshav)*. Thus though
the weight of evidence would seem to require the use only of ritually
slaughtered meat, this law can also be viewed as limited only to domestic consumption. This interpretation confers on one's *moshav* a
special sanctity. As in the similar interpretation that will be given to
the law prohibiting kindling in the chapter on the Sabbath, the home
consecrated by observance of the strict meaning of the Mosaic Law
becomes transformed into a Temple space, a sacred space set apart
from the outside profane world.

The meaning of the third dietary commandment can be much
disputed:

The first of the firstfruits of thy land thou shalt bring into the house
of the Lord thy God. Thou shalt not seethe a kid in his mother's
milk. (Ex. 23:19)

On the last half of this verse, and its two later identical repetitions
(Ex. 34:26 and Deut. 14:21), a vast structure of traditional laws has
been reared involving the separation of meat and dairy products. But
there seems no reason not to take this commandment literally. In its
biblical context it is concerned with sacrificial offerings, in which
young goats had a specific function. This was to serve as a personal
offering to atone for inadvertent sin, for a king a male kid (Lev. 4:23)
and for a commoner a female kid: "If his sin, which he hath sinned,
come to his knowledge: then he shall bring his offering, a kid of the
goats, a female without blemish, for his sin which he hath sinned"
(Lev. 4:28–30).

The most important use of such a "scapegoat" is, of course, on
Yom Kippur, where it is assigned to atone for the sins of the community. But there is another stipulation involving the sacrificial use of

kids that is significant here:

> When a bullock, or a sheep, or a goat, is brought forth, then it shall
> be seven days under the dam; and from the eighth day and thence-
> forth it shall be accepted for an offering made by fire unto the Lord.
> And whether it be cow or ewe, ye shall not kill it and her young
> both in one day. (Lev. 22:27–28)

A kid, as with a calf or lamb, shall be nursed by its mother for seven
days and shall not be slaughtered and burned as an offering during
that time; neither shall it be later slaughtered with its milk-bearing
mother. In no case, then, shall you "seethe a kid in his mother's milk,"
burning it while it is still nursing and so is with its mother's milk or
with its mother and her milk. All these stipulations seem clearly enough
to point to a literal reading of this commandment, which would make
it Temple-dependent and so abrogated.

Of course it is possible to accept the rabbinical interpretation of
this law and all the halakhic details of Kashrut. But there seems good
reason to interpret this law literally and therefore as having no real
dietary significance. A symbolic significance there may be. It may instruct us not to atone for a sin too early, before we have fully understood and accepted our responsibility for it. In other words, we should
not claim exonerating causes for this sin, but accept it as an independent expression of our own will, however inadvertent. Finally I would
suggest that a way of handling this law in terms of a personal *karet*,
the attempt to bring a close reading of the Mosaic laws into closer
accord with the Halakhah, would be simply to give up dairy, an aspect
of diet that is a congestant to the system and could be eliminated in
the interest of greater health. Vegetarians, of course, have no trouble
at all with the dietary laws. This brief consideration of the dietary
laws can serve as a model of the type of Torah interpretation appropriate to Covenantal Judaism, one that would observe the absolute prohibition of certain foods, would probably use kosher meats, at least in
the home, and would either not pay any regard to the separation of
meat and dairy, whether in the home or in restaurants, or give up
dairy completely, again at least in the home.

The same three levels of applicability, from clear and applicable,
through ambiguous but applicable, to clearly capable of abrogation,

can be seen as well in the laws regarding sexuality. An absolute prohibition of adultery is the sole sexual restriction legislated in the Ten Commandments and thus the one to be most respected. The Written Torah adds to it such other absolutely forbidden practices as incest in its various degrees, rape, animal sodomy, and prostitution, the latter two affecting both males and females. But the whole area of sex between consenting single or divorced individuals is left unspecified except for the seduction of unengaged virgins, in which case the male partner must be prepared to bear a financial responsibility and, if demanded, to marry the female (Ex. 22:15). The law is also silent about female homosexuality, and about male homosexuality it is capable of an interpretation that may render it less absolute than might at first appear. This law reads "Thou shalt not lie with mankind, as with womankind: it is abomination" (Lev. 18:22), and it can be interpreted as prohibiting only homosexuality that employs distinct gender roles.

Similar ambiguity affects the law on transvestism: "The woman shall not wear that which pertaineth unto a man, neither shall a man put on a woman's garment" (Deut. 22:5). Though this would seem to absolutely forbid men to wear "drag," it is not so clear regarding women. A literal translation of the first clause is, "No male vessel [keli] shall be on a woman," and this need not be interpreted as forbidding women the wearing of slacks, whose open-ended nature would hardly qualify them as vessels, but a variety of other possibilities. In addition to such possible prohibitions as lesbianism or male contraception, traditional interpretations would also include the bearing of arms (Nazir 59a), since the term for male here, gever, could be understood as "warrior," or the wearing of phylacteries, tefillin (Targum Yonatan, Eruvin 96a, Orach Chayyim 38:3),[16] whose boxes would seem to qualify best as male vessels and thus could restrict this whole commandment to men. Women could thus interpret this law as they choose, and men would have to take particular care not to engage in sex during their morning prayers while wearing tefillin. The final area of ritual uncleanliness requires somewhat fuller treatment.

The commandment that women atone for their menstrual periods (Lev. 15:19–31) seems to be subject to abrogation on the principle that there can be no determination of ritual uncleanliness for which there is no present means of ritual atonement. The rabbinical substitution of the ritual bath, mikveh, for the two turtle doves specified for Temple sacrifice has no Mosaic sanction whatsoever and simply perpetuates practices that, if literally followed, would make it impossible for men to function in a society in which women are not sequestered during their menstrual periods and the period of the following seven days. For during this period, "whosoever toucheth any thing that she sat upon shall wash his clothes, and bathe himself in water, and be unclean until the even" (Lev. 15:21). Not only can a man not share a toilet with his menstruous wife but he cannot sit on any seat in any public conveyance or restaurant, for all such seats may have been sat upon previously by an unclean woman.

While the death of the human potential represented by the unfertilized egg may be deplored, to focus excessively upon this "death" is to violate the prime commandment to "choose life," to be cursed, rather, by the constant specter of "death and evil" (Deut. 30:15, 19). It is important to recognize, therefore, that the laws concerning uncleanliness are Temple-dependent, not only regarding the Temple procedures for the atonement of such uncleanliness but also in their very purpose: "Thus shall ye separate the children of Israel from their uncleanliness; that they die not in their uncleanness, when they defile my tabernacle that is among them" (Lev. 15:31). As Kaplan points out in his note to this verse:

> The laws of purity thus deal with the Tabernacle and the Holy Temple. That is why today, when the Temple no longer stands, we are not careful regarding these rules. However, it is still forbidden to enter the area of the Temple Mount if one is ritually unclean.[17]

Some women will surely wish to continue the rabbinical practice of abstaining from sexual relations for a full week following their last emission of blood and then going to a ritual *mikveh* for purification, a practice whose discipline has tended to sanctify the sexual experience of observant couples. However, the Covenant of Love should be understood not to require any practices that depend on the sacrifices and sanctification of the Temple.

Observance of the still operative provisions of the Written Torah can thus be made fully consistent with the demands of modern society for those individuals who wish to enhance the spiritual dimension of their lives. The covenantal relationship may be said to have three levels of commitment and reward, none of which exactly conforms to the divisions within contemporary Judaism. The two main biblical covenants within the Written Torah of Moses have been defined here as the Covenant of Holiness, comprising just the Ten Commandments and including the commandment of Sabbath observance, and the Covenant of Love, the all-inclusive Mosaic Covenant, which emphasizes ritual prayer. But between these two another level may be discerned, not so much defining the covenantal relationship of the children of Israel to God as the relationship of the individual Jew to his or her Jewish heritage and people. This is the level of *karet*, of those laws whose violation involves the penalty of excommunication from the communal practices of Israel: "that soul shall be cut off from his people" (Gen. 17:14). Here applied to circumcision, it also is a subtle distinguisher of those minimal observances by which one can identify oneself as a Jew. Of the Mosaic holidays, the principle of *karet* applies only to the abstention from leavened bread during the seven days of Passover (Ex. 12:15) and that affliction of soul on Yom Kippur traditionally interpreted as fasting. The greater penalty of death for performing work during the sacred times applies only to the Sabbath and to Yom Kippur. One can thus make a personal Covenant of Holiness with extensions to the laws associated with *karet* that permit a further identification with Jewish communal practice and history. Or one may finally make that full commitment to the Covenant of Love that can so lift one's spirit as to overcome the chronic condition of anxiety endemic to modern man:

> If ye . . . will not do all my commandments, but that ye break my covenant. . . . I will even appoint over you terror . . . that shall consume the eyes, and cause sorrow of heart . . . and ye shall flee when none pursueth you. (Lev. 26:15–17)

Such a covenant to observe the complete Written Torah need not become a hardship as long as its laws are interpreted "that thou mayest do it," including a willingness to abrogate all the laws that can be demonstrated to be Temple-dependent. Among these latter may be included the pilgrimage holidays of Shavuot and Sukkot, not Passover since its ordination before the giving of the Torah on Shavuot makes it Temple-independent. This does not mean that the festivals of early and late fruits cannot be observed according to rabbinical practice or completely restructured. This is particularly true for Shavuot. A kabbalistic custom adopted by some elements of rabbinical Judaism is to spend the entire night of Shavuot studying Torah. For Covenantal Judaism this could well become the most important of holidays, the time when one can make a personal commitment to observe a chosen form of covenant by the light of one's own understanding, determining for oneself how to perform each *mitzvah* and assured that it will be a covenant still transmitting the divine power channeled to it through Moses.

This introductory chapter has attempted to define a new mechanism of Jewish Torah observance called Covenantal Judaism, which is based upon an individual commitment to observe the whole of either the greater or lesser covenant in light of one's own understanding of its laws. Understanding the Torah as a transmitter of divine holiness to the observant is offered here as the basis for a modern Covenant of Power that returns to the Sinai rituals as originally empowered through the agency of that greatest of spiritual masters, Moses. For a spiritual master is one who can infuse his spirit directly into a holy community and into the rituals he has established to maintain its communion with the source of his power. Such a community will retain the efficacy of his living spirit both through memory of his teachings and the sacramental reenacting of these rituals. The sanctified function of an ordained priesthood is to serve as the curator of the living spirit that founded its lineage and of the rituals that continue to transmit that spirit when properly empowered. In the case of Israel, it is the entire community that has been divinely sanctioned to serve as priests of the covenant. Thus any individual Jew who makes this covenant becomes a priest of its rituals, capable of reactivating the Mosaic channel through which the divine can become present during their performance. The next three chapters will be devoted to a reexamination of the mechanisms of kabbalistic meditation, of Sabbath observance, and of liturgical prayer that can bring one into the Promised Land of higher consciousness in communion with God.

CHAPTER 2

Kabbalistic Meditation: Beginning the Path of Jewish Covenant

Basic Concepts of the Kabbalah

In developing a graded method of Torah observance based upon the correlation of Jewish spiritual practices with the biblical covenants, the Jewish practice of meditation may be correlated with what can be called the Patriarchal Covenant because its first biblical practitioner was Father Isaac: "And Isaac went out to meditate in the field at the eventide" (Gen. 24:63). Since meditation may be associated with the patriarchal covenantors, it can be considered the form of spiritual practice with which we can make the most basic of personal covenants with the God of Abraham, of Isaac, and of Jacob. Such a commitment to spiritual development in terms of this most unstructured of Jewish covenants can begin a process of covenantal relationship with the divine that can lead to the ever more demanding and rewarding covenants made through Moses at Sinai and Moab, which involve the practices of Sabbath observance and liturgical prayer. Those who are already practicing these major *mitzvot* of Torah should find the power of such observance to increase as a result of meditation since meditation produces a level of spiritual experience that can make one more sensitive to the presence of the subtle energies transmitted through religious ritual. But it is especially recommended for those who have

40

never begun such observance or have discontinued it because it did not seem to convey spiritual power. The power was always there but it requires a certain degree of spiritual development to be able to receive it, and the quickest and most efficient means of developing this spiritual sensitivity is through meditation. Though its practice has been largely forgotten in the more traditional forms of Jewish observance, the spiritual awakening many have achieved through forms of Eastern meditation has led them and other defenders of the Jewish religion like Aryeh Kaplan and the Lubavitcher Hasidim to seek evidence of meditative techniques in the Jewish esoteric tradition. This chapter contributes to this collective effort by developing a three-part meditation, all of whose techniques are based on classic Jewish texts.

In an effort to bring the Jewish practice of meditation within the sanctity and power of Torah, the kabbalistic mode of meditation to be developed in this chapter will be introduced by suggestions for a simplified but effective method of performing the Sh'ma, the Mosaic core of Jewish ritual prayer beginning, in its usual translation, "Hear, O Israel." This treatment will contribute as well to the full discussion of liturgical prayer in the fourth chapter. A mode of attunement to meditation will then be developed, derived primarily from that seminal first extant text of the Kabbalah, the *Sefer Yetzirah*, and it will incorporate the previously developed method of performing the Sh'ma with this *Sefer Yetzirah* technique in a larger meditative attunement process involving a "Kavanah of Creation" based upon Genesis. The techniques presented in this section are designed to bring the practitioner into the meditative state. But the nature of kabbalistic meditation does not end with the simple achievement and perpetuation of this state, as in much Eastern meditation, especially in the forms being exported to the West. It is a directed mode that uses a method of verbal instruction together with revisualization to manifest such ends as healing and knowledge. In the full analysis of major kabbalistic texts on meditation in the next section, on which the guided meditation presented in the last section of this chapter is based, it will be shown that this directed mode is the classical form of meditation practiced by Kabbalists from at least the time of Abraham Abulafia in the thirteenth century. Though those who go to prayer service would probably wish to begin their meditative practice with the attunement technique I have derived from the *Sefer Yetzirah*, I hope that, with or without the Sh'ma, the kabbalistic meditation shortly to be developed will help many to grow both in their own spiritual development and to a greater appreciation of the Jewish religious heritage. Before turning to this practice, however, we should first survey the major kabbalistic texts on meditation that will give sanction to its various features. This, in turn, will need to be prefaced by a summary of kabbalistic concepts, particularly as related to the Tree of Life Diagram.

In the earlier discussion of this diagram, the concept of the ten Sefirot was briefly traced from the *Sefer Yetzirah* to the *Bahir* and related primarily to the divine attributes, particularly as associated with the body of the original cosmic man, Adam Kadmon. But in addition to their identification in the *Bahir* with a single anthropomorphically described divine body, some references in this text also identify the Sefirot with a group of divine personalities (Partzufim, the plural of Partzuf), an ambiguity continuing in the most important of kabbalistic works, the *Zohar*, appearing near the end of the thirteenth century in Spain.

It was not until the sixteenth century that this ambiguity was fully resolved in the cosmology expounded by Isaac Luria, known as the Ari, in Safed, Palestine. This cosmology assigns the ten separate Sefirot to the original form of the emanated cosmos, which marks the first of the three stages in the Lurianic cosmic drama, and assigns their reconfiguration into the Partzufim to the third stage called Tikkun. Between these stages of Emanation and Tikkun is the Shevirah—the breaking of the vessels of the Sefirot—which was Luria's version of the mythic loss of Edenic perfection. Luria reoriented the Kabbalah from its past emanationist perspective to the futurist focus that also marks the future form of kabbalistic cosmology. His concern was with the process of cosmic rectification he called the Tikkun, whereby human spiritual development and devotions would make possible the final transformation of the originally inadequate form of divine emanation into those multiple divine personalities that will fulfill the purpose of creation.

In the earlier anthropomorphic form of the Tree, Keter (Crown) is pictured above Adam Kadmon's head, Chokhmah (Wisdom) to the right of his head or brain, Binah (Understanding) to its left, Chesed (Mercy) on his right arm, Gevurah (Judgment) on his left arm, Tiferet (Beauty) on his heart, Netzach (Eternity) on his right knee, Hod (Splendor) on his left knee, Yesod (Foundation) back up on his genitals (a problematical position that suggests an original cross-legged, sitting posture rather than the standing form traditionally pictured), and Malkhut (Kingdom) below his feet. These identifications have led to the association of the upper triad of Sefirot with the mental faculty, the middle triad with the emotions, and the lower triad or tetrad with the instincts. There is also an eleventh non-Sefirah Da'at (Knowledge) sometimes associated, instead of Keter, with Chokhmah and Binah to form a balanced triad of mental Sefirot. In another understanding, the upper six Sefirot have been identified with the divine and the lower four with the human, with Tiferet serving to unite the finite with the infinite. Such identifications have also been variously associated with the three major soul levels in kabbalistic spiritual psychology. In the case of the three triads, the upper mental triad is associated with the Neshamah soul, the middle emotional level with the Ruach soul, and the lower instinctual level with the inborn Nefesh soul. In the second case, all of the upper six divine Sefirot are associated with the Neshamah soul, understood to be the divine higher self, and the lower human four are variously apportioned between the Ruach and Nefesh soul levels.

Various attempts have also been made to correlate the four kabbalistic worlds of emanation with the Tree. In the Lurianic Kabbalah, all ten Sefirot are assigned to the first world of Atzilut (Emanation), but in another more popular version, only the upper triad is so assigned, the middle triad being correlated with the second world of Beriah (Creation), the lower triad with the third world of Yetzirah (Formation), and the final Sefirah with the fourth world of Asiyah (Action or Making). There is also a slightly different correlation of cosmic worlds to Sefirot based upon a vertical form of the Tetragrammaton arranged to resemble the human body, Keter and Chokhmah now being identified both with the head-resembling Yod and Atzilut, Binah with the arms-resembling upper Hey and Beriah, Chesed to Yesod with the torso-resembling Vuv and Yetzirah, and Malkhut with the legs-resembling lower Hey and Asiyah. The purpose here seems to be the desire to establish cosmic world parity between the soon-to-be-defined masculine and feminine Sefirot. In addition, the four cosmic worlds have been related to the geometric dimensions of the point, line, plane, and solid, the fourth world of Asiyah being identified with our world of three-dimensional matter.

In the Lurianic version the Sefirot are reconfigured by the Tikkun into the Partzufim. Keter is now identified with the Partzuf of Arikh Anpin (Long Face), Chokhmah with Abba (Father), Binah with Imma (Mother), the six Sefirot from Chesed to Yesod with Ze'ir Anpin (Short Face), and Malkhut with the Nukvah (Female). Abba and Imma are derived from the originally androgynous Ancient One, Arikh Anpin. Their continuous sexual coupling, Yichud, is understood both to sustain the world and to result in the conception of their initially androgynous son, Ze'ir Anpin, from whom the Partzuf of the daughter and his mate-to-be is later separated. The intermittent subsequent coupling of this lower pair is held responsible both for the functioning of Providence and the conception of the higher human souls. To these last two Partzufim were also applied the major terms defining the transcendent and immanent forms of the divine in the Talmud—the Holy One, blessed be He, and the Shekhinah.

It is Tiferet that is the defining Sefirah of the six-Sefirot Partzuf of the son, and its position as the bridge between the finite and infinite also defines the cosmic function of this most important divine personality. His six Sefirot may similarly be viewed as uniting his upper divine triad of Chesed-Gevurah-Tiferet with his lower human triad of Netzach-Hod-Yesod. A curious element in Lurianic cosmology is the view that, unlike the four single-Sefirah Partzufim who are each understood to contain the whole Tree from the time of their emergence, the originally conceived six-Sefirot Ze'ir Anpin must return to the womb of Imma after his nursing phase to become such a ten-Sefirot Partzuf. In the major work of Lurianic cosmology, the Etz Chayyim (Tree of Life) of Chaim Vital, the author feels called upon to express our astonishment over this originally Zoharic detail:

And now we will explain what the Zohar says in Chapter Acharei Mot, p. 65: After Ze'ir Anpin's nursing is finished, he returns to the womb of Imma for a second pregnancy in order for him to get his brains, even though he had already completed for himself a whole Partzuf of six Sefirot in the days of his nursing. And in order not to be astonished over the idea of a second pregnancy after the period of nursing, does it not say: "From my flesh will I see God."[1]

The divine personality of the son can be considered, then, to be twice born, and from a variety of perspectives would seem to be the paradigm defining the goal of human spiritual development. For the hidden message of the Lurianic Kabbalah would seem to be that the purpose of creation, that cosmic conversion of the original creative source into the multiple divine personalities that define the Tikkun, is not only to be facilitated but fulfilled by man.

The Lurianic Kabbalah can thus take its place in the larger Jewish esoteric tradition going back to the biblical statement: "Thus saith the Lord, Israel is my son, even my firstborn" (Ex. 4:22). Although I have deferred to a later work a comprehensive treatment of the textual history supporting my understanding of this esoteric Hebraic concept of the divine son,[2] I should here summarize its main points, beginning with the suggestion that it probably had its origin with the ancient Hebraic priesthood. For the seeds of this mystery would have informed its central cultic practice of animal sacrifice, that ritual drawing down of divine holiness into the sacrifice and its communication to the celebrants through ingestion which signified and could be experienced as the God within. The implications of such a secret doctrine were first divulged by the prophet-priest Ezekiel, called "son of man" (Ezek. 2:1) eighty-seven times in his book, which establishes the same dyadic concept of such a humanly derived divine son as that further elaborated under this same term in the biblical Book of Daniel and the apocryphal Book of Enoch. This is a dyad that unites a human prophet with the human-appearing divine form he sees in mystic vision seated upon the Throne of Glory. Where the Kabbalah differs in its understanding of the divine son from the earlier tradition of mystical ascent deriving from Ezekiel is only in its sexualizing of the genesis of this cosmic son. The earlier dyadic concept, still reflected in the two primary Partzufim of Arikh Anpin and Ze'ir Anpin before their further division into sexually distinguished pairs, now becomes triadic with the Partzuf of the son unifying in his own divine personality the transcendent and immanent forms of the divine through which he was conceived. It is this same threefold synthesis of the transcendent and immanent forms of the divine, here those of the lower couple, with the human soul that is consistently maintained by the Hasidim to be the true purpose of prayer. The collective membership of the Community of Israel proclaimed by God as his son can be considered, then, to be composed of those highly developed seers who could recognize their unity with their divine higher selves and thus themselves be considered divine personalities, achieving that ultimate unification of the human and divine which can effect both the personalization of the divine and complementary divinization of the perfected human through which the cosmic process is to be redeemed. How this goal of divine personality can be thus achieved we will see in the final chapter on prayer, but now we must turn to our survey of classic kabbalistic texts on meditation.

Kabbalistic Texts on Meditation

Aryeh Kaplan's *Meditation and Kabbalah* is a remarkable compendium of relevant kabbalistic texts on meditation that makes the whole tradition of kabbalistic meditation available for study and practice as never before. As this book makes abundantly clear, the major technique for achieving the meditative state in the kabbalistic tradition involved written, visualized, and spoken permutations and unifications (*Yichudim*) of Hebrew letters and divine names. But beyond this initial technique, the texts quoted by Kaplan provide an understanding of the deepest levels and purposes of meditation. We shall start with a discussion of the Yichudim.

There are two main purposes to all techniques involving the visual and auditory inner senses. The first is to *alter* the consciousness, in terms of the kabbalistic concept of soul levels lifting it from Nefesh constriction to Ruach expansion, and the second is to *train* the expanded consciousness to use its verbal and visual perceptual modes properly. The verbal mode is taught to combine the spoken or mental pronunciation of divine names and other letter combinations with controlled breathing and, in Abraham Abulafia's system, specific head movements. Even more important is the training of the visual imagination. This is necessary for all higher spiritual work and not normally as well developed as the linguistic capability. Such training can be accomplished by the distinctive kabbalistic practice of letter permutations, a practice going back at least as far as the third century *Sefer Yetzirah* and its most overt meditative technique, one later developed into a fine art in Abulafia's system and still later in the yet more elaborate Yichudim of Isaac Luria.

In its very simplest form, this involves the four-letter holiest Name

of God termed the Tetragrammaton. This practice is discussed in the
Lurianic writings as follows:

> It is very good for a person to depict the letters of the name YHVH
> before the eyes of his mind. . . .

> It is especially fitting and necessary that you meditate in this man-
> ner when you pray. Through this, your prayers will be accepted and
> you will be answered. Through such meditations, you bind all the
> Universes together, and the Highest Holiness then rests on you and
> pertains to you.[3]

In this teaching we can see how visualization and a verbalized focusing of intention can be unified to ensure a desired result, the answering of one's prayers. Whether verbal, visual, or both, the Yichudim, by
the more usual and elaborate technique of combining and thus unifying two divine names, primarily the Tetragrammaton with Adonai,
symbolize and facilitate the unification not only of the upper and lower
worlds and human faculties but, as importantly, of the mental functions identified with the right and left sides of the Tree, in this context the visual and the verbal, respectively.

The *Zohar* tells us that the tradition of Yichudim goes back to
biblical understanding of the meditative function of the Sh'ma:

> This is the mystery of Unification *(Yichud)*. The individual who is
> worthy of the World To Come must unify the name of the Blessed
> Holy One. He must unify the upper and lower levels and limbs,
> uniting them all and bringing them all to the necessary place, where
> the knot can be bound.

> This is the mystery of, "Hear O Israel, God is our Lord, God is
> One." . . .

> Yod is the mystery of the Holy Covenant. Heh is the chamber,
> the place in which the Holy Covenant, which is the Yod, is con-
> cealed. And even though we have stated [elsewhere] that this is the
> Vav [in the Tetragrammaton, YHVH] here it is a Yod. The mystery is
> that the two are united as one. . . .

> One must elevate the mind so as to bind them all in one knot,
> and then, one must elevate the mind with awe and love until it

reaches the Infinite Being *(Ain Sof)*. At the same time, however, one must not allow the mind to leave all the other levels and limbs. But the mind should ascend with all of them, binding them so that all of them are a single knot in the Infinite Being *(Ain Sof)*.

This is the Unification *(Yichud)* of the Elder Rav Hamnuna. He learned it from his father, and his father learned it from his master, who had a tradition from the lips of the Prophet Elijah.[4]

The *Zohar* here provides two unifications of the Name. There is the vertical unification of the lower limbs—the *vav* signifying the torso and the Partzuf of Ze'ir Anpin while the lower *heh* signifies the legs and the Nukvah—as well as of the upper limbs—the *yod* signifying the head and Abba with the upper *heh* signifying the arms and Imma. Then we have a more sexually graphic depiction of the upper Yichud. Here the identification of the *yod* with the "Holy Covenant" is an allusion to circumcision and the revealed glans, and if the letter *heh* is turned around to face the *yod*—such a face-to-face position as signifies the Tikkun in the later Lurianic Kabbalah—it can be seen that the *yod* can be "concealed" in the space between the attached upper portion and the unattached line of the reversed *heh*: ה.

All of this sexual symbolism is related to the Zoharic interpretation of the Sh'ma as a Unification. For what it tells us Israel is meant to hear *(Sh'ma Yisrael)* is that YHVH *Eloheinu*, the personal Lord our God, and YHVH, the level of the Godhead beyond all qualifications, are one *(echad)*. In this twice-daily declaration of Judaic faith, the Tetragrammaton, normally vocalized as Adonai (the Lord), is thus associated first with a form of the divine name Elohim and is then given without such qualification. Now since Elohim is a plural designation of the divine, it would seem to specify the manifesting aspect of the Tetragrammaton in the world of multiplicity, that identified with the feminine Shekhinah, in contrast to its transcendent state, equated with the Holy One, blessed be He. Thus what is being unified is the God immanent within and relating to cosmic multiplicity with the transcendent God of unity. As earlier suggested, in this Yichud the meditative consciousness unifies "the upper and lower levels and limbs" of the Tetragrammaton in its vertical arrangement, a traditional arrangement suggestive of the anthropomorphic divine body but also understood to represent the upper and lower male and female Partzufim, and binds itself to it "in one knot." It then must elevate itself to the Infinite while still being bound to its finite body, realizing in the human mind and body the same unified duality as that understood to be expressed in the Sh'ma. If this is correctly accomplished, the soul will experience its ultimate Yichud of particularity with infinitude, recognizing itself, in what is surely one of the greatest definitions of Devekut (the "clinging" to the divine that signifies communion), as "a single knot in the Infinite Being."

We have thus far been considering the most basic kabbalistic techniques of achieving the meditative state, those that involve pronouncing or visualizing divine names, in particular that of the Tetragrammaton. Although both the Lurianic and Zoharic discussions go beyond the simple elucidation of initial techniques to depict the ultimate results of meditation, they do not specify what one is to do to achieve these results beyond the various techniques of attunement. Their techniques are all aimed at establishing the initial conditions for the expansion of consciousness and are directed, for the most part, to activating the meditative switching mechanism into expanded consciousness. But there are a few kabbalistic texts that do take us further, and we shall now turn to these for the illumination they can afford into the more advanced techniques of kabbalistic meditation.

The most important of these is the *Chayyei ha-Olam ha-Bah* (Life of the Future World) of Abulafia, a work later quoted in an unpublished section of Chaim Vital's *Sha'arei Kedushah* (Gates of Holiness) some three centuries later and an accepted guide to meditative practice in kabbalistic traditions continuing to the present day.[5] Abulafia begins with the process of attunement through letter permutations, which affects the emotional system centered in the heart. He then takes us to the higher spiritual work that may be accomplished after the Shefa, the spiritual influx, is experienced:

> Meditate (*hitboded*) alone . . . begin to permute a number of letters
> . . . until your heart is warmed as a result of these permutations. . . .
> The influx will then come, bestowed to you. . . .
> Then prepare your inner thoughts to depict God and His highest angels. Depict them in your heart as if they were human beings,

sitting or standing around you. You are in their midst, like a messenger whom the King and His servants wish to send on a mission. You are ready to hear the words of the message. . . .

After you have depicted all this, prepare your mind and heart so that your thoughts should understand the many things that come to you through the letters that your heart imagines. Understand each concept and its reasons, both as a whole and in its parts. Ponder them, like a person who has a parable or example revealed in a dream, or like one who delves into a very deep concept in a book of wisdom.

Take each concept that you hear, and interpret it with the best and closest interpretation that you can. Judge yourself according to what you understand from it. And what you are told can also relate to others.

All this will take place after you have cast the tablet from your hand and the pen from between your fingers, or after they have fallen of their own accord because of your many thoughts.[6]

Once the Shefa comes, the real work of the imagination can commence. And in this text we can see Abulafia guiding the meditative process toward a precise imaginative projection of an astral scene containing God and his angels that is meant to facilitate the reception of a divine message. In this state of prepared readiness for higher knowledge, the message will be transmitted through what the "heart imagines." This may come as letters, concepts, or symbolic images as in a dream. But the imaginative reception of the symbolic message is only half of the process. What is next required is that the image be interpreted, and this is a function of the rational mind.

In writing that the meditatively received symbolic image be interpreted as one would a dream, Abulafia was undoubtedly assuming in his readers a knowledge of the midrashic discussion of dreams. The Midrash tells us that in Jerusalem there were twenty-four schools of dream interpretation and that all the interpretations were fulfilled, whatever the school. Its summary statement, "all dreams follow the mouth," contains the surprising understanding that a dream means whatever one says it does, that the dream will become a reality in accordance with the interpretation given to it, whether for good or ill, and that, therefore, the interpreter has a certain power.[7] It might be pointed out that the talmudic understanding of dreams explains the success that the various schools of psychoanalysis have had with psychic healing through dream interpretation despite their rival interpretations of dream symbolism. But just as a positive construction of dream symbolism can aid in healing, so a negative construction can be injurious, for the combination of image with idea is very powerful and can affect reality.

Thus after Abulafia's instruction to "interpret it with the best and closest interpretation that you can," he concludes: "Judge yourself according to what you understand from it." If one can rightly judge what one's condition and prospects may be from the way one interprets such imaginatively projected material, the implication is that this mental process can impress itself on reality with the force of truth, that it can determine one's own reality and also that of others to whom it is applied: "And what you are told can also relate to others." Abulafia's method can be taken as a model for psychic healing, both of oneself and others, and I shall shortly expand upon this topic in conjunction with a full model of kabbalistic meditation. But there are two further kabbalistic texts whose concepts will aid in the development of this final model.

The first of these is a work contemporaneous with those of Abulafia, the *Sha'ar ha-Kavanah la-Mekubbalim ha-Rishonim* (The Gate of Kavanah of the Early Kabbalists), attributed to Rabbi Azriel of Gerona, a disciple of the Provençal Kabbalist Isaac the Blind. This short work is quoted in its entirety in the unpublished fourth section of Vital's *Sha'arei Kedushah*, and it merits the closest study. In the following I shall not enter into the details of the light meditation it gives, the varieties and positions of the lights to be visualized, but focus rather on its basic methodology. Unlike the previous techniques examined, which emphasize the pronunciation or visualization of divine names, this moves directly to the power of meditating on light:

When a person sets his mind on something, its essence returns to him.

Therefore, if you wish to pray, or if you wish to grasp the true nature of an idea, do the following:

Imagine that you yourself are light, and that all of your surroundings, on every side, are also light.

In the middle of this light is a Throne of light. . . .

This is the light that crowns the desires of the mind and illuminates the paths of the imagination, enhancing the radiance (zohar)
of the vision. This light has no end. . . .

When there is no other thought or desire intermingled with
[his concentration] it can become so strong, that it can transmit an
influence from the Infinite (Ain Sof).[8]

The text tells us that a focusing of the will powerful enough to elevate
an object of desire to the Infinite becomes a channel by which a reciprocal influence powerful enough to fullfill that desire can be transmitted from the Infinite. Concentration on this objective is facilitated by a visualization of oneself as a center of light surrounded by
the Infinite Light (Or Ein Sof). Such a visualization reveals the essential unity of the self with the Infinite, since all is light, while it main-
tains the distinction between the inner light of the self and the surrounding Infinite Light.

Maintaining this distinction is of the utmost importance for the
next and most vital step in this spiritual process, and it is this that
truly distinguishes the practice of a spiritual master:

An individual thus ascends with the power of his concentration
from one thing to the next, until he reaches the Infinite (Ain Sof).

He must then direct his concentration in a proper manner so
as to perfect it, so that the Highest Will should be clothed in his
will, and not only that his will should be clothed in the Highest
Will.

The highest influx does not descend except when the individual does this correctly. . . .

The Highest Will and the lower will are then unified. The individual identifies himself with his attachment to the Unity. The
divine influx can then be transmitted in order to perfect him.

The lower will is not perfected when the individual approaches
for his own needs. Rather, one must approach while clothed in the
will and desire to reveal the identification that is hidden in the
concealed Mystery.

When one approaches in this manner, the Highest Will then
brings itself close to him. It increases his power and motivates his

will until he can accomplish anything. This will even include things that he himself desires, in which the Highest Will does not have any portion.[9]

Whereas most spiritual teachings are directed only to the attainment of Devekut, to that communion with the divine that clothes the individual will in the Highest Will, the practice taught here retains and so directs the master's will "that the Highest Will should be clothed in his will." Rather than dissolving his will in the bliss of the Infinite, the aspirant to spiritual mastery is taught to perfect his will by attaching itself to Unity not as final consummation but "to reveal the identification that is hidden in the concealed Mystery." As the work later concludes: "This is one of the ways of prophecy. One who accustoms himself to it will be worthy of attaining the prophetic level."[10] The master is one whose words and deeds "reveal the identification" of such an individual with the divine power, and his purpose is to perfect himself into an instrument of divine revelation. Such an instrument "can accomplish anything" but only so long as he does not use his power of concentration "for his own needs." Yet if his will is properly directed toward revealing the Highest Will working through all his words and deeds, his purified personal desires will also be fulfilled and all his needs met. The spiritual master is one who can perform miracles through the power of his concentration, his Kavanah. Abulafia also speaks of "the mystery of the true discipline, through which you can alter the laws of nature."[11]

For both Abulafia and the author of the *Sha'ar ha-Kavanah*, the mystery of this true discipline involves three things—influx, symbols, and words: first, a process of attunement that can initiate the divine influx, then a process employing both visual symbols and words. The concluding discussion of the *Sha'ar ha-Kavanah* defines these three elements of master meditation and relates them to the description of the spiritual practices of the early Hasidim in *Mishnah, Berakhot* 5:1:

The individual must be clothed in spirit *(ruach)*, expressing his concentration with words, and making a symbolic act. According to how he does this, the influx will be transmitted from potential to potential, from cause to cause, until the result is completed according to his will.

It was in this manner that the early [saints] would linger an hour before praying [alluding to *Berakhot* 5:1]. During this period, they would dispel all other thoughts, fixing the paths of their concentration and the power of its direction.

They would then spend an hour in prayer, verbally expressing this concentration with words. Finally, they would spend an hour after their prayers, contemplating how the power of their verbally expressed concentration would have a visible effect.[12]

The sentence with which this extract begins defines the three essential elements of what can be called "transformational meditation." To change the course of events or "alter the laws of nature," the master must be filled with spirit and focus this spirit with words while "making a symbolic act." This last phrase can be understood in two ways. The first way is that suggested by the last sentence, the use of the imagination to symbolize visually the desired result. But another possibility involves the creation or reenactment of an empowering ritual. For this is precisely the way in which ritual originates. A charismatic master sacramentalizes a certain way of doing something, be it the way he cleanses his body before the Sabbath or piles up the loaves of bread on the Sabbath table, so that by repeating his words and actions, a symbolic ritual is performed that transmits the spirit of the master. The creation of ritual is, then, one way in which the spirit of a master can work in the world and continue to transmit to the participant in such a ritual the highest influx he, himself, has received. But if the phrase is understood in its first suggested meaning, the use of the symbolic imagination during meditation, it defines the more general technique by which the master accomplishes his will in the world.

According to how powerfully he is able to focus his spirit through words, whether original or formulaic, and visible symbols, whether imagined or ritually enacted, "the influx will be transmitted from potential to potential, from cause to cause, until the result is completed according to his will." From this it seems clear that the spiritual master can alter the workings of causality by effectuating certain potentialities that might otherwise have remained dormant but are still available within the realm of possibility. His power involves a mastery of the higher dimension of Providence, a dimension that influences the apparent randomness of events to bring about a desired result consistent with justice and that may operate through the improbable possibilities at the farther limits of the curve of probability.

In the first paragraph of the last quotation, the three elements appear to be simultaneous. With a properly attuned spirit, the master visualizes a desired result and decrees its manifestation with such words as "Let there be. . ."[13] But the description in the *Sha'ar ha-Kavanah* of the three-hour meditative practice of the early Hasidim, in correlating these three elements with a three-stage process, appears to add a step. Here the visualization does not accompany the verbal affirmation but appears in response to a verbal prayer, as a symbolic answer to a question and guide to future action. As the *Sha'ar ha-Kavanah* opens with instructions for visualizing light, it is clear, however, that it also understands the first stage of the process, where the Hasidim spent an hour "fixing the paths of their concentration and the power of its direction," as involving a visual focusing of the imagination toward a specific purpose. It would seem, then, that there are two separate visualizations, a first visualization of a problem, whether internal or external, that impedes spiritual perfection, a verbal carrying of this visualized problem to the Infinite, and a revisualization of the transmitted solution that, Abulafia tells us, must then be verbally interpreted to give it potency. Abulafia also presents the initial visualization of God and the angels as an aid to reception of a divine message, which would come through what the "heart imagines," that is, as a second visualization.

But the clearest treatment of the magical power of meditative revisualization appears some five hundred years later with the modern Hasidim, in particular in the writings of Dov Baer, the Mezhirecher Maggid and chief disciple of the Baal Shem Tov, the founder of the hasidic movement. In Dov Baer's works the concept of Ayin, "nothingness" or, more precisely, "no-thingness," is developed. Ayin is identified with the first kabbalistic world of Atzilut, Emanation, and is the goal of a meditative technique that begins with letter permutations and carries the spirit up through all the supernal worlds to the highest level of Ayin. In the thought of the Mezhirecher Maggid, it is only through such an ascent to Ayin that the alchemy of transformation can be explained:

If you consider yourself as "something," and ask for your own needs, then God cannot clothe Himself in you. God is infinite, and no

55

vessel can hold Him at all, except when a person makes himself like Nothing.[14]

Nothing can change from one thing to another [without first losing its original identity]. Thus, for example, before an egg can grow into a chicken, it must first cease totally to be an egg. Each thing must lose its original identity before it can be something else.

Therefore, before a thing is transformed into something else, it must come to the level of Nothingness.

This is how a miracle comes about, changing the laws of nature. First the thing must be elevated to the Emanation of Nothingness. Influence then comes from that Emanation to produce the miracle.

When a person gazes at an object, he elevates it into his thought. If his thought is then attached to the supernal Thought, he can elevate it to the supernal Thought. From there it can be elevated to the level of Nothingness, where the object itself becomes absolute nothingness.

This person can then lower it once again to the level of Thought, which is somethingness. At the end of all levels, he can transform it into gold.[15]

The alchemical process by which lead can be transformed into gold is here explained as a wholly spiritual exercise. Beginning with concentration on an actual physical object, the person visualizes this leaden object imaginatively. If this visualization can be properly attached to the supernal Thought, it can then be further elevated to that state of Nothingness beyond all visualization in which the image is dissolved. At this stage the true mastery of the spiritual alchemist is tested. For rather than resting in this state of Ayin, his will must actively revisualize the original object as transformed into gold. This is in the world of Creation, Beriah. He must then lower this image through Yetzirah to Asiyah, the world of physical manifestation, with such power of concentration as can carry "Influence . . . from that Emanation to produce the miracle," the physical object transformed into gold when he opens his eyes.

But such physical alchemy is only a sign of the more profound personal transformation that the master has undergone prior to performing such miracles. He must first dissolve his own ego and make "himself like Nothing." In the words of the Mezhirecher Maggid: "To enter the Universe of Thought where all is the same, you must relinquish your ego, and forget all your troubles. You cannot reach this level if you attach yourself to physical worldly things."[16] But he does not remain in this state of Nothingness. He must then lower himself transformed into a vessel of divine power, clothing God. As the *Sha'ar ha-Kavanah* had said, "The Highest Will should be clothed in his will." Once he has so transformed himself, he can perform all miracles through the same process of visualization, dissolution, and revisualization. All the masters of kabbalistic meditation whose works we have examined convey the same essential understanding of meditation as a discipline not aimed solely at spiritual purification for the purpose of eternal union with God but at purification for the purpose of channeling the divine energy back into the human realm as a means of perfecting that realm. It is aimed not at the dissolution of personality as an end in itself but as a means toward the achievement of the transformed personality of the master who, in the words of the *Sha'ar ha-Kavanah*, "can accomplish anything." This study of the advanced classic texts of kabbalistic meditation should lay the foundation for the following development of a kabbalistic model of mediation suitable for the Aquarian Age, one that will here be prefaced by suggestions for a mode of performing the essential Sh'ma that, when used to introduce this meditative technique, can bring it within the sanctity of Torah.

Combining the Practice of Meditation with Prayer

We have seen that support for such a practice combining meditation and prayer can come from the early Hasidim, who are credited by the Mishnah with spending one hour of meditation before prayer, and that this time period was extended to a three-hour practice in the *Sha'ar ha-Kavanah*, one hour devoted to meditation before prayer, one hour to prayer, and one hour to meditation after prayer. Such a combined practice may also be inferred from the writings of Abulafia, the thirteenth-century Kabbalist most concerned with the practice of meditation and a major influence in its propagation. This inference will, however, require some development and will lead to a new analysis of these practices in kabbalistic terms.

We can begin with the following passage, which focuses upon two divine names in relation to the highest path of mystical illumination:

> The seventh path is a special path and it includes all others and it is
> the holy of holies and it is fitting for prophets only. . . . It is impossible to disclose this to anyone, not even the main points, unless in
> his yearning he has learnt as a preliminary, in a direct communication from a teacher, the forty-two and the seventy-two letter names
> of God.[17]

Though Abulafia refuses to disclose the nature of this highest practice, he does provide a key to it, suggesting that it is somehow related to "the forty-two and the seventy-two letter names of God." Understanding the nature of these Names will help in the possible reconstruction of this practice. It will also provide a fitting conclusion to the preceding analysis of kabbalistic meditation as well as an introduction to the following section on how the Sh'ma may be effectively included in the practice of meditation.

It is generally agreed that the name of forty-two letters is either derived from or exemplified in the ancient prayer Ana Bekhoach, ascribed to the second-century figure Nechunya ben ha-Kana. The significance of the name of forty-two letters seems to be given in the form of this prayer. It is composed of seven lines containing six words apiece, each word beginning with an initial of the name of forty-two letters. The significance of this name would thus seem to be attached to the multiplication of the numbers six and seven. This numerical coding also seems to distill the understood purpose of prayer, the unification of the finite and transcendent identified with the numbers six and seven, numbers associated most importantly with the sixth and seventh days of creation. Thus the first of these numbers can signify the six workdays of creation or just the sixth, that in which man was created, while the second can signify the Sabbath, their multiplication symbolizing the fruitful unification of the Infinite with the finite creation and particularly with man. As the Sabbath is characterized in later kabbalistic thought with the Shekhinah, the feminine-characterized divine Presence, the multiplication of six by seven could also be understood to signify the generative unification, Yichud, of man and the Shekhinah, a theme of much kabbalistic Sabbath imagery. But if the forty-two letter name, both incorporated in and exemplifying the mystical purpose of prayer, can be associated with prayer as a spiritual practice, what of the name of seventy-two letters that Abulafia couples with it as the core of the highest mystical path?

This name also dates from ancient times and its composition was explained in the eleventh century by Rashi. It is derived from Exodus 14:19–21, each of whose three verses are composed of exactly seventy-two words. The seventy-two triplets derived from these verses are formed by taking the initial letters of the first verse in normal order, those of the second verse in reverse order, and those of the third verse again in normal order.[18] Let us now look at these three biblical verses, each so carefully composed of exactly seventy-two Hebrew letters:

> And the angel of God, which went before the camp of Israel, re- moved and went behind them; and the pillar of the cloud went from before their face, and stood behind them:
>
> And it came between the camp of the Egyptians, and the camp of Israel; and it was a cloud and darkness to them, but it gave light by night to these: so that the one came not near the other all the night.
>
> And Moses stretched out his hand over the sea; and the Lord caused the sea to go back by a strong east wind all that night, and made the sea dry land, and the waters were divided. (Ex. 14:19–21)

What this passage tells us is that the angel and cloud, which before had preceded Israel, now went behind it, separating the camp of the Egyptians from the camp of Israel; that the cloud appeared to the Egyptians as dark but to the Israelites as a light in darkness; and that after these events, Moses showed mastery over the elements as the instrument of God. The significance of this sequence of events seems to concern a reversal of the cosmic positions of angel and man. The angel no longer leads but follows that man who has achieved enlightenment. The angel is now positioned between the camps of the ignorant and the enlightened, at or below that of the divine cloud which, like the firmament of Ezekiel's vision, appears as darkness even to the

Chayyot or cherubs beneath it but reveals man on the throne to the prophetic eye. The culmination of the reversed position of enlightened man comes with Moses' display of master power in the service of God, the climactic dividing of the Red Sea that shows him to have passed beyond the cloud of unknowing to that state of knowledge which is power.

As we have seen, this is the state to which the practice of kabbalistic meditation aims—not that emptying of self to become a vessel of divine unification, which we will later see to be the mystical intention of prayer, but a focusing of the purified self into an instrument of divine power. If, then, the practice involving the name of seventy-two letters is either derived from or encoded in these verses of Exodus, it would seem to be a form of meditation. And if the analysis up to this point is correct, then the seventh path to enlightenment described by Abulafia, which uniquely combines practices involving the forty-two- and seventy-two-letter names of God, would have to entail both prayer and meditation. We will now briefly explore how these two complementary practices may be more theoretically related in terms of the Kabbalah.

Beginning with the premise that the two practices related to these two names are intimately connected within one theoretical framework, we can understand more concerning the name of seventy-two letters by reviewing what was earlier deduced concerning the name of forty-two letters. As we saw, this number forty-two signifies the product of the number six multiplied by the number seven, numbers that can refer not only to the sixth and seventh days of creation but also to the sixth and seventh Sefirot, to that unification of Tiferet with Netzach that would accomplish the unification of the double heart. Though the traditional understanding of the double heart involves its good and evil inclinations, *yetzer tov* and *yetzer ha-ra*, I would like to suggest another way of looking at this concept. We have seen that Tiferet was identified both with the heart of Adam Kadmon and with the central Sefirah of Ze'ir Anpin, which can also be considered the level of the Neshamah soul. And as Tiferet may thus be identified with the higher heart of the Neshamah soul, so may Netzach be identified with the lower human heart of the Ruach soul centered in the gut.[19]

Now if these two names are part of a single framework of reference, and the meaning of one involves the multiplication of two numbers identified with Sefirot, then the same should be true of the other. As forty-two is the product of six times seven, so is seventy-two the product of eight times nine. When one now tries to correlate these numbers with the positions of Sefirot on the Tree of Life Diagram, one gets a less than satisfactory result with the normal numbering, namely Hod and Yesod. Though both may be related to power or potency, these are Sefirot that cannot be naturally associated with the concept of Yichud involved in multiplication. But if we reverse the order, counting not down from Keter but up from Malkhut, then we do get such a natural association of Sefirot, Binah (Imma-Mother) and Chokhmah (Abba-Father), the Sefirot-Partzufim whose upper union represents the completion of the Tikkun. If the unification of Netzach and Tiferet can be understood to represent the integration of the double heart, the unification of Binah (Understanding) and Chokhmah (Wisdom) would represent the integration of the double mind. This is most appropriate since the heart is the instrument of prayer as the mind is the instrument of meditation. As prayer can accomplish the vertical union of the upper and lower centers of feeling located in the upper and lower torso, so can meditation add the horizontal union of understanding with wisdom, the mental faculties located in the left and right brain hemispheres. It is such a meditative integration and focusing of mental faculties that may well be associated, as Abulafia appears to suggest, with prophecy.

The way of numbering the Sefirot just adopted, going down with reference to prayer and up with reference to meditation, can be taken to reflect the complementary natures of these dual practices. As we will see in chapter 4, prayer involves a downward movement of the divine into the human heart, and we can now say that meditation involves an upward movement of man to spiritual mastery. These dual movements may also be seen in the prime Jewish symbol of the Star of David, the descending triangle representing the direction of divine concern and the ascending triangle the direction of human spiritual growth.

Though the association of these two number-defined and unpronounceable divine names with the Sefirot of the Tree of Life Diagram may not have extended as far back as the first records of these names, it would have been possible by the time of Abulafia, and it is certainly

available for such a current kabbalistic interpretation of the significance of these names as I have attempted here. This interpretation
supports the understanding that the double practice of prayer and
meditation can effect a further unification of the integrated heart and
mind into a pattern of spiritual response in which each has its necessary part to play. With this understanding, we can now turn to a consideration of the Sh'ma, the core of Jewish prayer, which will develop
a simplified form of this prayer that can be used to introduce, and so
bring within the sanctity of Torah, the kabbalistic meditative practice
to be later developed in this chapter.

The Sh'ma

The high point of Jewish spirituality for both weekdays and the Sabbath is the saying of the Sh'ma, the only mode of ritual prayer commanded in the Torah. As will be shown in chapter 4, the tradition of
liturgical prayer incorporating the Sh'ma goes as far back as the liturgy developed by the priests for the prayer services they held within
the Temple as an adjunct to the ritual sacrifices. As cited in Mishnah
Tamid 5:1, the commanded twice-daily recitation of the Sh'ma had
taken a particular form in the Temple prayer services marked by two
degrees of expansion. The Sh'ma proper was extended to include "paragraphs" taken from three separate portions of the Torah: Deuteronomy
6:4–9; Deuteronomy 11:13–21; and Numbers 15:37–41. And these
three "paragraphs" of the Sh'ma were incorporated into a surrounding liturgy of benedictions for both the morning and evening prayer
services. The further expansion of the liturgy over time by the rabbis
is given in the Siddur, the prayer book used for both synagogue and
private worship. Indeed, it is the recitation of the Sh'ma within these
services that gives them the sanction and power of Torah. Since it
has become traditional in Orthodox practice to "Daven" the evening
service right after sundown as a quasi-continuation of the afternoon
service normally performed just before sundown, many halakhically
observant Jews will also say the simple three paragraphs of the Sh'ma
a third time just before retiring to ensure strict conformity to the rules
for saying the Sh'ma prescribed in Deuteronomy 6:7: "when thou liest
down, and when thou risest up." While this method of observing the
Torah commandment for ritual prayer has certainly been successful

for millennia in the sanctification of Israel as a holy nation unto God
and of its people into empowered priests, I would like to suggest an
additional way of saying the Sh'ma that may release its power for those
not as skillful in traditional observance. As with the later suggestions
regarding the Sabbath, this will involve a return to the text in accordance with the divine instruction for its interpretation: "The word is
very nigh unto thee, in thy mouth, and in thy heart, that thou mayest
do it" (Deut. 30:14).

Let us begin by studying the Sh'ma in its context: Deuteronomy
6:4–9, which is traditionally considered its "first paragraph":

4 Hear, O Israel: The Lord our God is one Lord:
5 And thou shalt love the Lord thy God with all thine heart, and
with all thy soul, and with all thy might.
6 And these words, which I command thee this day, shall be in
thine heart:
7 And thou shalt teach them diligently unto thy children, and
shalt talk of them when thou sittest in thine house, and when
thou walkest by the way, and when thou liest down, and when
thou risest up.
8 And thou shalt bind them for a sign upon thine hand, and they
shall be as frontlets between thine eyes.
9 And thou shalt write them upon the posts of thy house, and on
thy gates.

It becomes immediately clear upon studying the text that verses 6–9
are instructions for the proper observance of what was given in verses
4–5, "these words" as defined in verse 6. Verses 6, 8, and 9 tell us
where the words in verses 4–5 should be put: in the heart (v. 6), in the
tefillin (v. 8), and in the *mezuzah* (9). Verse 7 distinguishes the times
and locations where saying of the Sh'ma is appropriate. It commands
us to teach the words of verses 4–5 to our children and to say them
when we are lying down and rising up—the times of our devotions—
whether we are sitting meditatively at home or walking meditatively
in the divine Way, whether our devotions are in the passive or the
active mode, of the Sabbath or the weekdays.[20]

The text seems to stipulate that it is specifically verses 4–5 that
must be said at the prescribed times, a stipulation that differs from

traditional practice in two regards. Instead of either the whole of the Siddur service or a minimum of the Three Paragraph Sh'ma, it restricts the content of the prayer to only two verses, and it does not contain the extra line that has traditionally been inserted between verses 4 and 5 in the Siddur: "Blessed be the name of his glorious majesty forever and ever." Further, it gives verse 5 a force almost equal to that of verse 4, the quintessential affirmation of the divine unity or unification. That the Sh'ma was once understood to comprise just these two verses and that the second of these verses was recognized to have enormous spiritual importance is shown in the words of Jesus:

> And Jesus answered him, The first of all the commandments is Hear, O Israel, the Lord our God is one Lord: And thou shalt love the Lord thy God with all thy heart, and with all thy soul, and with all thy mind, and with all thy strength: this is the first commandment. (Mark 12:29–30)

Jesus was presumably not the only Jewish leader who preached observance of the Sh'ma in its strictest sense, one that would limit it to just verses 4–5 and that recognized the importance of verse 5.

It has become traditional to give special importance to the saying of verse 4, which begins with the word *Sh'ma*, and its words are often held longer, whether said or sung to a traditional melody. But it has not been recognized that the words of verse 5 have a special formulaic quality in Hebrew, forming five rhyming lines. Understanding the structure of verse 5 can help us to formulate a new way of delivering both verses 4 and 5 by which they can become ritually empowered to transmit holiness. Verse 5 can be broken down into the following five rhyming phrases:

Ve-ah-hav-ta	*And you shall love*
Et A-do-nai E-lo-he-kha	*The Lord your God*
Be khol le-va-ve-kha	*With all your heart*
Uh ve-khol naf-she-kha	*And with all your soul*
Uh ve-khol me-o-de-kha	*And with all your might*

What is most interesting about these five phrases concerned with the loving of God is that they each end with the sound "ah," a sound that will be shown in chapter 4 to have a special resonance with the heart.[21] It would thus seem that this second verse of the Sh'ma contains a power to open the heart to the divine when properly delivered and that perhaps it was for this reason its twice-daily performance was commanded.

If the opening of the heart to God is to be aided by producing the "ah" sound in the twice-daily repetition of what might be called "the second line of the Sh'ma," then it would seem that the best way to let the "ah" frequency affect the heart, to which it is in special attunement, is to allow this sound to resonate through the body. This can be accomplished by taking a full breath for each of the five phrases and chanting the phrases so that the last "ah" sound in each is drawn out for as long as possible. This method of delivering the second line is in keeping with one traditional way of delivering the first line of the Sh'ma, which is to draw out the final vowel of each of its six words, taking care to pronounce the final consonant of the last word at the close:

Sh'ma Yisrael Adonai Eloheinu Adonai echad.

In this method of delivering the two lines of the Sh'ma, one would take a complete breath for each of the six words of the first line and a complete breath for each of the five phrases of the second line, eleven full breaths in all.[22]

There are two particularly effective ways of producing the six assorted vowel sounds of the first line (ah, eh, eye, oo, eye, aw) and the five "ah" sounds of the second line. The first is to chant the six words and five phrases containing them on a low monotone, as in Zen chanting, drawing out each of the last vowel sounds. The second is to sing them in the same drawn-out fashion, though melodically. For the first line there already is a famous melody. As there is no traditional melody just for the second line, I would like to offer a new melodic setting for its words. Before doing this, however, it is necessary to consider the status of the second and third paragraphs of the Sh'ma in relation to such daily practice.

The second paragraph, as contained in Deuteronomy 11:13–21, would also seem to specify twice-daily repetition of "these my words" (11:18), the words given in verses 13–17. But the operative instruction given in verse 11:19 differs significantly from that given in verse 6:7 of the first paragraph. This difference is masked in the King James Version for the first portion of these verses:

> And thou shalt teach them diligently unto thy children, and shalt talk of them when . . . (Deut. 6:7)

> And ye shall teach them your children, speaking of them when . . . (Deut. 11:19)

The more accurate rendering is given in the Aryeh Kaplan translation,[23] which preserves the crucial difference in the verb forms related to speaking:

> Teach them to your children and speak of them when. . . (Deut. 6:7)

> Teach your children to speak of them, when . . . (Deut. 11:19)

In verse 6:7 the significant word used is *vedibbarta*, meaning "and you shall speak," while in verse 11:19 it is *ledabber*, the infinitive "to speak." Now if you are to teach your children to speak the words given in verses 11:13–17, on a logic paralleling that for the first paragraph that reduces the speaking portion to verses 6:4–5, then you would be doing this teaching during the times specified for saying the Sh'ma, in this interpretation just the aforementioned two verses of chapter 6. That is, you would be teaching them the meaning of the special Providence attending obedience to the commandments by your own daily repetition of the two lines of the Sh'ma when lying down and getting up. The second paragraph does not, then, stipulate any additional words that you are to say at these times, just that you are to set an example of the rewards of obedience to the commandments by the quality of spirit you develop through twice-daily repetition of the Two-Line Sh'ma. Nonetheless, I would like to suggest the addition of the first word of this second paragraph to the two lines from chapter 6 in token of the stated importance of this chapter 11 portion to daily practice and in virtue of its unique character.

This first word is *vehayah*. Composed of the same letters as the

Tetragrammaton but in a different order, not YHVH but VHYH, it is usually translated in the King James Version as "and it shall come to pass." But it is more than this. As a transposed form of the Tetragrammaton, *vehayah* cannot be considered to be just a grammatical signifier of future eventualities; it names the force through which all things come to pass, the empowering force that can translate will into manifestation. The power of the word *vehayah* to bring the divine unity into manifestation is supported by a most significant passage in which it is juxtaposed to the Tetragrammaton. This is in the crowning epiphany of Moses:

> And he said, I will make all my goodness pass before thee, and I will proclaim the name of the Lord [YHVH] before thee; and will be gracious to whom I will be gracious, and will shew mercy on whom I will shew mercy. And he said, Thou canst not see my face: for there shall no man see me, and live. And the Lord [YHVH] said, Behold, there is a place by me, and thou shalt stand upon a rock: And it shall come to pass [VHYH], while my glory passeth by, that I will put thee in a cleft of the rock, and will cover thee with my hand while I pass by: And I will take away mine hand, and thou shalt see my back parts: but my face shall not be seen. (Ex. 33:19–23)

The parallelism in God's first statement seems to equate the passage of His goodness before Moses with the proclamation of the divine Name. This goodness is then defined as double aspected, with a front that cannot be seen and a back that can. An interesting interpretation of these two aspects is given in the translation by Aryeh Kaplan, which is here nonliteral:

> I will then remove My protective power, and you will have a vision of what follows from My existence. My essence itself, however, will not be seen. (Ex. 33:23)[24]

In this interpretation the "face" (*panim*) is understood to refer to the nonmanifest "essence" of the divine, the "back parts" (*achorim*) to what "follows" from this, the existential, manifesting form of the divine in the process of time, in what "shall come to pass," (*vehayah*). Thus the form of the name that Moses sees through "a cleft in the rock" would seem to be not YHVH but VHYH, not the forward but the reversed arrangement of the divine letters, through which all the glory of the creative power can pass.

I would argue that in most biblical passages where it is used, *vehayah* should not be translated but taken as a noun denoting some relationship to the divine power of manifestation, as in the epiphany of Moses where it can be taken to activate and inform the very process of protected revelation that it introduces. For analysis of its biblical contexts from this perspective strongly suggests that *vehayah* was a magical word widely used throughout the Bible to focus the divine power into manifestation, for *influencing* what shall come to pass.

I hope that this new understanding of *vehayah* can reclaim it as an apparently potent spiritual tool from the natural oblivion or forced suppression to which it has been subject. Though the use of *vehayah* as a power word may well have been suppressed as part of one of the many drives against magical practices that has marked the long history of Judaism, as well as other religious traditions, the practice itself has either survived or returned in another form. It is a common practice in Orthodox circles to reinforce one's pious intentions by adding the phrase "Barukh ha-Shem," meaning "Blessed be the Name." And it may well be that just as a pious fence was built around the pronunciation of the Tetragrammaton by substituting the term *Adonai*, the Lord, so the same may have been the case with pronunciation of the potent power word *vehayah*. But since there is no law or statute, written or oral, specifically condemning use of *vehayah* as a power word, and since it can be demonstrated to have been in general use as such throughout all the books of the Hebrew Bible, including its spectacular use in connection with the most powerful of biblical figures, Moses (Ex. 17:11) and Elijah (I Kings 18:24), there seems no reason not to attempt to tap the power of this word once more as an aid to spiritual development both of one's self and the world.

In view of the potential importance of this new understanding of *vehayah*, a word used throughout the Hebrew Bible, I have added an appendix to this work that gives a comprehensive treatment of its always significant usage. This analysis also proves to be a survey of the major levels of spiritual empowerment that appear in the Bible—those utilizing the four means of prayer, covenant, sacrifice, and the transcendent power of the spiritual master or Tzaddik. As such it can also provide a culminating vision of that spirituality which is both past and future. This appendix should not only make a contribution to biblical studies but suggest various ways in which *vehayah* may be used once more as a tool of spiritual empowerment to access the vital current of spiritual power animating the Jewish religious tradition.

One such usage is as a conclusion to the Two-Line Sh'ma, where it provides, at the very least, a benediction much like Amen to the increased capacity to love God, at once commanded and given through the Sh'ma. Used as a reference to the second paragraph of the Three-Paragraph Sh'ma, it can draw its further power into the two line recitation, ensuring that obedience to the commandments will bring the promised rain and inspire the same obedience in one's children. A close reading of Deuteronomy 11:13 shows, moreover, that all the promised blessings will come from a proper harkening to the commandments specifically given in the second line of the Sh'ma:

> And it shall come to pass [VHYH], if ye shall hearken diligently unto my commandments which I command you this day, to love the Lord your God, and to serve him with all your heart and with all your soul, That I will give you the rain of your land in his due season. . . . (Deut. 11:13–14)

Not only does *vehayah* introduce the second paragraph of the Sh'ma but it also introduces the operative section of its third paragraph, which states the purpose of the *tzitzit* (fringes):

> And it shall be [VHYH] unto you for a fringe, that ye may look upon it, and remember all the commandments of the Lord, and do them; and that ye seek not after your own heart and your own eyes, after which ye use to go a whoring: That ye may remember, and do all my commandments, and be holy unto your God. (Num. 15:39–40)

It should be pointed out that the full third paragraph, Numbers 15:37–41, makes no reference to daily repetition of any words but rather commands the wearing of the *tzitzit* as an aid to remembering the commandments and being holy. It has been traditional to wear a *tallit* (prayer shawl) containing such ritual fringes while saying the Sh'ma, and this is a practice it is well to continue even if the instruc-

tions for wearing them are only alluded to at this time in the concluding *vehayah*. Not only would this be a fitting tribute to the traditional
third paragraph of the Sh'ma in the nontraditional mode of delivering it being developed here, but it would add an extra ritual power to
the opening and redirection of the heart toward which repetition of
the Sh'ma is also directed. Wrapping oneself in a prayer shawl while
chanting divine names or words is a recognized method in all spiritual
traditions for concentrating and amplifying the spiritual and physical
resonances produced through chanting. It provides an enclosure that
transforms any place of sitting, of meditation, into a sacred space, a
Temple. Looking at the fringes, especially when praying, is a special
ritual means, like the Sabbath itself, for the transmission of holiness.

Adding v*ehayah* to the Two-Line Sh'ma would increase its length
by another full breath, also ending with the "ah" heart sound, for a
total of twelve full breaths. Constituting what might be called the
"third line of the Sh'ma," it transforms the nature of the Tetragrammaton given in the first line, bringing its transcendent unity into
the manifesting process of time, into what "shall come to pass." Thus
the addition of *vehayah* to the Two-Line Sh'ma or to any prayer or
verbal affirmation is more than just a benediction; it adds the divine
power of manifestation. In the case of the Sh'ma, it empowers the will
to reach a true understanding and love of God. Because of its unique
manifesting power, *vehayah* will also be used in the Master Meditation
that will close this chapter, and it will be an essential feature of the
attunement process that will link the reformulated Sh'ma to this guided
Master Meditation.

We have just seen that use of the prayer shawl while chanting the
Sh'ma is a ritual means for the transmission of holiness, for being "holy
unto your God" (Num. 15:40), that is, for turning the soul from Nefesh
to Ruach consciousness. With this we come to a matter of deep im-
port to the meaning of the Sh'ma. If we turn again to the Hebrew of
the Two-Line Sh'ma, two points are of great significance. The first is
the shift from *Eloheinu* (our God) in verse 4 to *Elohekha* (your God) in
verse 5. The second is the restriction of the soul reference in verse 5,
nafshekha (your soul), to the Nefesh soul level. The implication of
these two factors is that the speaker and the listener of these words are
not the same even though one person is performing both activities.
And, indeed, the Sh'ma has always been a sounded form of prayer in

which hearing the words is as important as producing them vocally. A resolution of the apparent paradox between the first person plural speaker and the second person listener may lie in the definition of the listener as the Nefesh soul. For if the speaker can be distinguished from the Nefesh soul as a superior spiritual guide and yet identified with the Nefesh in worship of a God beyond both, this speaker would seem to have a special correspondence to the Ruach soul—the Ruach and not the Neshamah since the latter would be identifiable as the divine form of both the Nefesh and Ruach soul levels.

It follows, then, that in the Sh'ma it is one's higher Ruach soul that is calling upon one's innate Nefesh soul to "hear," to move from the particularizing perceptions of sight to the harmonizing perceptions of sound, to rise to that ultimate perception of the unity within all things by which they are related. This higher soul calls for a radical attunement of Nefesh consciousness to the subtle energies vibrating throughout its field in accordance with the harmonic laws of sound. Thus it is most important that the sound element of the Sh'ma be skillfully performed to produce the proper quality of resonance that can purify the bodily senses of their grossness and give them a crystalline conductivity. For it is through such conductivity that the subtle impressions arising from the all-containing reservoir of cosmic experience can convey their information to the elevated individual consciousness.

In the preceding pages, I have suggested how the Sh'ma may be skillfully performed so that it becomes ritually empowered to transmit the original energy of the Mosaic Law while still drawing upon the accumulated additional energy of the priestly and rabbinical traditions. We saw that the power of the Sh'ma is contained in the two verses proclaiming the divine unity and commanding Israel's whole-hearted love of God. And we saw that this is all that need be said when lying down and rising up but that elements from the traditional second and third paragraphs of the Sh'ma might be added because of their special capacity to amplify the essential power of the Two-Line Sh'ma: adding the first word of the second paragraph to conclude the sounded Sh'ma and continuing the traditional wearing of the ritual garment commanded in the third paragraph while the Sh'ma is chanted or sung.

We come finally to the musical setting of the Sh'ma in the form I have been suggesting:

Figure 2. "The Three Line Sh'ma"
With Additional Music by Leonora Leet

In the above musical setting the first line is given with its traditional melody and the remainder with a melody of my own composition, one whose fermata signs above the "ah" sounds indicate that these sounds should be prolonged. But whether one uses this melody for performance of the Sh'ma or prefers to chant it in a low monotone, it is important to try to produce the purest of tones, listening as well to any possible overtones that may be thus produced. The production of such tones in conjunction with the precisely specified vowel sounds and the sacred words in which they are contained has a power to purify the body and lift the consciousness regardless of the understanding with which one says them. But one can add to this power by using various Kavanot— the "mystical intentions" with which the saying can be informed.

We have already considered one such Kavanah, that through which the sounding of the Sh'ma can be understood to be produced by the Ruach level of one's soul and the hearing by the Nefesh level. Another still more profound involves a triple unification of the immanent and transcendent forms of the divine with the highest form of the praying soul. Though this meaning will be more fully developed in the later fourth chapter on prayer, a brief summary is pertinent here. The concept of such a triple unification builds upon the previously noted Zoharic recognition that the unity proclaimed in the Sh'ma really signifies a unification (Yichud) of the divine feminine immanence (YHVH Eloheinu) with the divine masculine transcendence (YHVH). I now propose to add a third member to this divine unification. This is the soul's own highest form as a member of the supernal Community of Israel whose realization in the very process of unifying the immanent and transcendent aspects of the divine is the true purpose and reward of mystical prayer. Thus the Sh'ma both means, and is a means of achieving, that threefold divine unification of the ideal Community of Israel with the divine immanence and divine transcendence revealed in the following partial translation of the Sh'ma:

Hear: Israel, YHVH Eloheinu, [and] YHVH [are] one.

As it is best to defer further consideration of this deepest Kavanah to the fuller treatment of Jewish prayer in the fourth chapter, I will only say here that it can certainly be utilized in the minimal form of the Sh'ma defined here. But I would now like to suggest an additional

Kavanah practice involving the Tree of Life Diagram that can be used with the extended attunement prelude to the Master Meditation to be developed in the next section. Though this should normally be a morning practice, one can also choose to extend the evening Sh'ma with this attunement procedure without continuing past it to the more active phase of the Master Meditation, thereby further resonating and relaxing the body as a preparation for sleep. In the next section we will see how the biblical Sh'ma can be joined with a kabbalistic meditation technique derived from the *Sefer Yetzirah*.

A Kabbalistic Attunement

Just as kabbalistic cosmology has its source in the *Sefer Yetzirah*, so can a source for kabbalistic meditation be found there. Such a meditative practice would appear to be encoded in the first chapter of the *Sefer Yetzirah*, that which defines the first ten numbers, named "Sefirot Belimah." Through these definitions the *Sefer Yetzirah* can be understood to explain not only how God created Adam but also how man can meditatively recreate himself in the divine image. The names given to the first four of these Sefirot numbers are: Ruach Elohim Chayyim (Breath of the Living God), Ruach me-Ruach (Breath from Breath), Mayyim me-Ruach (Water from Breath) and Esh mi-Mayyim (Fire from Water). The final six Sefirot are identified with the six directions: Up, Down, Forward, Back, Right, and Left. In the third chapter of the *Sefer Yetzirah* the elements identified with the first four Sefirot are further associated with the three "mother letters" *aleph, mem,* and *shin.* These are the functions through which the universe was created and which it continues to manifest in all its aspects, including the three psychic centers of the soul. *Aleph* is associated with the element of breath or air and with the principle of mediation centered in the chest, both of which can be related to the second stage, Ruach me-Ruach. *Mem* is similarly associated with the element of water centered in the lower torso, and can be related to Mayyim me-Ruach. *Shin* is assciated with the element of fire centered in the head, and can be related to Esh mi-Mayyim. We can thus identify the elements in the first four Sefirot names with psychic centers in the subtle body of man on the basis of the associations of the mother letters: Ruach me-Ruach with the air and the chest of *aleph*, Mayyim me-Ruach with the water and lower torso of *mem*, and Esh mi-Mayyim with the fire and head of *shin*. Once we have done this it becomes possible to read verses 9–12 of the first chapter as providing hidden instructions for a meditative technique combining mantra with special breathing.

The ninth verse gives the name of the first Sefirah as Ruach Elohim Chayyim and identifies this divine name with the Ruach ha-Kodesh, the Holy Spirit. The meditator begins, then, inspired like Adam with that divine breath by which he becomes a "living soul" (Nefesh Chayyah) and silently pronounces the divine name Ruach Elohim Chayyim. The breath is then slowly exhaled from the chest while silently repeating Ruach me-Ruach, an exhalation completed with an abdominal contraction expelling the last of the breath with the silent words Mayyim me-Ruach. A full new breath is now inhaled to the head, accompanied by silent repetition of Esh mi-Mayyim. The breath is then held for the divine influx through the crown, which reinspires the consciousness with the Holy Spirit as the empowering name Ruach Elohim Chayyim is again silently repeated. As this breathing pattern becomes a continuous flow, the mantralike names of the first four Sefirot begin to form a rhythmic and rhyming pattern:

> *Ruach me-Ruach*
> *Mayyim me-Ruach*
> *Esh mi-Mayyim*
> *Ruach Elohim Chayyim*

At a point to be later defined, when the full influx has occurred, the procedure can be simplified, the breath becoming shallower and accompanied only by silent repetition of the essential mantra containing the divine name. One method of relating breath to mantra would be to inhale the breath while repeating Ruach, hold the breath to Elohim, and exhale it without abdominal contraction to Chayyim. While this shallower breathing is regulated by the silent, rhythmic repetition of the divine name Ruach Elohim Chayyim, a visual unification (Yichud) can also be practiced based upon the cube whose psychic construction is defined by the last six of the Sefirot numbers. Where the first four Sefirot become a means of reestablishing contact with one's creative source and recreating one's three psychic centers, the last six Sefirot become a means of building one's spiritual body.

Before pursuing the nature of this later meditative work, we should return to the pattern of complete breathing defined by the first four Sefirot of the *Sefer Yetzirah* and see how it can be related to the performance of the Sh'ma with which such kabbalistic meditation should properly begin.

In the previous section, a method of performing the Sh'ma was developed based upon the taking of twelve complete breaths. But since the Sh'ma contains the holiest of the divine names, the Tetragrammaton, it seems possible to draw its power more fully into the attunement process by making use of its numerical value (Gematria), twenty-six, also the value of *vehayah*. This number is formed by adding up the numerical equivalent of each of its four letters as they appear in the Hebrew alphabet: 10 for *yod*, 5 for *hey*, 6 for *vav*, and 5 again for *hey*. Increasing the number of attunement breaths from twelve to twenty-six, the number of the Holy Name, could be accomplished by following the twelve-breath Sh'ma with fourteen repetitions of the complete four-part *Sefer Yetzirah* breath-mantra cycle. This would have the further effect of unifying the Holy Name with that divine name most suitable for meditative breathing, Ruach Elohim Chayyim (Breath of the Living God), the ultimate kabbalistic mantra of the *Sefer Yetzirah*.

But an additional Kavanah, can be introduced into this attunement process by reconceiving the fourteen repetitions of the *Sefer Yetzirah* breath-mantra cycle in terms of a further relationship of both the twelve- and fourteen-breath divisions of this attunement to the *Sefer Yetzirah*. We have thus far been largely concerned with its first chapter, which defines the ten basic numbers. But the remainder of this short book is devoted to defining the structure and power of the twenty-two letters of the Hebrew alphabet, of which the main divisions are into the twelve single letters and the seven double letters (those letters like *bet/vet* that have a different pronunciation when a dot is added to them). The third division of the three mother letters—*aleph*, *mem*, and *shin*—we will return to shortly. But it is clear that the main divisions can be related to the breath numbers thus far defined by identifying the twelve-breath Sh'ma with the twelve single letters and by regarding the fourteen-breath continuation beyond it as consisting of the seven double breaths that can be identified with the seven double letters.

Once one conceives of the continuation to the Sh'ma in terms of seven double breaths, one can begin to see the whole of the twenty-six breath attunement process in a new light. For the number seven is clearly to be associated with the days of the week, and these with the creation. Further, the seven days, both of the week and of creation, have been kabbalistically associated with the lower seven Sefirot of the Tree of Life Diagram. Now if these seven double breaths are to be associated with the lower seven Sefirot of the Tree, the question arises whether the Sh'ma itself can be correlated with the upper three Sefirot and the Partzufim they also represent, as reviewed at the beginning of this chapter. I believe it can.

Such a correlation can best be made not in terms of the twelve-breath formula I have devised but of its division into three lines. Thus the essential first line of the Sh'ma, traditionally translated as "Hear, O Israel, the Lord our God is one Lord," can be correlated with Keter, the second line with Chokhmah, and the one-word added third line, *vehayah*, with Binah. Support for such a correlation can be found in the opening words of the *Etz Chayyim*, the central work of the Lurianic Kabbalah written by Chaim Vital:

> When it arose in His will, blessed be His name, to create the world in order to do good to those He created, and that they should be able to recognize His greatness and to merit being a chariot of the supernal to be attached to Him, the Blessed One, He emanated one point, which included ten, and they are the ten Sefirot of the points that were in one vessel, and they were invisible. . . . And know that when the ten dots mentioned above spread out, Keter was able to absorb this light but Abba and Imma were not equal because Abba received the light face-to-face from Keter and he had within him the ability to absorb the light but Binah only received the light from Chokhmah back-to-back because she could not absorb it.[25]

In Luria's cosmology, it is only Keter that is able to accept the power of the divine unity directly and incorporate its light, a capacity by which Keter may be associated with the proclamation of the divine unity in the first line of the Sh'ma. The face-to-face relationship of Chokhmah, or Abba (Father), to Keter is, moreover, precisely the proper position for the love commanded in the second line of the Sh'ma: "And thou shalt love the Lord thy God with all thine heart, and with all thy soul, and with all thy might." Finally, the back-to-back position of Binah, or Imma (Mother), to Chokhmah is also precisely that which can be correlated with *vehayah*, "and it shall come to pass," the forward direction of the infinite light into the process of cosmic creation, a process to be carried out through the seven lower Sefirot from Chesed to Malkhut and in the days of creation that they may be individually said to inform.

With such an understanding, one can now perform the twenty-six-breath attunement process with a Kavanah by which one's consciousness is enabled to reenact the whole process of its creation, from the divine unity to the first Sabbath, in a descent through the ten Sefirot of the Tree of Life Diagram. In the first six breaths of the first line, the consciousness would be placed in the supernal unity of Keter, the Crown. During the next five breaths of the second line, the consciousness would be drawn from the crown of the head to Chokhmah, Wisdom, a Sefirah that may be associated with the right hemisphere of the brain and which expresses the expansive power of the supernal love. During the final twelfth breath of the added word *vehayah*, the consciousness would move to Binah, Understanding, that may be associated with the left hemisphere of the brain, the agency of manifestation. Thus Binah, the cosmic mother, is also understood to contain the seven lower Sefirot within her, which descend from her in seven streams. The following seven double breaths, during which the four-part *Sefer Yetzirah* mantra cycle is silently repeated, may be considered as manifesting the creative power of Binah contained in that word *vehayah* whose letters, *vuv-hey-yod-hey*, form a back-to-back transposition of the letters in the Tetragrammaton.

The way in which the fourteen-breath cycles can best be transformed into cycles of seven double breaths would be through alternate hand counting, going first through one four-part cycle marked by the little finger of the right hand, then through one marked by the little finger of the left hand, then two such cycles marked by the right and left ring fingers, and so on through the thumbs and back to the middle fingers.[26] Going through the seven days of creation while engaged in such a form of breath counting produces a totally new understanding of the creation account in Genesis that, once discovered, seems to be part of its intrinsic structure. This is especially true if one further associates the hands doing the counting with the opposite brain hemisphere that controls such hand movements, the right hand being an extension of the left brain and the left hand of the right brain. For in the seven days of creation there also appears to be a division of each day into two stages of the creative process, the first stage being associated with the more contractive, left brain functions, and the second stage with the more expansive, right brain functions. The following chart clarifies and illuminates the connections among these various features.

DAY	SEFIRAH	LEFT BRAIN	RIGHT BRAIN
1	Chesed	Chaos and darkness	Supernal light
2	Gevurah	Firmament to divide the waters	Firmament called Heaven
3	Tiferet	Dry land and seas	Plant life
4	Netzach	Sun	Moon
5	Hod	Fish and fowl	Blessing of them
6	Yesod	Animals	Blessed man
7	Malkhut	Divine rest	Sanctification of the Sabbath

As can be seen, the left brain stages begin in chaos and division, are associated with matter, solar power, and the lower animals, and end in divine inactivity. In contrast, the right brain stages begin with the hidden light, and are later associated with lunar power and the night and continue to be associated with life in its nonanimal forms, man and the plants that are to be his proper food, with blessing and the transmission of holiness. As one goes through the seven double breaths of the mantra cycle, it is well to keep these associations at least in the back of one's mind. When one has completed the twelve chanted or sung breaths and the fourteen breaths of alternate hand counting these twenty-six full breaths should have placed one deeply into a meditative state. If one has accomplished these twenty-six breaths with the Kavanah of Creation, one's imaginative condition at its close will be that of unfallen Adam in the Garden of Eden of the supernal world of Yetzirah. One's meditative task from this point on will be the construction of one's higher soul bodies, thus fulfilling the original divine plan for man's spiritual perfection in an unfallen world.

There is one final correlation that can be made regarding the twelve single and seven double breaths of the attunement process, and that is to the development of these numerical divisions in the *Sefer Yetzirah* itself. Following upon the first chapter definition of the ten basic numbers, chapter 2 distinguishes its three major divisions: the three mother letters, the seven double letters, and the twelve single letters. Chapter 3 defines the three mother letters—*aleph, mem,* and *shin*—that exemplify the cosmic functions of expansive fire *(shin)*, contractive water *(mem)*, and the air that mediates between these opposed forces *(aleph)*. Chapter 4 defines the seven double letters, associating them with "the seven days of creation" (4:12),[27] the seven planets, the "Seven gates in the Soul" (4:12)—which are the two eyes, two ears, two nostrils, and the mouth—seven principles and their inverses, and, most important for our later purposes, the seven extremities—the six directions "and the Holy Palace precisely in the middle [that] upholds them all" (4:3). Chapter 5 defines the twelve single letters, associating them primarily with the twelve astrological signs and months, with the limbs and internal organs, and most important for us with the "twelve diagonal boundaries" (5:1) whose defining directions have puzzled commentators because they appear to describe the edges rather than the diagonals of a cube. Finally, chapter 6 shows how all three groups of letters work together in space, time, and the soul, closing with a reference to Father Abraham and how he was able to use them successfully to achieve the divine revelation and embrace.

We have seen how the twenty-six-breath attunement process just described can be correlated with the basic constituents of creation defined in the *Sefer Yetzirah,* the twelve single breaths with the twelve single letters and the seven double breaths with the seven double letters. But we can now also see how both of these breath groupings may be said to contain the three mother letters. Their elements of breath, water, and fire are contained in the words accompanying the seven double breaths and they can also be related to the three supernal Sefirot associated with the twelve single breaths, Keter with the fire of the infinite light, Binah with the fertile waters of creation, and Chokhmah with the force that mediates the transfer of the limitless light from the hidden source of Keter to the manifesting form of Binah. As can also be seen, the Kavanah of Creation through the Tree of Life Diagram and the whole structure of the attunement process as developed here depend upon the innovative addition of the single word *vehayah* to the Two-Line Sh'ma. The very fact that this addition makes possible the development of such a rich meditative process seems justification enough for its inclusion and suggests something of the power of this word.

Before we turn to the Master Meditation, we should discuss the geometric enigma that the *Sefer Yetzirah* has seemed to contain, since my solution to this enigma will be featured in the manifesting meditation that follows. The *Sefer Yetzirah* has been understood to allude to a cube because of its definition of the six directions of space at the end of its first chapter. It has hitherto proved impossible to explain the exact nature of this construction, however, because the definitions it provides for the twelve diagonals of this cube seem rather to define its twelve edges:

> Twelve Elementals: HV ZCh TY LN SO TzQ. . . . Their measure is the twelve diagonal boundaries: the north-east boundary, the south-east boundary, the upper-east boundary, the lower-east boundary, the upper-north boundary, the lower-north boundary, the south-west boundary, the north-west boundary, the upper-west boundary, the lower-west boundary, the upper-south boundary, the lower-south boundary. They continually spread for ever and ever. They are the arms of the universe.[28]

The solution I would offer is that the "twelve diagonal boundaries" refer not to the edges of a cube but to the edges of its dualing solid, the octahedron, in geometry an intervening means by which the cube can be doubled.

For the octahedron has an upper point, a lower point, and four additional points at the four corners of an intermediate square that can be identified with the four compass points of North, East, South, and West. The directions of these six points allow the octahedron to dual the cube exactly. The six vertices of the octahedron correspond to the six sides of the cube, just as the eight vertices of the cube correspond to the eight triangular sides of the octahedron. The two solids can thus dual each other in the sense that each can exactly contain the other: when the octahedron is within the cube its vertices touch the center of the cube's sides and when the cube is within the octahedron its vertices touch the center of the octahedron's sides. Both solids, however, have twelve edges that can be defined by the same twelve letter names given for the twelve diagonals in the *Sefer Yetzirah*. If these be rearranged to correspond to the on-point form of the octahedron, that of two pyramids meeting at a square, we can then identify the four edges going from the upper point to the intermediate square as UE, US, UW, and UN, the four edges going from the lower point to the intermediate square as LE, LS, LW, and LN, and the four edges of the square as NE, SE, SW, and NW. What is also significant, is that, unlike the right-angled edges of the cube, the edges of the octahedron are all diagonals. They are all also the sides of equilateral triangles, the other sides of which they meet individually at oblique or diagonal angles of sixty degrees. Thus even the edges of the intermediate square, which divides the octahedron into two facing pyramids, are also diagonal sides of triangles and reveal their diagonal nature as soon as the octahedron is turned on another of its points. With this in mind, we should now return to the phrasing of the *Sefer Yetzirah* regarding the twelve single letters: "Their measure is the twelve diagonal boundaries: the north-east boundary, the south-east boundary," etc. The reference here seems clearly to point to the diagonal edges or boundaries of the octahedron. And it suggests that its author was well aware of the octahedron method of enlarging the cube.

The *Sefer Yetzirah* further specifies that these diagonals are infinite: "They continually spread for ever and ever" (5:1). This suggests that it is through the diagonals of the octahedron that the cube of the Adamic spiritual body, whose construction seems to be implied at the end of the first chapter, can expand to its ultimatly infinite size. But since Yetzirah is the two-dimensional cosmic world, the form of the diagram that is suggested, presumably as a meditative aid or mandala, in this Book (Sefer) of Yetzirah should also be two-dimensional. In such a two-dimensional representation, the octahedron will appear as a hexagram within a hexagon and the cube as a Y within such a hexagon. A virtue of plane geometry is that on this level the cube and the octrahedron can thus become interpenetrating. It is the three-dimensional projection of such an interpenetrating cube and octahedron that I would now offer as the solution of the mysterious *Sefer Yetzirah* Diagram in the following Figure 3, which also identifies these interpenetrating forms with the sexually distinguished Partzufim—the cube with Abba and the octahedron with the Imma:

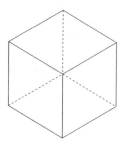 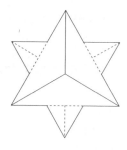 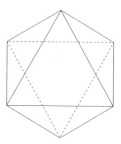

The Cube of Abba   *The Yichud*   *The Octahedron of Imma*

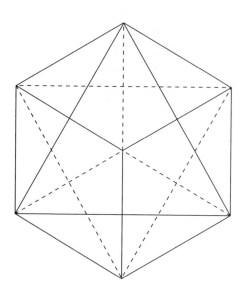

The Sefer Yetzirah Diagram

Figure 3.

Figure 3 also shows the tetrahedron formed by the interpenetration of Abba and Imma within the heart of Arikh Anpin, the hidden form of God in which the Yichud or coupling of Abba and Imma is eternally taking place. This union is understood kabbalistically to be responsible not only for the continuous creation of the cosmos but also for the originally androgynous cosmic child, Ze'ir Anpin, the model for human spiritual perfection.[29] Meditation on this minimal *Sefer Yetzirah* diagram can thus be a means of integrating the masculine and feminine, the right- and left-brained aspects of one's personality, and it is included in the meditation to be given shortly.

After the twenty-six-breath attunement is completed, one should be in a high state of resonant energy and ready to begin the process of creative revisualization that is the essence of Master Meditation. Since the effectiveness of this process depends upon one's capacity for visualization, part of it must be devoted to training the higher Ruach visual center, the "imagination of the heart." Although the major kabbalistic technique for such training has been the visualization of Hebrew letters and the unification of divine names containing them, in what follows I will recommend the visualization of cubes and octahedra in both three- and two-dimensional forms as effective means of improving one's power of visualization while at the same time contributing to the construction of the spiritual bodies that they will be representing throughout the meditation. In addition to the two-dimensional forms just given, it is good before beginning the meditation to have a clear idea of the form of the three-dimensional octrahedron and of its spatial relationship to the cube. As recently explained, these two solids are said to be dualing because each can exactly contain the other: The six points of the octahedron touch the center of the six faces of the cube, and the twelve points or vertices of the cube touch the center of the twelve faces of the octahedron. The octahedron is best pictured as two pyramids joined together at their square bases; it is composed of eight equilateral triangles, four above and four below, meeting at a square. One should also be familiar with the form of the three letters in the Tetragrammaton and the three mother letters since the infinite cube to be visualized will be sealed by these letters, as specified in the *Sefer Yetzirah*, which has been both source and inspiration for the meditation shortly to be given. To aid this visualization, the following Hebrew letters are here reproduced:

ʾ *(yod)*, הֵ *(hey)*, וֹ *(vav)*, אֵ *(aleph)*, מִ *(mem)*, שֵׁ *(shin)*. After these visualizations of geometric forms and Hebrew letters, the meditation will move into its main phase with forms of visualizations and affirmations that continue the techniques of meditation specified in the classic kabbalistic texts studied earlier. Each affirmation will conclude with the biblical power word *vehayah*, which can strengthen and channel the manifesting power of these affirmations, as it can also be added to every good wish and carry every prayer into the manifesting work of time.

In the following section, the meditator will be taken through four levels of higher consciousness in a guided meditation addressed directly to the meditator. This meditation is performed most effectively after the process of attunement outlined earlier, which not only should ensure the Shefa, the divine influx of energy, but also bring the meditator imaginatively to the point of his or her original creation in unfallen Eden. From this point the following guided meditation will take the meditator forward to his or her recreation as a divine personality. The spiritual progress through this meditation may be said to have four stages. In the twenty-six-breath attunement process, one is still functioning from the Nefesh soul, the primary function of this attunement being to lift the Nefesh soul up to the Ruach level. In the subsequent work of geometric soul-body construction and healing visualizations, the Ruach soul becomes activated but still functions in conjunction with a continuing Nefesh presence as long as its focus is on the individual. The consciousness then moves fully into the Ruach soul-body with the shift to relational vision, and one begins to experience as well the emerging presence of the Neshamah soul in the increase of information being filtered down. This presence continues to grow until it finally becomes dominant in the last phase of the meditation, a phase filled with the element of its light.

The Master Meditation

Breathe softly, regulating your breath with the mantra *Ruach Elohim Chayyim* silently pronounced so that you breathe in with the word for breath, *Ruach*, hold the breath for the divine name *Elohim*, and exhale the breath to *Chayyim*, the word for the living process made possible through the Ruach Elohim Chayyim, the Breath of the Living

God. As you feel yourself filled by the divine breath, begin to build
the permanent spiritual body of your Nefesh soul, visualizing it in the
form of a cube of light. First imagine its upper plane above your head,
then its lower plane below your feet or cushion, then fit into them the
planes in front of you, behind you, to your right, and to your left. As
you experience yourself expanded into this resonant, crystalline body
of light, imagine that the cube is lifting you a few feet into the air.
Now imagine the octahedron, the visualized form of your Ruach spiritual body, and see it enclose the cube in which you are seated, the
upper pyramid coming down to join with the inverted pyramid rising
to meet it, whose lower point may be imagined as just touching the
floor. Visualize all the triangles of the octahedron and be careful that
all eight vertices of your cube are exactly touching their centers before finally clamping the two pyramids together. As you begin to feel
the concentrated force of this pyramid power, let it lift you out of your
earthly space, guiding your octahedron chariot forward through your
nearest window and swiftly up to the center of the galaxy. In this star-
lit darkness of outer space, construct the divine spiritual body of your
Neshamah soul. From the Or Ein Sof, the Limitless Light, draw down
the upper plane of your infinite cubic body, seeing it as composed of
the same light as that which extends beyond it to infinity and sealing
it to the upper point of your Ruach soul body with the letter yod. You
should draw this light down while inhaling your breath to the word
Ruach, seal it with the yod while holding the breath to the word Elohim,
and then direct this light down through the yod point of your octahedron Ruach body into your Nefesh and physical bodies while exhal-
ing the breath to the word Chayyim, repeating this breathing rhythm
for all six directions. From the lower direction, draw the lower plane
of your body of Limitless Light, sealing it to the lower point of your
octahedron body with the letter aleph. From the forward direction,
draw the forward plane of your Neshamah body so that it fills the
extent between your upper and lower planes and seal it to the forward
point of your octahedron body with the letter hey. Follow the same
procedure for the rear plane of the forming infinite cube and seal it to
the rear point of your octahedron Ruach body with the letter mem.
Finally, draw the right and left planes to complete the cubic form of
the Neshamah soul body, the right plane first being sealed to the right
point of the octahedron body with the letter vav, and the left plane

lastly sealed to the octahedron's left point with the letter *shin*.

With your consciousness now centered within the layered light of your three progressively higher soul bodies and extending out through them to the ends of the universe, draw a beam of light down from the Limitless Light through the *yod* and into your crown until it reaches your heart, bringing this light as well into your heart through the *hey* and chest and the *vav* and right side. Let the force of this light build until you feel it shatter your heart, throwing off the shackles of your restrictive ego so that your heart can become a conduit between the transcendent power of the divine name and the cosmic functions through which its purposes may come to pass. Now feel the androgynous power of the divine unity flowing through you from the *yod* above to provide the balancing force for the *aleph* below, the feminine power of the *hey* being similarly transformed through you into the contractive function of the *mem* as is the masculine power of the *vav* into the expansive function of the *shin*. Feel and understand that it is only through this higher development of your heart that the transcendent wisdom and power can be translated into cosmic form.

As the infinite power streams through you from the letters of the transcendent Name to the mother letters of the cosmic functions, a unification, Yichud, of these letters is accomplished in your heart, the transcendent becoming enclothed in the cosmic, the unspeakable Name in works of the imagination. It is with this new imagination of the heart that the next level of spiritual work should now be undertaken. To begin the process of creative revisualization that marks the higher levels of Ruach spiritual work, first focus your visual imagination in your heart center and take a two-dimensional cross-section picture of your higher soul bodies from this vantage point. You will see the heart-level square of your Nefesh spiritual body within the diagonal square of your Ruach spiritual body, the plane at which the upper and lower pyramids of the octahedron meet, within the straight square of the Neshamah spiritual body parallel to that of the Nefesh body.

Once you are able to visualize this two-dimensional cross section of your three subtle bodies spread out around you at your physical heart level, take this image and bring it up to your inner eye, projecting it forward as a reduced image containing the twelve lines of light that form these three squares, enclosed one within the other with the middle square being at a diagonal angle to the other two. The next step in the process is to reduce these twelve discrete lines to a small ball of light and then revisualize the original image as a three-dimensional projection. First take six of the lines of light out of this ball of light and arrange them as an on-point hexagon. Next take three additional lines of light from the ball and arrange them in a Y-shape whose points meet alternate points of the hexagon, in this way forming an orthogonal projection of a cube. To this cube add the infinite diagonals of the inverted triangle formed from the remaining three lines of light, the points of this triangle touching the same points of the hexagon as do those of the Y-shape. By itself this triangle within the hexagon becomes an orthogonal projection of an octahedron; interfaced with the cubic projection, it becomes the diagonal means for the infinite expansion of the cube. Together they may be regarded as the visual manifestations of the supernal Partzufim, the divine personalities of Abba (Father), Imma (Mother), and Arikh Anpin (Long Face, the long-suffering, hidden face of God). Concentrate on this image, which is the *Sefer Yetzirah* Diagram, understanding the projected cube to represent Abba, the projected octahedron to represent Imma, and the whole, which contains their coupling, to represent the androgynous Arikh Anpin, who contains and harmonizes their duality. The next and final step in this stage of the meditation is to take this image of the supernal Partzufim and place it within the inner eye in the center of your head.

You have just completed the initial work necessary for your soul development and should visualize the whole. Your psyche should now resemble the retinal afterimage of a flame. At the center is a small, brilliant image of light, the divine inner radiance composed of the interfaced Abba and Imma within Arikh Anpin. Surrounding this is the darkness of your physical body, which is surrounded, in turn, by the layered light of the three higher soul bodies representing your discrete personality. Try to keep the awareness of this initial geometric work of soul body construction throughout the remainder of this meditation, of your divine inner radiance and of the subtle bodies that enclose and empower you. For though their construction is a mode of training the higher imagination for its later work of manifestation, it also begins to accomplish that very manifestation of the higher soul bodies that is the ultimate purpose of Master Meditation.

Seated within your complex body of light, you are now ready to begin perhaps the most important phase of meditative work, that of healing. Begin by drawing another beam of light down through the *yod* point of the Limitless Light and into your crown. As the single beam of light goes down through your head, divide it into three beams, the left beam going down your left shoulder and arm, the right beam down your right shoulder and arm, and the central beam through your torso, at the base of which it should divide again into two, the left beam going down the left leg and the right beam down the right leg. Throughout the whole previous process of visualization and continuing to this point, you should have been repeating the mantra and doing all the imaging to its rhythm. In the present process it is good to draw the light down through the crown and into the image of your divine center, while inhaling the breath to the word *Ruach,* holding the light there with the breath to the word *Elohim,* and then sending the light down through your body to the word *Chayyim.* As you continue to do this with successive breaths, your physical body will begin to feel more and more charged with light.

Now send your consciousness down with this light, exploring all aspects of your body and spirit with it to see if there is any evidence of dis-ease and sending back a visual image of your inner condition to your imagination. Now diagnose it. Once you have diagnosed this image with your higher intelligence and by this means discovered what is required for its cure, revisualize your self-image in its already cured and perfected form and reinforce the power of this revisualization with the following silent affirmation:

> Let me be transformed into that body of light, radiating the psychic and physical vitality that arises from a willing conformity to the laws of creation, the compassion to love all that is produced by those laws, and the wisdom to understand both the nature and the higher purpose governing the cosmic Law, that I may make my creative contribution to that higher purpose which will fill my own life with meaningfulness while transmuting it into an instrument of divine revelation. VEHAYAH.

Continue to breathe the light in through your crown and let your exhalation carry it down throughout your body. Your consistent use of the mantra in association with your rhythmic breathing will have ended with the silent verbalization of the affirmation and should not be re-

sumed, from this point to the end of the meditation, to allow the
verbal center to participate in the higher work of manifestation. It is a
good practice, however, to end every affirmation with the manifesting force of the word *vehayah* and you can, if necessary, repeat this
three-syllable word a few times both to reestablish the regularity of
your breathing and to direct its psychic energy into manifestation.

The work of self-healing and inner direction that you have just
completed marks the first level of Ruach spiritual power, and in the
remaining work of this meditation, you will ascend through levels of
Ruach power to the final spiritual height of the master. The next higher
level of this power is developed as one begins to direct this energy
outward. As you have been breathing in the light and directing it
down into the body for self-healing, you will begin to feel your body
swell with this energy like a balloon, and just at the point at which it
feels ready to burst you should begin to direct the light you breathe in
through the crown to go out through your heart at each exhalation.
At the same time, project the image of someone you have chosen to
work with in this meditation, directing the light flowing through you
out to that visualized person. You will now repeat the same process
with this chosen individual that you earlier used on yourself. First
diagnose the image you have projected in terms of any psychic or physical malady it may disclose and then discover the specific cure you can
prescribe for this condition. Finally, revisualize that person in terms of
your image of his or her perfect realization and repeat the same silent
affirmation previously used for yourself though with the substitution
of that person's name and the appropriate pronouns for those by which
you referred to yourself:

Let _____ be transformed into that body of light, radiating the
psychic and physical vitality that arises from a willing conformity
to the laws of creation, the compassion to love all that is produced
by those laws, and the wisdom to understand both the nature and
the higher purpose governing the cosmic Law, that he (or she) may
make a creative contribution to that higher purpose which will fill
this life with meaningfulness while transmuting it into an instrument of divine revelation. VEHAYAH.

Since one biblical usage of *vehayah* is to begin the "second paragraph" of the Sh'ma, in which you are commanded to teach your children the meaning of divine Providence while or through performing the Sh'ma, it is a good practice to add to this affirmation the words "to my children as well." The whole of the conclusion can then be thought of as signifying in translation: "And it shall come to pass to my children as well." Thus even when one of your children is not the specific subject of your meditation on this day, you can include all of your children in your daily Sh'ma meditations as commanded. If you do not have children, you might wish to add these or similar words to indicate that all the world's population can be considered your children, the subject of your special concern and protection.

After you have completed sending these healing and perfecting energies to the other person in your meditation, address the perfected image of that person from the level of your own visualized perfection with the invitation:

> Let our souls now embrace, recognizing that you are the other who completes my being as I am the other who completes yours. Together we form the higher unity of our relationship, which has a purpose requiring both our complementary natures.

Allow yourself to feel that soul embrace "with all your heart, and with all your soul, and with all your might" so that you can experience the true unifying force that binds the two of you together. For anyone who is sufficiently present in your consciousness to become the subject of your meditation is someone with whom you are significantly involved, and it is the significance of this involvement to your life that you will now be meditating upon. Try to vary the outer directed subject of your healing meditation from day to day, going through the members of your immediate family and anyone else who may be in immediate need of healing. On the Sabbath morning it is best to meditate upon the person you have been most intimately involved with during that Sabbath. But once a week or so it is also good to meditate upon something other than a specific person, a problem area associated with your work, family, community, or world, and to subject it to the same method of diagnostic visualization and prescriptive revisualization. In this case the concluding affirmation should, however, be simplified in the following manner:

Let _____ be transformed into that body of light, radiating the
vitality, compassion, and wisdom through which it can make its
creative contribution to the higher purpose governing the cosmos.
VEHAYAH.

You should then engage in the same embrace with the informing soul
of this situation or condition as you would with a single individual
and with the same verbal invitation. Whoever or whatever the partner of this soul embrace may be, whether an intimate or a stranger,
you should feel the embrace deeply enough to experience the force
that binds the two of you into a unity, for it is through this experience
that you can rise to the highest level of Ruach power.

This is the level that can take you above the two-dimensional
world of Yetzirah to the higher energies emanating from the one-
dimensional world of Beriah, the linear world of Creation. Where
before you were contemplating only separated individuals, yourself
and others, now you begin to see them in their connectedness. The
next step is perhaps the most important one of the whole meditation
and the most difficult. It requires a shift of consciousness from the
individual aspect of yourself as a part of a relationship to the unity of
that relationship of which you are a part. It is a shift from your lower
ego consciousness to that larger or higher collective consciousness
from which you can witness your ego-self as part of a larger whole. If
and when such a shift to what has been called "witness consciousness"
is truly accomplished, you will also experience a qualitative change
that signals the movement into a higher soul body. From the heavier,
fluid energies that signified the continuing psychic environment of
the Nefesh soul body, you will now move decisively into a lighter
element, the more "spaced out," ethereal environment of the true
Ruach soul body.

The most immediate work at this highest level of Ruach power
does not seem to be so different from the work at the lower levels of
this power, the work of creative revisualization. Thus again you will
project an image of the relationship in which your ego-self is involved
and diagnose its strengths and weaknesses—those that bind you two
together and those that are a source of stress and withdrawal. You will
come to understand what function this relationship is serving for both
its partners and what can be prescribed to cure its wounds, increase its

health, and restore it to that creative purpose for which it was initially contracted. Most importantly, you will determine what energy your single self can contribute to the life of that larger whole of which you are a part to transform it into conformity with your higher vision. Such transformative work most characterizes this final level of Ruach power, and its nature supports the old truth that the only thing one can ever really change is oneself. Thus one's ego-heart can only know what it needs to contribute to transform a larger whole when it has so expanded that it can identify itsef with this whole. Just as the heart is the organ through which transcendent vision can be transformed into the physical products of this cosmos, so too is it the organ by which the dualities of this world can be again transformed to reflect their higher source and purpose. It is only when the heart of an individual becomes as identified with the welfare of a larger whole as it is with its own self that its transformational work will serve the best interests of that whole, as well as the still larger cosmic whole of which it is also a part, rather than turning that other person, group, or cause into an unhealthy extension of its own ego. When you have completed this work of understanding and creatively revisualizing your relationship, conclude with the silent affirmation:

> Let this relationship be transformed into such a source of mutual empowerment. VEHAYAH.

We come at last to the final phase of the meditation, that in which you pray to be uplifted into the Neshamah soul body for communion with the nondimensional source point of all, the world of divine Emanation that is Atzilut, an ascent that can be invoked by the following affirmational prayer:

> Let me be enlightened by the Ruach ha-Kodesh, the Holy Spirit, to recognize myself as a centering point of the Limitless Light, with access to all knowledge, and may I rest in that state of blissful being that informs me of all I need to know (especially _____). VEHAYAH.

In this phase you should experience a state of spontaneous meditation and it should, if possible, be without seed, without the aid of any mantra. Whether or not you specify a particular problem you would like to have resolved in this final meditative experience, you should wait in a state of readiness for any answers that may emerge in your consciousness. Your previous work during the earlier phases of the meditation may have left a residue of unresolved or imperfectly resolved issues that may now begin to cohere into more instructive patterns. But whether or not this phase affords you any specific insights in answer to a stated or unstated question, its blissful state is answer enough to the soul's true needs. After five to ten minutes of such wordless meditation, start to return to normal consciousness, concluding your meditation with this final affirmational prayer:

Let me return transformed by this crowning experience, my individual will ever enclothing the higher will. Let me draw its wisdom and power down with me into the world of relationships that I may see and reveal the unifying force within all dualities. And as I reenter the physical plane of my body, let me ever walk in the way that is perfecting me into a body of light, the layered light of my personality surrounding a divine inner radiance, the image of a twice-born, divine personality. VEHAYAH.

CHAPTER 3

The Sinai Sabbath and the Covenant of Holiness

The Three Mosaic Laws of the Sabbath

Introduction

For Judaism the concept of sacred time is centered in its most holy institution, the Sabbath. The laws governing its ritual observance proclaim its holiness and its power to convey that holiness to the observer: "Remember the sabbath day, to keep it holy. . . . Verily my sabbaths ye shall keep: for it is a sign between me and you throughout your generations; that ye may know that I am the Lord that doth sanctify you" (Ex. 20:8, 31:13). But this Covenant of Holiness depends upon the precise enactment of certain ritual stipulations—laws of the Sabbath with the power to focus and transmit the holy spirit.

In his remarkable study of religion from the perspective of its archaic origins, Mircea Eliade has shown that such ritual empowerment of time is among the oldest legacies of religious man. His treatment of sacred time has special relevance for understanding the nature of the Sabbath.

> *By its very nature sacred time is reversible* in the sense that, properly speaking, it is *a primordial mythical time made present.* Every religious festival, any liturgical time, represents the reactualization of a

95

sacred event that took place in a mythical past, "in the beginning."
. . . it is the time that was created and sanctified by the gods at the
period of their *gesta*, of which the festival is precisely a
reactualization. . . . Hence religious man lives in two kinds of time,
of which the more important, sacred time, appears under the para-
doxical aspect of a circular time, reversible and recoverable, a sort
of eternal mythical present that is periodically reintegrated by means
of rites.[1]

This concept of sacred time as a ritual return to the time of begin-
nings can be assimilated to that of the Sabbath despite the fact that
Eliade not only omits any reference to this central feature of the Jewish religious calendar but specifically rejects any such possible appli-
cation:

It is this archaic conception of mythical time that is of chief concern to us. We shall later see how it differs from the conceptions
held by Judaism and Christianity. . . . For Judaism, time has a beginning and will have an end. The idea of cyclic time is left behind.
Yahweh no longer manifests himself in *cosmic time* (like the gods of
other religions) but in *a historical time*, which is irreversible.[2]

Certainly the God of Judaism manifests Himself in history; but to say
that therefore He does not or cannot manifest Himself in cosmic time
shows far less understanding of Jewish religious observance on Eliade's
part than of the archaic religious practices from which he derived
such a profound interpretation of the sacred.

Nor is such understanding of Jewish religious Law far to seek:

For this commandment which I command thee this day, it is not
hidden from thee, neither is it far off. . . . But the word is very nigh
unto thee, in thy mouth, and in thy heart, that thou mayest do it.
(Deut. 30:11, 14)

What shapes the Sabbath period of time into a chalice for the reception of the spiritual wine of holiness is the observance of three Mosaic
laws, the laws prohibiting work, leaving of one's place, and kindling
of fires. In what follows, an attempt will be made to interpret these

three defining laws of the Sabbath in the spirit of the above Mosaic passage, understanding in as direct a fashion as possible how they may be observed so that they become transmitters of the covenantal holiness of the Sabbath. For as the only ritual stipulated in the Ten Commandments that mark the Sinai Covenant, it is the vehicle precisely designed and designated to convey the power of sanctification that is the aim of this central covenant between God and Israel, that by which Israel is to become "a kingdom of priests, and an holy nation" (Ex. 19:6). It has this unique power because "the Lord blessed the sabbath day, and hallowed it" (Ex. 20:11).

In this chapter a mode of observing the Sinai Sabbath will be developed through an interpretation of the Mosaic laws as direct and unmediated as possible. This may not be as attractive to those long schooled in halakhic observance as to those who have never experienced the power of Sabbath devotions, but even the Orthodox should find their practice illuminated by this fresh understanding of the central Torah laws of the Sabbath and of the stages through which the Sabbath progresses. For it can provide new Kavanot through which traditional observance can be made to yield some of its hidden mystical power. But those who do practice the Sinai Sabbath will find it to be a way of directly tapping the Sabbath holiness with its original Sinai energy. The following treatment will be addressed primarily to those for whom Sabbath observance will mark the first stage of their commitment to Jewish ritual practice. It will assume that their interest in such observance has been fueled by spiritual experiences resulting from meditative practice and that they will, in fact, be incorporating the Kabbalistic meditation developed in the last chapter into their Sabbath observance. But I also hope that this form of observance will not represent the conclusion of their spiritual development and that if and when they do progress to the highest form of Jewish practice—the mystical prayer that will be the subject of the next chapter—they will include the prayer services within their observance of the day of rest.

We shall follow this study of the Sabbath laws with a consideration of the four stages of the Sabbath, giving special attention to such subjects as the nature of Sabbath sexuality and the Sabbath sunset experience as well as to forms of its festivities and devotions. And we will conclude with an analysis of the difference between the Sabbath, the Temple in time, and the Temple designed to occupy space, considering the difference between the holiness of the Sabbath and the holiness of the other Mosaic holidays and suggesting some Kavanot to heighten their celebration. But it is the biblical *mitzvot,* the sanctifying commandments, which must first be studied to understand how they may be most skillfully observed, for it is only such observance that can ever newly empower ritual to perform that sanctification of our lives by which we can become purified vessels of the divine. The Sabbath is the great vehicle of divine grace through which we can every week become filled with a holiness whose presence we invoke through our ritual acts but whose power is beyond our conjuring. The most important of the three Mosaic laws, whose observance alone can still shape the immaterial time of the Sabbath into a unique and potent conveyer of holiness, is the commandment to rest, and to this we now turn.

The Commandment to Rest

The Sabbath as a day of rest is first defined in the creation story: "And God blessed the seventh day, and sanctified it: because that in it he had rested from all his work" (Gen. 2:3). The Fourth Commandment stipulates only one rule by which one can "remember the sabbath day, to keep it holy": "thou shalt not do any work," and this because "in six days the Lord made heaven and earth . . . and rested the seventh day" (Ex. 20:8-11). The holiness of the Sabbath is directly related to a divine state of rest. Work is to cease not just for relaxation but as an imitation of God, to bring man back to the unfallen perfection of his creation "in the image of God" (Gen. 1:27).

Though the meaning of *melakhah,* the forbidden Sabbath work, is not specifically defined in the Fourth Commandment, it can be deduced from the linguistic and contextual peculiarities of later renderings of the Sabbath law. A new way of viewing *melakhah* can be gained if one follows Aryeh Kaplan's illuminating translation of another phrasing of this law: "You may work during the six weekdays, but on Saturday, you must stop working, ceasing from all plowing and reaping" (Ex. 34:21, AK).[3] In the more familiar versions, the terms here translated as "plowing and reaping" are interpreted not as modes but as times of work. The King James Version renders this last phrase as: "in earing time and in harvest thou shalt rest." But the two terms *charish* and *katzir* can be translated as either types or times of work, and it is Kaplan's choice that makes the most sense in terms of the other archetypal definitions of work given in the Bible.

The first of these is man's initial assignment of work in the garden: "And the Lord God took the man, and put him into the Garden of Eden to dress it and to keep it" (Gen. 2:15). Man the gardener, whose work it is to tend the earth, is an extraordinary concept, for it makes man the true "husband" of the earth, one whose work is primarily concerned with maintaining the healthy ecology of the system. It was man's inability to abide within the given limitations of this ecological system that ruined the land and made his labor on it hard and unsatisfying: "Cursed is the ground for thy sake; in sorrow shalt thou eat of it all the days of thy life" (Gen. 3:17). But man can return his world and his life to its original Garden state by learning to treat whatever work he does as husbandry, by considering whether the products and ideas he is putting out into the world will pollute or cleanse the garden earth, and dedicating himself to accepting only that work which will dress it and keep it, beautify and maintain it.

The other major locus that defines man's work in gardening terms is the Torah portion recited twice daily in halakhic observance and referred to as the "second paragraph" of the Sh'ma. This begins:

> And it shall come to pass, if ye shall hearken diligently unto my commandments which I command you this day, to love the Lord your God, and to serve him with all your heart and with all your soul, that I will give you the rain of your land in his due season, the first rain and the latter rain, that thou mayest gather in thy corn, and thy wine, and thy oil. And I will send grass in thy fields for thy cattle, that thou mayest eat and be full. Take heed to yourselves, that your heart be not deceived, and ye turn aside, and serve other gods, and worship them; and then the Lord's wrath be kindled against you, and he shut up the heaven, that there be no rain, and that the land yield not her fruit; and lest ye perish quickly from off the good land which the Lord giveth you. (Deut. 11:13–17)

Here is given the great karmic lesson, also stated in gardening terms, that as you sow so shall you reap, that there is a Providential order operating within nature that provides abundantly for those content to live within its bounds and serve its purposes but that turns against those deceived persons who think no such higher order exists and who worship the gods of their own appetites, repeating anew the original sin of the Garden. The Promised Land is no other than that Garden state renewed through rededication to God's law, the law that earthly existence is only possible through limitation, and such love of this existence as recognizes its source in something greater than the human will and wishes to serve that higher will with all its heart and soul. The good husbandman will have blessings rain upon his head while he who violates the ground of his being will perish in a dry wasteland.

Thus the law that tells us that on the Sabbath one must cease "all plowing and reaping" defines the work of the six weekdays in terms that complement rather than contradict the Sabbath rest. It repeats the law governing the use of Manna that contains the two complementary aspects of the week, six days of gathering "bread from heaven" (Ex. 16:4) and a seventh day of rest from such gathering, both aspects equally determining "whether they will walk in my law, or no" (Ex. 16:4). The Fourth Commandment not only ordains the Sabbath but also the six days of work:

> Remember the sabbath day, to keep it holy. Six days shalt thou labour, and do all thy work: But the seventh day is the sabbath of the Lord thy God: in it thou shalt not do any work. (Ex. 20:8–10)

It tells us that to keep the Sabbath holy, one must also remember it during the six days of work, remember the divine creation of the world and that all that we gather is divinely given. We will thus not come to the Sabbath from a week of cheating and exploitation but from one we have also tried to keep holy, recognizing God as well in the flow as in the stillness and as contained in both the in- and outgoing breath of the living God. Once we have so regulated our work life that our plowing and reaping can contribute to the health of our society and planet as well as earning us a personal profit, we can then cease on the Sabbath all those activities connected with our individual means of reaping a profit, whatever they may be. And we should also take care to observe Exodus 34:21 in its literal as well as figurative sense, ceasing from all activities associated with farming or gardening, however relaxing we might find the latter.

Where linguistic reinterpretation of Exodus 34:21 can give us an understanding of *melakhah* as devoted to maintaining the healthy ecology of the system, contextual interpretation of the sixth and final restatement of the Sabbath law in Exodus can take us beyond such maintenance of healthy Being to the additional work necessary for Becoming. Exodus 35:2, which again prohibits work on the Sabbath, not only introduces the further prohibition of Sabbath kindling in the next verse but is set in a meaningful context for this final understanding of *melakhah*, the work prescribed for the six days and prohibited on the seventh. This context, the Torah portion known as *vayakhel* (Ex. 35:1–38:20), describes Moses' assembling of the entire people to instruct them on the work of building the Temple. Only the law of Sabbath rest is restated in this context of commanded work and this is the basis of the talmudic interpretation that the forbidden Sabbath work is precisely the work of constructing the Temple. In this traditional interpretation, the Temple in time, which is the Sabbath, is constructed by deliberately refraining from those activities involved in building the Temple in space. What these activities are may be determined from the tasks summarized in Exodus 35:11–19 and detailed throughout this Torah portion. They primarily involve crafts associated with making cloth (for the Tabernacle tent), carpentry (for the tent beams and other Tabernacle furniture and objects), metal working (for the Menorah and other objects) and working with gemstones (for the breastplate).

But just as it is important to know from which crafts to refrain on the Sabbath, so is it important to know how the great work of Temple building is to be pursued on the six workdays, since that too is commanded in this as in each restatement of the Sabbath law: "Six days shall work be done" (Ex. 35:2). It would appear that contributions to the construction of the Temple depend upon both attitude and capacity. But whatever one's capacity, one's contribution must come from the heart. The King James Version is more accurate than some more modern translations in always preserving the Hebrew references to the heart in its renderings. Thus contributions of monetary value were brought by "both men and women, as many as were willing hearted" (Ex. 35:22) while actual work on the Temple was contributed by the "wise hearted" (Ex. 35:10). These two heart categories, *nadiv* ("willing," in the particular sense of a willingness to give) and *chakham* ("wise"), appear in the same verse with slight rephrasing: "And they came, every one whose heart stirred him up, and every one whom his spirit made willing" (Ex. 35:21). The identification of the *chakham lev*, the wise heart, with the stirred up heart is made clear in the following parallel references:

> And all the women that were wise hearted did spin with their hands . . . (Ex. 35:25)

> And all the women whose heart stirred them up in wisdom spun . . . (Ex. 35:26)

The wisdom of the heart arises, then, when the heart is stirred up or, more properly translated, lifted up, and what lifts it up is the spirit of God:

> [God] hath filled him [Bezaleel] with the spirit of God, in wisdom, in understanding, and in knowledge, and in all manner of workmanship. (Ex. 35:31)

Such divine inspiration is not restricted to this chief artificer but given to all the Temple workers, men and, as we have seen, women:

> Then wrought Bezaleel and Aholiab, and every wise hearted man, in whom the Lord put wisdom and understanding to know how to work all manner of work for the service of the sanctuary, according to all that the Lord had commanded. (Ex. 36:1)

Work on the Sanctuary is action in accordance with divine commandment, with Torah, and such correctly perfomed action can only arise by remembering the divine source of one's power. Of this Moses was later to warn Israel:

> Beware that thou forget not the Lord thy God, in not keeping his commandments . . . the Lord thy God, which brought thee forth out of the land of Egypt, from the house of bondage . . . who fed thee in the wilderness with manna, which thy fathers knew not, that he might humble thee, and that he might prove thee, to do

thee good at thy latter end; And thou say in thine heart, my power and the might of mine hand hath gotten me this wealth. But thou shalt remember the Lord thy God: for it is he that giveth thee power to get wealth, that he may establish his covenant which he sware unto thy fathers, as it is this day. (Deut. 8:11–18)

Israel was brought forth from bondage not for unstructured, individualistic freedom but to prove worthy to make a Covenant of Power through law. On Sinai, the six workdays were to be spent in two activities that are actually one, gathering Manna and working on the Temple. Since what one took in for sustenance and what one gave forth with wise or willing heart could be seen to derive from the same heavenly source, rather than from the power of one's own hand, such work could become a refining process, freeing one from the bondage of ego for that "service . . . according to all that the Lord had commanded" in which empowerment and gratitude are one.

To wish to construct a Temple requires a willing heart, and to know how to construct it so that it becomes a magnetic focuser of higher energies requires a further wisdom of heart. Both are powers derived from spirit, that Ruach dimension of soul that lifts the heart up to a level of cosmic connectedness. It should be remembered that when God asked Solomon what he would like to be given, he replied: "Give therefore thy servant an understanding heart to judge thy people, that I may discern between good and bad" (I Kings 3:9). And with a *lev shome'a,* similar to the *chakham lev* we have been considering, Solomon proceeded to build the Temple in Jerusalem. Temple building is the proper work of Ruach consciousness and it is the joint work of the two complementary elements in even the most ideal of societies—the spiritual master and the populace, the wise and the willing.

I suggested earlier that gathering Manna and building the Temple were modes of work that could be identified because both taught the soul to recognize the divine source of its power. But they can also be distinguished, and it is in this distinction that we can understand the need for both. We have seen that gathering Manna, the Sinai form of plowing and reaping, was a mode of work that in its Sabbath inversion could take one back to the Garden. Temple building, however, involves a step forward. It is the work of Tikkun, the Lurianic rectification of that shattering that can be associated with the loss of Eden, and this does not merely return the soul to its original vulnerable condition but carries it forward to a new perfection higher than what was lost. It does not reject the hard-won knowledge of good and evil but, with Solomon, seeks to inform such knowledge with the saving grace of a wise and understanding heart. It restores the soul to an innocence before God, now disentangled from the ignorance of His way that had once burdened its innocence. In like manner the Passover celebration rejoices in liberation from the evil of Egyptian bondage while also clinging to the memory of that bitterness. For it is through the memory of that experience that the Hebrew soul can achieve its necessary compassion. Thus on the Sabbath one is told "that thy manservant and thy maidservant may rest as well as thou. And remember that thou wast a servant in the land of Egypt" (Deut. 5:14–15). The Exodus will have been in vain, Elijah never come again to herald the Messianic Age with a sip of our Passover wine, unless the bitterness of bondage is made to yield that wise heart in whose compassion a foundation is being laid for the Temple of Messianic consciousness.

It is not enough, then, simply to gather Manna, however blissful such a perfected walking in the divine Way may be. One must also make a personal contribution to its ongoing process based upon the fullest realization of one's God-given and God-inspired talents. As Emerson said, we must "build altars to the Beautiful Necessity."[4] To build a Temple is to make a pledge to the future. It is to go beyond the ever recurring present of the agricultural cycle, never enduring though always reviving with its original freshness. It is to add the creative work of man to the forces of cosmic evolution, an evolution that is impossible without the contribution of human creativity and the reason for man's creation. As the highest work of man is to build the Messianic Temple on God's Holy Mountain, so in its Sabbath inversion it is the Temple of higher consciousness that is being constructed, the Temple of the higher soul bodies constructed through conscious spiritual discipline.

If the six days of work have been properly directed toward the dual tasks of gathering Manna and building the Temple, then the Sabbath rest can convert these energies into pure modes of consciousness that reflect and fulfill their spiritual intentions, carrying us at the same time back to the Garden and forward to the Messianic Temple. As the Sabbath increasingly teaches us this integration, so are we more and more able to achieve such integration of energies during the six work-days, earning the Manna that sustains us from the Temple work by which our own uplifted spirits can raise the energy level of the whole. For as Robert Frost has said so well:

> *Only where love and need are one,*
> *And the work is play for mortal stakes,*
> *Is the deed ever really done*
> *For Heaven and the future's sakes.*[5]

In such creative labor as Temple building always is, work is redeemed from the curse and becomes transformational. As Manna is transformed into the products of intelligence, so gifted man becomes spiritually transformed in the very exercise of those talents that serve the world as a redemptive transformer of divine energy. His work is but another mode of the same divine encounter he experiences on the Sabbath and is the best preparation for it. For the Sabbath brings us to a condition within and beyond time where the Temple and the Garden are one. And when the Temple is thus found in the Garden, the weekly return to Being can reinforce the discipline of Becoming—of becoming a spiritual master.

If Eliade is right in distinguishing the Hebraic from the archaic concept of sacred time, it is only in this, that in the return to primordial time, which characterizes the religious festival, this original time is transformed to contain a complementary vision of future perfection. The Sabbath represents, in the words of T. S. Eliot, "time future contained in time past."[6] Just as the Passover Seder takes us from the memory of Egyptian bondage to the promise of Messianic redemption, so the Sabbath takes us from night to day. It returns us to the Garden with the new strength of obedience to the Law derived from the very observance of the Sabbath laws that transmit its holiness, a strength that cancels our exile from the Garden and permits us to build a Temple of redeemed consciousness "eastward in Eden" (Gen. 2:8). It is the special power of the Sinai Sabbath to achieve such a synthesis of time past with time future as can build that Garden Temple, and this power develops from the conversion of the outgoing energies of Sinai melakhah. For the two modes of work commanded at Sinai—gathering Manna and building the Temple—were precisely designed to move the spirit simultaneously backward to the beginning and forward to the end of time. During the Sinai experience past and future became one in work and rest, and this same union can inform our present workdays and Sabbaths if we attune ourselves to the spirit of Sinai *melakhah* and of the laws of the Sinai Sabbath.

In the recurring present of the Sinai Sabbath, the past Garden and the future Temple are both manifested and unified through the power of the primary law of the Sabbath, the prohibition of work. The function of the two subsidiary laws of the Sabbath is to reinforce the two spiritual movements back to the Garden and forward to the Temple initiated by the Sabbath inversion of the two modes of Sinai *melakhah*. As we shall now see, the law of place may be viewed as a further empowerment of the Temple aspect of the Sabbath, the law of nonkindling as a further empowerment of its Garden aspect.

The Law of Place

If the prohibition of work on the Sabbath provides a time for holiness, the second law of the Sabbath defines its sacred space. This appears in the context of the second biblical Sabbath, that of the Manna: "Abide ye every man in his place [*tachtav*], let no man go out of his place [*mekomo*] on the seventh day" (Ex. 16:29). Two different Hebrew terms are translated here as "place." *Makom* is the general Hebrew word for "place." *Tachtav*, used here as a synonym of *makom*, has the additional connotation of "underpart." The term *makom* is particularly interesting because, with the definite article, this word becomes one of the standard ways of referring to God—Ha-Makom. *Mekomo*, "his place," is thus related to Ha-Makom, God, with the implication that the place one is not to leave on the Sabbath is a sacred God place or Temple, the form of consciousness divinely given with the Sabbath: "The Lord hath given you the sabbath . . . so the people rested on the seventh day" (Ex. 16:29–30). But the difference between *mekomo* and Ha-Makom, between man's place and that ultimate substance that is God, is defined by the alternate term for one's place, *tachtav*. Man's place is to take the "underpart"; his proper cosmic position is beneath the sovereignty of God. The nature of Sabbath consciousness is this awareness of one's dependent and limited, but divinely given and blessed, existence, the choice of that life which is God: "for he is thy life, and the length of thy days" (Deut. 30:20).

The deepest sense of *makom* as a state of Sabbath consciousness is revealed through linguistic analysis, but context again provides another dimension of meaning, in this case a particularizing dimension that seems to restrict its literal reference to the home. If on the most spiritual level the place we are not to leave on the Sabbath is the Temple built in our consciousness, on the physical level it is the home that becomes the Sabbath Temple. One can adopt the spiritual rather than literal interpretation of this law, an interpretation consistent with synagogue worship, but observing it in its literal meaning provides a channel for what may well be the most potent transmission of Sabbath holiness, one in which the home can become a Temple space for a spiritual retreat. Such retirement from the world, as from its work, allows for an uninterrupted concentration of consciousness, which is the proper function of the Temple and seems intended by the biblical context. As with the Passover feast commanded shortly before (Ex. 13:6), the Sabbath as given at Sinai was a family-centered home observance. In both cases, the principal instructions involve food, unleavened bread in the former case and previously cooked food in the latter. As the law prohibiting cooking on the Sabbath is clearly related to the later enunciated prohibition of kindling, it is best to consider it in the context of this third law of the Sabbath, to which we now turn.

The Law Prohibiting Kindling

Where the first two Sabbath laws define the sacred nature of its time and space, the law against kindling is most important in defining and enhancing the special quality of its holiness. This is simply given as: "Ye shall kindle no fire throughout your habitations upon the sabbath day" (Ex. 35:3). Let us first try to understand the meaning of this law in its most absolute terms.

It is clear that living without man-made fire would bring man back to the natural condition in which he was created. Without the artificial light that upsets man's diurnal rhythm, he can return to his original harmony with nature, lying down and rising up with the sun, the light made "to rule over the day" (Gen. 1:18). Without the heat of man-made fire, he can likewise return to the diet for which he was originally ordained: "And God said, Behold, I have given you every herb bearing seed, which is upon the face of all the earth, and every tree, in the which is the fruit of a tree yielding seed; to you it shall be for meat" (Gen. 1:29). If man returned during the Sabbath to this original diet of fruits and vegetables, it would provide a weekly cleansing of his body that would greatly enhance his spiritual sensitivity to the higher energies transmitted by the Sabbath. Thus the main intent of the law against kindling is to effect a spiritual return of man to a precivilized condition of harmony with God and His creation. With Thoreau, it calls upon us to "Simplify, simplify."[7] And as with the myth of Prometheus, which enshrines a view of man's improper use of this great civilizing agent as a theft of divine fire, it shows how this harnessing of the power of the sun can make man feel like a petty god and can cause him to forget his true dependence. "Remember" is the first word of the Fourth Commandment, and all the laws and lore of Sabbath observance are designed to bring man to remembrance of that first Sabbath when he shared in the holiness of the divine rest. As man's invention of fire translated the light of intelligence into a material process, so his refraining from kindling can reverse the direction of his psyche from absorption in the materialism of the world to a new vision of that spiritual light by which all things were created. On the seventh day, then, both God and man can remember and return to the first condition of creation, "the day that the Lord God made the earth and the heavens" (Gen. 2:4). Where observance of the Sabbath rest from work can bring man back to his unfallen condition in the Garden, observance of the prohibition of kindling on the Sabbath can bring him still further, to a divine state of spiritual illumination.

To explore how this prohibition can be meaningfully incorporated into a modern Sinai Sabbath, we must now consider the somewhat ambiguous instruction regarding cooked food for the Manna Sabbath:

> To morrow is the rest of the holy sabbath unto the Lord: bake that which ye will bake to day, and seethe that ye will seethe; and that which remaineth over lay up for you to be kept until the morning. (Ex. 16:23)

Though the words "to day" are added by the translators to clarify the sense, it is clear that only leftovers are to be eaten from the morning of the following day and that therefore all cooking for the Sabbath would have to be done on the day he is speaking, Friday. If it was understood that the Sabbath began at sundown, as in the days of creation, then three time periods are indicated with reference to food: today or Friday, when all Sabbath cooking is to be done; tomorrow, the Sabbath, beginning with evening, when the still hot food prepared before sundown is eaten; and the following morning of the Sabbath, Saturday, when, if only leftovers are to be eaten, they would have to be eaten cold.

This distinction between the two halves of the Sabbath, those corresponding to the hours of Friday evening and of Saturday before nightfall, has relevance to the question of proper Sabbath lighting as well as cooking. The tradition has been that both lighting and cooking are activities to be completed prior to the onset of the Sabbath so that the Sabbath evening meal need not be eaten cold and in darkness. As currently practiced, the Sabbath is a twenty-five-hour day, normally beginning eighteen minutes before sunset on Friday and ending forty-two minutes after sundown on Saturday. It is in that last sunset hour beyond time, before the appearance of three stars in the night sky signals the return to the profane time of the week, that the sacred energies of the Sabbath reach a culminating holiness. We shall consider this holy hour more fully later in this chapter, but at the moment it is sufficient to point out that the most critical effect of the Sabbatical time scheme may be its power to sensitize the relaxed and reverent psyche to the special quality of sunset and, by so doing, effect that reattunement of the psychic system with the solar rhythm that can return it to its original condition of cosmic harmony. Since this also seems to be the purpose of the prohibition against kindling, the allowance of previously kindled fire for cooking and lighting need not be considered a violation of the spirit of this law—of the letter it certainly and carefully is not—as long as the form of this cooked food and lighting is such as may serve to facilitate the psychic return intended by the law against kindling.

A return to the Garden by way of the Sinai Sabbath need not reject the whole of the intervening tradition, which for millennia has carried the pure Mosaic spirit into a ritual poetry of great beauty and power. If it is adherence to the three Mosaic laws of the Sabbath that produces this blessed and hallowed chalice of time, it is specific traditional practices that, like an aged and mellowed wine, can best fill such a vessel. These are practices whose true attunement to the holiness of this time is revealed by their capacity to be conveyors of spiritual energy. The most important of them involve the lighting of Sabbath candles, the blessings of the wine and bread, the special character of Sabbath sexuality, and the reading of a specific portion of the Torah. These four practices bring to the Sinai Sabbath the added power of long and devout observance. The first in importance as well as in sequence is the woman's act of candle lighting, which initiates the Sabbath.

In this ritual, the dualism of the week is lifted into a Sabbath harmony by the three circular hand motions the woman makes over the two candles she has lit. This harmony is consciously directed into her being by the sanctification of the blessing and prayers she utters while she holds her hands over her closed eyes. When she opens her eyes to see the candlelight, she has become filled with the light of the Sabbath and embodies its spirit.

It is important that women observing this mitzvah do so not mechanically but with a Kavanah, mystical intention, fully aware of the power that can be present in this ritual if skillfully practiced. Most important must be their intention to invoke the presence of the Neshamah Yeterah, the additional soul that tradition insists can enter their spirits at this time. But this higher power is one that must be consciously invited to enter them. If women know what they are doing they can experience this highest level of Shefa, a level of spiritual influx so powerful it is desirable that they practice this mitzvah privately. With no distraction and the ability to relax for at least the eighteen minutes between candle lighting and sundown, they should be able to experience something of this Sabbath holiness. Such effects are nearly impossible with the usual practice of lighting candles at the dinner table with the family present and ready to eat. In Orthodox families where the men attend Maariv services at the synogogue, women do have an opportunity for such private and prolonged candle lighting if they would but take it. Women living and observing the Sabbath alone have the best opportunity for experiencing this weekly miracle of grace. But all women should set aside the time of candle lighting and at least a twenty- to thirty-minute period of reclined relaxation after it to experience the bliss of the Beloved who has entered their being and filled it with an inner radiance.

The illumination of the Sabbath has, then, a double character. It is feminine in spirit—bride and queen, Shekhinah and Malkhut, an ingoing receptivity, the soft passivity that is the Sabbath rest—and it is candlelit. In this last circumstance we have what is probably the best solution to a mode of Sabbath lighting that will not violate the spirit of the law against kindling. In what follows I shall present suggestions for new ways of observing this law that, while not in strict accord with present halakhic practice, are not in violation of any rabbinical *mitzvot*. They seem rather to provide a balance between more extreme forms of interpreting this law. If the Karaite practice of a completely darkened home on the Sabbath eve represents a Gevurah spirit of interpretation, rabbinical practice displays its Chesed spirit just as markedly. For not only are previously lit candles deemed acceptable on the Sabbath but also previously turned-on electric lighting. Not that electric lighting is any more of a violation of the letter of the prohibition against kindling than previously lit candles, and it can certainly be employed if desired. But I would suggest that electric lighting is not in as close an attunement to the spirit of the Sabbath. Unlike the soft receptivity of candlelight, electric lighting is so powerful that it completely overwhelms and annihilates the darkness. Where the healing, harmonizing energies of firelight have the capacity to absorb the surrounding darkness and fill it with a magnetic radiance, the garish glare of electric light not only annihilates the surrounding darkness but overwhelms even the blessed light of the Sabbath candles, their function extending no further than a ceremonial symbolism.

If the Sabbath is, indeed, to time what the Temple was to space, then it can best be enhanced by the same mode of illumination—the candlelight that emanated from its divinely appointed Menorah (though use of a seven-branched candlestick is to be avoided on ritual grounds). Once one has determined that candlelight will have primacy on the Sabbath eve, such lighting can become a spiritual guide to the activities proper to this portion of the Sabbath by revealing which are in harmony with, and which opposed to, its spirit. It will be found that the activities most enhanced by this type of lighting are those appropriate to the dining room, the living room, and the bedroom, while the activities most impeded by this lighting are those involving any form of Sabbath preparation—such as bathing, dressing, cleaning, and cooking—as well as the reading of extended liturgical passages or other works of even the most sacred character. These restrictions accord well with the general nature of traditional observance, since all preparations for the Sabbath should be completed before the time specified for lighting the Sabbath candles and since the Torah reading is reserved for the Sabbath morning, when natural light is usually available. But Maariv prayers can, of course, be said, either in the synagogue or near a specially prepared lamp at home. As the participants move through the various phases of a candlelit Sabbath eve, they will find that the special glow of its warmth and light releases a certain spirit into the air, surrounding them with a holy atmosphere that is more than the romantic quality contributed by candle- or firelight to profane occasions. The sanctification of the Sabbath converts such mood enhancement into a special instrument of its peace.

In moving from the Friday night to the Saturday portion of the Sabbath, one is not only moving from the activities appropriate for candlelight to those appropriate for natural light, but from a diet requiring heat preparation to one that should be as pristine as the light by which it is eaten. The law against Sabbath baking and boiling was not intended as a hardship to be circumvented by complicated procedures, such as that by which food previously cooked on Friday afternoon is maintained at a simmering temperature until served the following noon. Its true intent can only be discerned in the attempt to abide by its spirit. As indicated earlier, the intention would seem to be to return man to a cold vegetarian diet, thus bringing his digestive system back into the original harmony with its creation that can open his spirit to the more subtle vibrational level of the Sabbath.

The Torah defines four different spiritual levels of food. Lowest of all are, of course, the forbidden foods, primarily pork and shellfish. These are as forbidden on the Sabbath as on any other day. Next are the animal meats created on the sixth day. Such animal foods are not only permitted but, as we have seen in the second paragraph of the Sh'ma, they are considered an earthly reward for obedience to the commandments: "I will send grass in thy fields for thy cattle, that thou mayest eat and be full." This touching description of physical satiation through the eating of animal meat carries, however, an additional negative suggestion, of a total absorption of the human spirit in the animal physicality of which it has partaken. Such satiety may be considered as both a provision and reward for the rigors of weekday labor, but its grossness is more conducive to after-dinner stupor than to that lightness of spirit needed to receive the "Neshamah Yeterah," the additional soul said to enter one during proper observance of the Sabbath. On the next higher level are the foods created on the fifth day, the fish and fowl that, unlike the animals, were blessed by God in their creation. Though the pious person will try to sanctify all food and drink by blessing it in God's name, fish and fowl form a special class of naturally blessed foods. As such, they would seem the most appropriate to the holy feast of the Sabbath eve, and this meal has traditionally featured an appetizer of gefilte fish and a main course of roast chicken. We come finally to the food for which man's digestive system was created, the fruits and vegetables created on the third day and ordained as unfallen man's food on the sixth. It is such a diet that seems both best suited to the day portion of the Sabbath and intended by the dietary implications of the law against kindling.

The ranking of these four basic levels of biblically defined diet is consistent with the conclusions of most modern nutritionists concerned with optimal health as well as of other spiritual traditions concerned with the lifting of consciousness. If the purpose of the prohibition of kindling is to bring us by the two stages of the Sabbath, the Sabbath eve and the Sabbath day, to a return to higher stages of the creative process, then this would seem to be best accomplished on the dietary level by confining the foods of the evening to those created no later than the fifth day and the foods of the final day stage to those created on the third day. Dairy products, insofar as they involve no slaughtering, may perhaps be added to the latter group if they have not been eliminated from the diet for reasons of health or greater conformity to traditional Jewish Law.

In consideration of diet as well as lighting, the law against kindling on the Sabbath is most important in defining both the internal and external environment for the reception of Sabbath holiness, and it does so in the two stages corresponding to Friday night and Saturday before nightfall. It is most interesting that the two portions of the Jewish Sabbath should correspond to time periods whose English names convey exactly the same character as their Jewish counterparts. The prefix "fri" means "to love," "to be free," and "to be at peace." And Friday is the day of the Old Norse goddess of love and beauty, Freya, the counterpart of Venus. Saturday means, of course, Saturn's day. In its highest planetary significance the name implies the contemplative mood and in its significance as a Roman deity the name alludes to the god identified with the golden age. Thus the Sabbath eve is also Freya's night, the period of the Sabbath identified with the feminine, with love and peace. And the Sabbath day is also Saturn's day, the day of contemplative return to a golden age. These astrological associations derive from cultures completely divorced from the concept of the Jewish Sabbath, and yet they correspond with the exact period of the Sabbath. This correspondence reinforces the suspicion that the special character of the Sabbath does not result simply from what the observer invests in this time or even from his skillful performance of its prescribed rituals but is an inherent property of this time—a property whose nature the three laws of the Mosaic Sabbath are empowered to reveal in its highest potency.

The Four Stages of the Sabbath

Introduction

In addition to the major distinction between the dark and light phases of the Sabbath, it is customary to divide the Sabbath into three waking stages, those of Friday evening, Saturday morning, and Saturday afternoon. These time periods have been associated by Kabbalists with the Patriarchs, not so much because of their biblical personalities as their positioning on the Tree of Life Diagram, Abraham identified with the Sefirah Chesed, Isaac with Gevurah, and Jacob with Tiferet. The mood of the Sabbath is thus seen to move from the merciful Chesed spirit of Friday evening through the strict Gevurah spirit of Saturday morning to the serene harmony and balance that define the final Tiferet spirit of Saturday afternoon. These can be seen to correspond to the festive mood of Friday evening, the devotions and Torah reading of Saturday morning, and the special sense of holiness that crowns the final hours of the Sabbath afternoon. These three stages can also be associated with the progression through the three spiritual levels of the Nefesh, Ruach, and Neshamah souls, a progression that distinguishes the Sabbath from the six weekdays and reveals its true purpose. In what follows I shall attempt to provide a new understanding of the nature and distinction between Sabbath and weekday spirituality in terms of correspondences between the times of the day and the activation of the various levels of the soul.

During the working days of the week, the average person is normally operating at the level of the Nefesh soul except for his or her daily period of rest. This daily rest period, corresponding to the time from lying down to rising, that is, from Sh'ma to Sh'ma, provides a temporary lifting of normal consciousness to the Ruach level of the soul. It is a time for the higher and more fluid energies of prayer, sexual union, and the astral structuring of dream sleep. The lunar night world gives daily respite from the active particularizing energies arising with the sun, brings a touch of that deep rest that defines the Sabbath, and then returns the soul to the bustling world of earthly plowing and reaping. The Sabbath differs from this daily pattern in at least two respects. The Ruach portion becomes both more extended and consciously controlled and the soul, rather than returning to Nefesh functioning, ascends still higher with the Sabbath dawn to the Neshamah level of divine communion.

If we take the view that the period from Sh'ma to Sh'ma provides a daily overlay of Ruach spirituality to an otherwise continuous operation of the Nefesh soul, and that on the Sabbath this somewhat extended period provides a bridge between the Nefesh and Neshamah souls, then we may find a way to reconcile our previous divisions of the Sabbath into first two and then three periods. The period from sunset to sunrise, which we might call Freya's night, can thus be identified with the Nefesh part of the cycle while that from sunrise to sunset, which we can call Saturn's day, can be identified with the Neshamah portion. Overlaying segments of both, with its center at sunrise, would be the bridging work of the Ruach time span. Though more complex than the previous divisions into two or three phases, this fourfold division provides what may be the most precise description of the sequence of temporal moods through the Sabbath. In this conception, we begin with a purely Nefesh portion of Friday evening and then move to an overlay of the Ruach spirit on this Nefesh dimension for the remainder of the night. As dawn approaches the Nefesh element fades away to be replaced by an expanding Neshamah power, its morning development occurring within the context of continuing Ruach activity. Finally, as the afternoon progresses, the soul moves into a pure Neshamah state of bliss. The following discussion will provide a fuller exposition of these four Sabbath phases, correlating them both with these graduated soul levels and with the periods and activities of the Sabbath.

The Sabbath Evening Festivities

The Nefesh portion of the Sabbath corresponds to the feast, whose consecrated and shared wine and bread expand the animal Nefesh soul to a higher communion with both God and family. I have spoken of the Sabbath as a chalice for the reception of the spiritual wine of holiness. And as the symbolism of the Sabbath associates the female principle with the feast and festivity through the woman's two Sabbath mitzvot of challah baking and candle lighting, so does it associate the male principle with the Kiddush, the sanctification of the wine. Filling a special cup to the brim with the wine he has provided, the man blesses the wine and sanctifies the Sabbath, his ritual language recalling the original creation and the spiritual recreation of the Exodus. In the shared illumination provided by the woman's lighting and blessing of the candles, the blessing of the sparkling wine is now also shared. The final ritual of blessing before the commencement of the meal provides a synthesis of these two energies, as the challah baked by the woman is blessed by the man. The ritual sharing of the blessed wine and bread creates a Sabbath communion between all the participants in the ceremony, human and divine. And as the blessings draw the divine spirit into the light, the wine, and the bread, an additional soul, the Neshamah Yeterah, is thought to enter each individual breast, enlarging it through the successive phases of the Sabbath until its essence has been completely refined into holiness.

Between the conclusion of the feast and the normal retiring time for saying the evening Sh'ma, with its evocation of Ruach spirituality, is a specially blessed period of the Sabbath, a period in which the presence of the Neshamah Yetirah first becomes apparent to many. It would thus seem that on the Sabbath there is an earlier movement to the Ruach dimension, commencing shortly after the feast. Whether the participants remain at the dining table or move into a living area, the group becomes centered around the candlelight, which has a special power, like that of a great campfire in the chilly woods, to create a congenial community. In this relaxed and meditative atmosphere, a flow of creative and sympathetic energies is engendered that can lead not only to singing and the telling of tales but more importantly to a deeper form of human communication. At this time, the area illuminated by the candles becomes a people space. With no television or homework to distract or occupy them, satisfied by the feast, enlarged by the wine, but most of all lifted and hushed by the light, a space is cleared for a relaxed and rambling sharing of thought. Parents and children, lovers and friends, all find in this time a sympathetic attention that allows for personal communicating on a level normally lacking. In this mutually supportive atmosphere, openings and connections are made. The soul moves into the Ruach dimension of sensitivity to the subtle energies of those around it and learns how to adjust to these energies and enhance them.

This Nefesh-Ruach portion of the Sabbath night has various phases, a first period of family-centered relating that we have just considered, a second in which the Sh'ma is said, and the culminating time when the human relating of the first phase and the God relating of the second join in a sexual union of heart, soul, and might, of that love-engendering passion that, like the Sh'ma, can lift one to the divine. A new way in which to say the Sh'ma was proposed in the last chapter. So we shall now turn to a brief examination of the special association of sexuality with the Sabbath that both the talmudic and kabbalistic traditions stress.

Sabbath Sexuality

The association of the Sabbath with sexuality is defined in the *Shulchan Arukh,* the standard code of Jewish Law, as follows:

> One should not be unduly familiar with his wife, excepting at the time regularly appointed for the performance of his marital duty. . . . The time appointed for the learned men is from Sabbath Eve to Sabbath Eve.[8]

Where men of other occupations and dispositions are granted more frequent and even unspecified times for sexual union, it is traditional to view Friday night as "scholar's night," the night in which he is not only permitted but required, given certain conditions of ritual cleanliness on his wife's part, to perform his "marital duty." The laws concerning chastity begin with the statement: "It behooves a man to become accustomed to super holiness, purity of thought and proper frame of mind when having intercourse."[9]

Now, if it is appropriate to be accustomed to "super holiness" when having intercourse, the implication is that in its ideal form there is a holiness to sex. This potential can best be realized, the tradition holds, within the holy Temple of the Sabbath: a joining and mutual amplification of holy energies that can only be properly accomplished by a man whose spirit has been refined by deep thought and meditation. Such a man was the Baal Shem Tov, founder of the hasidic movement. One biographical account gives a most illuminating detail:

> Along with his bride, Rabbi Israel lived in a small mountain town
> . . . he spent his days and nights in study, worship, and meditation,
> coming home only on the Sabbath. Like the Ari [Isaac Luria], he
> spent seven years in such secluded meditation.[10]

Doubtless when the Baal Shem Tov performed his marital duty on the Sabbath, he did so because his meditations on the divine mysteries had instructed him in the holiness of Sabbath sexuality.

The nature of this holiness lies at the heart of the Lurianic Kabbalah. It is not necessary to enter here into an extended discussion of the sexual relations among the Partzufim in terms of which the ongoing processes of cosmic creation and Providential direction are explained. But there are two additional points that should be developed here. One involves the contribution of human sexuality to the supernal Tikkun. This is suggested in the *Etz Chayyim* of Chaim Vital, the major text of Lurianic cosmology, by the following:

> Just as the souls of the righteous raise the female waters for the
> purpose of uniting the Male and Female, in the same way the Male
> and Female can raise the female waters for the purpose of uniting
> Abba and Imma.[11]

On both the human and divine levels the cosmic process is defined by the division and unification of sexual energies, the energies of expansion and containment. There is, moreover, a sympathetic response on higher cosmic levels to unifications below. It is a central concept of the Lurianic Kabbalah that conjugal intercourse leads to a corresponding union between the lower Partzufim of Ze'ir Anpin and the Nukvah on the spiritual plane. This, in turn, leads to the higher coupling of Abba and Imma, each such union aiding the process of Tikkun above it. It is, then, the nature of properly attuned physical union to produce a spiritual union, an understanding enshrined in the popular expression for sex, "making love." The holiness of sex consists in two factors: It exemplifies and makes present the profoundest of divine mysteries and it spiritualizes the consciousness by lifting it into a realm of resonant sympathy beyond material discreetness. It is an act that brings the divine into immanence and leads the human spirit to transcendence.

The esoteric nature of human sexuality is further illuminated by a curious detail of Luria's sexual cosmology:

> And know that when reference is sometimes made to the Malkhut of Abba . . . the meaning is that [of] the glans of the Yesod of Abba [and this] is the mystery of circumcision and the uncovering, the Yesod and the glans. This glans we call the Malkhut of Abba.[12]

This seems to be saying that "the mystery of circumcision," its hidden purpose, is to expose the most sensitive portion of the male sexual organ and that this portion contains his feminine nature. For whereas the male sexual organ is symbolized by the Sefirah Yesod on the Tree of Life Diagram, the glans is symbolized by the feminine final Sefirah of Malkhut.

The first covenantal moment occurs when God changes the names of Abraham and Sarah to mark the new state of their relationship to him and institutes the rite of circumcision as a token of this covenant:

> Thy name shall be Abraham; for a father of many nations have I made thee. . . . Every man child among you shall be circumcised . . . and it shall be a token of the covenant between me and you. . . . As for . . . thy wife . . . Sarah shall her name be. And I will bless her, and give thee a son also of her: yea, I will bless her, and she shall be a mother of nations. (Gen. 17:1–16)

The sexual "mystery of circumcision" of which Vital spoke is suggested by the biblical context in which this rite was initiated, one in which the procreative function of Abraham and Sarah is insisted upon and the female partner is specially blessed. Thus the covenantal promise can only be transmitted to a child of Abraham's seed by passing through the blessed female vessel. But if the divine covenant enters into the procreative act and is marked by circumcision, then circumcision must serve a sexual function, one that contributes to the holiness of the act.

What this may be is suggested by the Lurianic identification of the glans with Malkhut, the lower female sexual Sefirah of the Tree of Life Diagram. This identification suggests, first of all, that circumcision was intended as a means of sensitizing the male to the sexuality of the female. But more than this, it suggests that the holiness of sex occurs when the male ceases to perceive the female as a sexual object or even sexual partner but rather experiences her as his female self. When Luria associates the male glans with the female soul, he provides a key for understanding the nature of higher Ruach sexuality. What characterizes Nefesh sex is the fact that each partner is imprisoned in the physical pleasure of his or her own body. It is the contrasting characteristic of Ruach sex that it lifts both partners into a shared passion in which they experience the other's pleasure in their own, a unity experienced not simply on a physical level, however exquisite, but in an ecstasy of the soul. Ruach sexual union is more than a physical coupling, then; it also contains a soul mating.

This is particularly true on the Sabbath, for on this day each partner is endowed with the Neshamah Yeterah, an additional soul that not only partakes in the sexual act but translates it to the supernal realm from which it came. The Kabbalah identifies the Sabbath with Malkhut, a female aspect of divine consciousness. And as the male attunes himself throughout the Sabbath eve to a feminine spiritual receptivity, so his consummate experience of Sabbath consciousness occurs in physically entering the female. If he has properly attuned himself in the earlier phases of the evening to the subtle Ruach energies of family interaction and prayer, then he will bring this spiritual sensitivity into the sexual act and endow it with a holy character. The Tzaddik, who generally engages in such Sabbath sexuality no more than twice a month, comes to it as to a sacred rite that can initiate him into the realm of higher energies and teach him how to work with them, how both to enhance and join their flow. This capacity to work on the subtle dimension of sexual energy is a key feature of Jewish mystical practice and is attested to in both talmudic law and kabbalistic cosmology. It provides the training ground and initial reward for the development of spiritual power and its lessons can be translated into many different spheres, social or supernal. The Ruach Master is he who can work with spiritual energy and, like the Baal Shem Tov, he delights in the crowning holiness of Sabbath sexuality.

The Sabbath Morning Devotions

The Jewish tradition of Sabbath sexuality, whether formulated in talmudic or kabbalistic terms, reflects a spiritual understanding strongly analogous to the tantric branches of Buddhism and Hinduism. A similar parallel to Eastern religious practice may be seen in the ideal time that Judaism stipulates for morning devotions. The *Shulchan Arukh* stipulates that

> the time to commence the reading of the *sh'ma* in the morning . . .
> extends to the end of the first quarter of the day . . . reckoned from
> daybreak. . . . The ideal fulfillment of the precept is to read as the
> pious of former days used to do. They were accustomed to begin
> reading a short time before morning dawn, in order to finish the
> reading of the *sh'ma* and the benedictions thereof at the morning
> dawn, and the prayer immediately thereafter. He who can manage
> to do so, his reward is very great . . . but one may read the *sh'ma* by
> itself even all day long.[13]

Though the Sh'ma may be said whenever one rises, the ideal time to rise for this purpose is before daybreak. As developed in the Mishnah, this is the hour from the dawn's early light, the point at which one can distinguish between the blue and white threads of the *tzitzit*, to the sparkling of the sun, the *netz ha-chamah*, as the sun first appears over the mountaintops. In the yogic tradition this is the time of the holiest *sattva* energies. By rising and cleansing oneself at least forty-five minutes before dawn, so that one is sitting in meditation during the ten minutes before dawn in which bodily chemistry is balanced and revitalized, yogis believe they obtain optimal health and the greatest benefits from disciplined meditation.

As we saw in the last chapter, Aryeh Kaplan has analyzed the two major biblical terms for meditation, *siyach* and *hagah*. Kaplan's analysis of *hagah* and related terms suggests that *hagah* signifies a directed mode of mantralike meditation:

> Rabbi David Kimchi states that the root H*agah* indicates a sound or thought that is repeated over and over. . . . What is immediately suggested here is a system very much like mantra meditation, where a word or phrase is repeated many times, either verbally or mentally . . . it is significant to note that the Hebrew word *Hegeh*, meaning rudder or helm, has exactly the same root letters as *Hagah*, meaning meditation. *Hagah*-meditation is therefore meant to provide the mind with a rudder and helm, so that it no longer drifts aimlessly in a sea of thought. . . . Another base closely related to *Hagah* is *Gah*, denoting "brightness.". . . The most important derivative of this base is the word *Nogah* . . . the primary meaning being the spiritual light that one experiences during meditation, a dawn-light shining through the darkness of the mundane world.[14]

Thus *hagah* meditation is a form of directed meditation that can be associated both with mantra repetition and the dawn. Since this is also the ideal time for saying the Sh'ma, it is possible to link the Sh'ma with *hagah* meditation in two respects. One can view the daily repetition of the formulaic Sh'ma, either by itself or in the context of the morning service, as constituting a form of this meditation. Or one can treat the Sh'ma as providing an introductory attunement to a guided Master Meditation such as that given in the previous chapter, a form of *hagah* meditation best performed in the dawn or early morning hours.

The Ruach-Neshamah portion of the Sabbath may be said to begin with the first light of the dawn and its first activity is the saying of the Sh'ma, which can serve as an introduction to a directed meditation. The significance of this introduction derives not only from what a skillful delivery can contribute to initiating the meditative state but also from its ritual power. As the only mode of prayer commanded in the Torah, the Sh'ma carries all the covenantal power that can be contained in prayer. Just as the prayer services derive their Torah status from their inclusion of the commanded Sh'ma, so a meditation introduced by the Sh'ma brings that meditation within the framework and power of Torah.

In a Sabbath observance that includes the full morning service, either at home or in the synagogue, one will normally have a light breakfast before the service. This meal does not count ritually as one of the three Sabbath meals, which are Friday night dinner, a large meal following the Sabbath morning service, and another light meal in the late afternoon. If one is following a less structured mode of observance, it seems advisable to begin the day with the Sh'ma and Master Meditation and then have breakfast. The period between a midmorning breakfast and a midafternoon main meal would then be taken up mainly with Torah reading and study.

So far we have discussed various conduits for the transmission of Sabbath holiness. To the main energy transformer of the three Mosaic laws, the additional means of heightening Sabbath holiness are the blessed candle lighting, whose ionizing of the air contributes a special spirit to the external atmosphere; the blessed wine drinking, which contributes its own "spirits" to enhance the feast and festivity of the evening; and the prayerful prelude of the Sh'ma to the crowning sexual consummation. If all this seems mildly Dionysian it is because the priests and curators of the holy have from archaic times recognized a spiritual content to various substances and activities that, when properly brought under the protection of the sacred, could lift the consciousness to transcendental experience. In addition to such natural substances and activities that can be ritually transformed for sacred purposes, there are also acts and artifacts of a wholly religious character that serve as direct agents of higher energies, and it is with these that the Sabbath morning is charged.

One might think that it is the Sh'ma, in prayer or meditation, that is the primary conveyor of the highest energies, but since this is or should be a daily practice, its Sabbath performance does not introduce a new energy but rather opens the soul to receive the specially holy energy that the next, more specifically Sabbath activity can convey. This is the prescribed reading from the Torah. In the first chapter it was noted that the priest Ezra restructured the covenant so that the divine presence and power could thenceforth be communicated through the physical book of the Torah, the ritual reading of its contents, and the private observance of its laws (Neh. 8–10). This priestly transfer of power from the Ark of the Covenant to the scribally duplicated Torah scrolls and books stands behind the present reverence for the Torah scrolls in synagogue worship, and with good cause. For the scrolls are still the respository of the same holy Presence that originally resided over the Ark in the Holy of Holies. It can be experienced by the spiritually sensitive just as it was by those sensitives who prescribed its central ritual use in synogogue worship.

The congregation always rises at the specified points in the service when the scrolls are shown and the culminating point in a service comes when the Torah is carried around the congregation and touched by its members. To carry the Torah or to be called up to the altar to read from it is the highest honor that can be awarded to a member. Many who have carried or touched the Torah scrolls during synagogue worship have been awed by the experience, and though this weekly experiencing of the holiness of the Torah scrolls is an important reason to attend Sabbath morning services, something of this same experience of the holy can be had in a private Sabbath-day reading of the prescribed Torah passage at home. For many the very act of picking up a printed Torah and reading the passage communicates a holy energy to the psychic system normally absent from such Torah reading at other times. And the fact that some passages may be more intellectually "interesting" than others seems to have nothing to do with the ritual effectiveness of the reading. From Ezra to the later rabbinical formulations of prescribed Torah readings for the Sabbath, the tradition has invested this commemorative covenantal act with the highest potency of Sabbath holiness, and it is available to all who keep the Sabbath. What is more, such ritual reading of the Torah every Sabbath can provide a familiarity with the Law that can enhance the interpretative skills of those who wish to follow the path of Covenantal Judaism.

Both the Sh'ma meditation and the Torah reading are characteristic of the Ruach-Neshamah portion of the Sabbath insofar as they are activities consciously directed to producing psychic openings to the divine spirit. What distinguishes the Nefesh-Ruach from the Ruach-Neshamah level of activity is that the former involves a conscious redirection to sacred purposes (Ruach) of normal animal and social functions (Nefesh) whereas the latter involves conscious rituals of attunement (Ruach) to the transcendent (Neshamah). As Friday night is devoted to lifting the Nefesh up to Ruach spirituality, so Saturday morning is devoted to opening this Ruach spirit to the wholly other energies of the Neshamah soul, the direction of spiritual evolution to which the Neshamah Yeterah has been guiding the observer throughout the Sabbath. On the Sabbath day, as on its eve, the Ruach period is extended beyond the saying of the Sh'ma, first to a period of meditation and then to the Torah reading or full prayer service. And as it participates in Ruach Torah study, the Neshamah soul is inspired to the deeper contemplation of the Torah passage by which it finally moves beyond the Ruach dimension of directed consciousness into its own higher space, a heavenly space in which the ascending soul and the setting sun can meet in a moment of shared radiance.

The Sabbath Sunset

The association of Jewish religious life, particularly on the Sabbath, with the sunset is so profound that it deserves a special section devoted to its significance. In recounting a crucial turning point in his spiritual life, Abraham Joshua Heschel tellingly reports: "Suddenly I noticed the sun had gone down. . . . I had forgotten God—I had forgotten Sinai—I had forgotten that sunset is my business."[15] The Jewish structuring of the day to begin at sundown focuses attention on the spiritual potentialities of this time, and it is a special virtue of Sabbath observance that it not only makes impossible such forgetfulness as Heschel once experienced but fully prepares the spirit to be receptive to the highest energies transmitted in the culminating time of the Sabbath sunset.

If properly prepared and permitted, the psychic system should move at this time into the state known today as spontaneous meditation. This is the state the Patriarch experienced when, as we are told, "Isaac went out to meditate in the field toward evening" (Gen. 24:63, AK). The word for "meditate" used here is *suach*, and this is its only occurrence in the Bible. But Aryeh Kaplan has given an important interpretation of its meaning as referring to the highest form of *siyach* meditation, the word *suach* being linguistically related to *siyach*. To greatly condense his precise and comprehensive analysis:

> The term *Siyach*, then, connotes spiritual elevation and growth, as well as referring to the Tree, which represents the spiritual ladder, and man's own spiritual essence. When the individual engages in *Siyach*-meditation, he clears his mind of all thought, and then

directs it on high, floating and soaring through the transcendental realm. . . . In general, the word *Suach* seems to have the same form as the roots . . . meaning "smooth" and "flat." *Suach*-meditation is therefore very similar to that implied by *Siyach*, but it is a mental state that is very "smooth," ultimately calm and tranquil. While *Siyach* can be said to denote climbing the Tree of Life, *Suach* would denote resting on its highest branches . . . [or] smoothly floating on the still waters at the Source.[16]

The priceless record of Father Isaac's meditative practice is most illuminating in specifying that it is "toward evening" that Isaac went out to *suach*, to achieve a state of ultimate tranquillity. It is of such a state that the poet Wordsworth also writes:

It is a beauteous evening, calm and free,
The holy time is quiet as a Nun
Breathless with adoration; the broad sun
Is sinking down in its tranquility;
The gentleness of heaven broods o'er the Sea:
Listen! the mighty Being is awake,
And doth with his eternal motion make
A sound like thunder—everlastingly.[17]

And I might add one of my own haiku on the subject:

Reverberating
Like a gong through my heart beat—
The chord of sunset.

It is particularly in the holy hour beyond time with which the Sabbath ends, from eighteen minutes before to forty-two minutes after sunset, that this powerful energy can be experienced by a receptive vessel. When a psychic vessel has been attuned for this moment by the spiritual exercises of the previous twenty-four Sabbath hours, it develops a crystalline resonance that can function like a radio receiver to pick up and amplify the subtle energy with which the sunset is endowed.

It is possible that this energy could be scientifically defined as predominantly or exclusively composed of low voltage, direct current, electromagnetic power, though no scientist has yet done so. But while the power of sunset has not been scientifically investigated, that of the aurora borealis has, and the result of that investigation can provide us with some intriguing clues to the energy function of the setting sun's color display. Bruce Brown has summarized the investigation of the aurora in his article "The Shining: The Mysterious Power of the Northern Lights":

> Geophysicists today see the space immediately beyond the earth's atmosphere—the magnetosphere—as a huge electrical generator, which develops power as the charged particles of solar wind pass through the earth's geomagnetic field. . . . The aurora is therefore the visible manifestation of great amounts of electrical power being "burned off." The power is direct current (D.C.) and can be drawn at any electrical ground below the aurora . . . the aurora must be produced by ionized particles from the sun striking atoms on the edge of the atmosphere . . . the particles strike atoms of oxygen, nitrogen and other gases, each of which gives off its characteristic color . . . there is no doubt that, up close, the aurora conveys a feeling of power that is not confined to colors in the sky.[18]

Though the color displays of the sun at its rising and setting appear to have a source other than the sunspot activity to which the aurora is attributed, the display itself serves as proof of electrical power generation. It is "the visible manifestation of great amounts of electrical power being 'burned off.'" Whatever causes the sun's rays at rising and setting to become ionized and accelerated toward the upper atmosphere—and I would speculate that it has something to do with the geometry of the sun's angle to the Earth at these times—the collision of solar particles with atoms of the various gases produces a colored by-product of the breakdown of atomic structure into more elementary particles and energy. The colored particles beautify the sky while the energy is discharged to the Earth in the form of direct electromagnetic current.

The work of Robert O. Becker and Andrew A. Marino has demonstrated that the human nervous system is designed to respond to such subtle though natural levels of energy. As they show, the central nervous system has properties of semiconductivity that can transmit

127

information by direct electromagnetic current, both self-generated and received from the environment.[19] Most interesting in the present context is the relationship of such information transmission from the external field to the establishment of circadian biological rhythm. Humans, honeybees, and homing pigeons are all able to respond to electromagnetic signals that seem to convey the same information provided by sun angle and polarized light. When shielded from light cues, humans continue to open and close their eyes just as oysters do their shells in synchronization with solar and lunar rhythms transmitted through electromagnetic currents.[20] The circadian sleep-wakefulness cycle is a similar general biological phenomenon and seems to indicate that the most powerful electromagnetic signals come when the sun is at or near an angle of 180 degrees to the Earth's horizon.

Modern chronobiology has yet to investigate the specific electromagnetic characteristics of sunrise and sunset, but the most recent research in geophysics and electrobiology suggests that they are powerful and independent of the color display also correlated with these phenomena. They have also been well attested by spiritual masters and poets in all traditions and are within the latent or conscious experience of all. There is, however, an important difference between the information transmitted at sunrise and sunset. The former awakens the psyche to activity while the latter composes it for rest. This information seems to be associated as much with the direction from which the sun appears as with its angle to the horizon, and these directions are associated not only with geography but also with cultures.

When Kipling said "East is East and West is West and never the twain shall meet," he was making an important correlation between cultural geography and the rising and setting of the sun, for East is, by definition, where the sun rises and West is where it sets. And it is most interesting that it is in the East that spiritual traditions emphasize the paramount importance of the sunrise while Western traditions emphasize the time of sunset. In the Far East lies Japan, which calls itself "The Land of the Rising Sun." And from Japan to India, the most spiritual hours are believed to be those just before dawn. The Western traditions deriving from Judaism for the most part follow Isaac in preferring the late afternoon and early evening hours for spiritual devotions. At this time the horns are sounded from minaret towers, Vesper bells chime from churches, and synagogues fill for Minchah and Ma'ariv, the afternoon and evening services that are nearly con-joined at sunset. Not that yogis do not appreciate the value of sunset nor Hasidim the value of sunrise, but they are less scrupulous in ob-serving the one than the other.

The reason may lie in a felt need for psychic balancing. It is a cliché to consider the East to be more right-brained and the West more left-brained, psychic orientations that may also be somehow linked with geography. Now if, on at least one level, this would make the right-brained East more passive and the left-brained West more active or aggressive, one can see why those from the East would need to be galvanized by sunrise while those from the West would need the relaxation granted by sunset. The most obvious proof of such a need lies in the Sabbath—the day of rest that has become universal in the West and has no indigenous counterpart in the East. It is not well known that until quite recently in modern Japan, industrial workers only had two or three days off after close to a month of steady work, and such practices were not an industrial invention but derived from Japanese culture.

The Sabbath is Judaism's gift to the world, but in its specifically Jewish form it is structured to take particular benefit of the tranquiliz-ing effects of the sunset: "From even unto even, shall you celebrate your sabbath" (Lev. 23:32). The scientific evidence for such a tran-quilizing effect—and there is further evidence for "the production of general anesthesia by electrical currents that traverse the brain"[21]—indicates that such effects are not simply subjective, though "the subject's state of arousal was an important element in determining the direction, and perhaps the existence, of a field-induced effect."[22] Be-cause these effects are subtle, they can easily be overpowered by any strongly motivated activity or concentration, but when prepared for and permitted they can be overwhelming.

Becker and Marino's electrobiological research has shown that "environmental electromagnetic energy mediates the transfer of in-formation from the environment to the organism,"[23] but scientific methodology can only investigate the medium, not the message. From the broad spectrum of response it elicits, it seems clear that it is a multidimensional message. Thus the message sent by the sunset causes flowers to close up, tired workers to chatter over cocktails, and Isaac to go out of his limited self in an experience of cosmic communion.

Again we must turn to Wordsworth for the words that can express this highest of sunset experiences:

> And I have felt
> A presence that disturbs me with the joy
> Of elevated thoughts; a sense sublime
> Of something far more deeply interfused,
> Whose dwelling is the light of setting suns,
> And the round ocean and the living air,
> And the blue sky, and in the mind of man:
> A motion and a spirit, that impels
> All thinking things, all objects of all thought,
> And rolls through all things.[24]

The information conveyed to Wordsworth by "the light of setting suns" was of a Presence, felt both within him and around him—"a sense sublime/ Of something far more deeply interfused." To attempt to reduce the source of such "elevated thoughts" to no more than electromagnetic currents is not even to explain the message that triggers somnolence in the lower animals. To assert that there are natural tranquilizing forces of great power operating on biological systems at sunset is not, then, to reduce such forces only to that constituent that can be scientifically measured. It seems, rather, that the information transmitted by such scientifically measurable forces has a complexity commensurate with the capacity of the receiving organ to decode its signals.

As we have seen, the Jewish tradition provides two models by which these energies can be utilized in their highest devotional form. The rabbinical approach is not to be simply enthralled by them but to convert their transcending power through the conscious discipline of liturgical prayer. The way of Isaac is to become one with this power, to Suach. The way of Suach may not be appropriate for everyone since it implies a degree of spiritual development beyond that of the Nefesh soul level. Some are so filled with tension that they are unable just to relax and watch or feel the tranquillity imparted by the sunset hour, or if they begin to feel it flooding their system they may become anxious at such an unaccustomed depth of response and break it off. But if permitted, it can become a great inner teacher, accustoming the soul to a previously unexperienced peace whose preservation and enhancement can lift it to the highest levels. As liturgical prayer will be fully treated in the next chapter, I shall confine my remaining remarks to the power of Suach.

Achieving the full state of Suach, or spontaneous meditation, normally requires a spirit that has already been rendered sensitive to subtle energies through conscious meditative work with these energies. It requires a certain familiarity with their somatic effects that can enable one to amplify rather than block their reception. With such readiness, however, the experience can become a fulfillment of the Sabbath command to rest, seeming to enter each cell with healing restoration. It is, as I have said in another haiku,

> *Balm in Gilead—*
> *Sunset splashing through the spine*
> *A quivering calm.*

It is an experience of being caught up and held by the embrace of a higher power to which one feels one belongs. Such an experience is not only healing to the body but to the soul, restoring it to that sense of harmony with the whole on which its own quality of harmony must rest. But this restoration is also transformational, not simply taking the soul back to cosmic unity but forward to that highest communion with the divine for which the soul is being perfected.

Though these energies are always present in the sunset, it is understandable that they would be greatly enhanced on the Sabbath. If ever the soul is properly prepared to receive the highest cosmic information, it is after such a period of sacred activities and with the aid of the Neshamah Yeterah. But the experience of Sabbath Suach can also inspire the soul to repeat this experience during the week, to strive to set this time apart every day for quiet meditation. The high tranquillity of sunset Suach can thus become part of one's daily life, relieving the rigors of labor with a touch of Sabbath rest. It can so keep one in the flow that one seems to float from Sabbath to Sabbath. As the culminating point of the Sabbath, the sunset Suach leads directly into the final sabbatical ceremony, that of Havdalah. In this ceremony of rekindling, the holiness of the Sabbath is drawn by the Havdalah torch into the profane week ahead, lighting its way and lightening its labor.

The Temples in Time and Space

The two great repositories of holiness in the Mosaic covenants are the Sabbath and the Temple, and the ceremonial rekindling that marks the conclusion of the Sabbath is a reminder of the inverse relationship of these two main pillars of the Sinai Torah. For where Sabbath holiness is defined by the law prohibiting kindling, Temple holiness is defined precisely by kindling, and on the Sabbath by that redoubled kindling required for the sabbatical doubling of the daily sacrifices (Num. 28:9–10). The Temple is exempt from the laws governing the Sabbath just as the Sabbath has been exempted from the laws governing the Temple, and yet both represent the highest containers of the divine Presence: "Ye shall keep my sabbaths, and reverence my sanctuary: I am the Lord" (Lev. 19:30).

God said, "Let them make me a sanctuary; that I may dwell among them" (Ex. 25:8) and then commanded that "ye separate the children of Israel from their uncleanness; that they die not in their uncleanness, when they defile my tabernacle that is among them" (Lev. 15:31). What defiles the Temple is contact with the dead, leprosy, and both male and female discharges. Sexual uncleanliness extends not only to masturbation and menstruation but even to normal intercourse: "The woman also with whom man shall lie with seed of copulation, they shall both bathe themselves in water, and be unclean until the even" (Lev. 15:18). Just as the people who came to Mount Sinai to receive the Ten Commandments were told, "Be ready against the third day: come not at your wives" (Ex. 19:15), so it would seem that any discharges associated with sexual maturity were sources of ritual uncleanliness that prohibited one's appearance at the Temple.

The main sources of defilement to the Temple involved, then, sex and death. These are two aspects of human existence caused or fundamentally altered by that mythic loss of immortal Edenic perfection for which we can adopt the more widespread Christian terminology of the Fall, though without its idea of Original Sin. As women were thenceforth to suffer in the labor of childbirth, so were men thenceforth to suffer in their farm labor, and both were now subject to death. Not only is contact with sex or death prohibited to those attending the Temple sacrifices, but work as well; for the days on which the people were to come to the Temple are specified holidays on which work is prohibited. In these prohibitions we may discern the essential function of the Temple: it is to provide a ritual means of atonement for that loss of perfection mythologized as the Fall. There is one further prohibition, involving only the priesthood, which makes this yet clearer:

> And the Lord spake unto Aaron, saying, Do not drink wine nor strong drink, thou, nor thy sons with thee, when ye go into the tabernacle of the congregation, lest ye die: it shall be a statute for ever throughout your generations: And that ye may put difference between holy and unholy, and between unclean and clean. (Lev. 10:8–10)

Drink is prohibited to the priests who enter the tabernacle so that they may distinguish between the holy and the unholy. This is also a distinction that entered creation with the Fall.

Now it should be clear that not only are those prohibitions involving sex and drink not forbidden on the Sabbath but that they have become special Sabbath *mitzvot* in the rabbinical tradition. In beginning the Sabbath meals with the sanctification of the wine and in specifying the Sabbath as the "scholar's night" for sex, the tradition has recognized, however silently, that what distinguishes the Temple in time from the Temple in space is the power of the Sabbath to sanctify and redeem the unholy for holy uses. Where the Temple in space "put difference between holy and unholy, and between unclean and clean," the inverse temporal Temple of the Sabbath lifts the spirit beyond its fallen condition into the world of Tikkun, the future time of redeemed consciousness. It does this through the greatest and most abiding revelation of the divine power, the sanctification of the very time of the Sabbath. In his beautiful book on the Sabbath, Heschel explores the manner in which this crowning commandment serves to sanctify time and transforms it into a special Temple:

> Judaism is a *religion of time* aiming at *the sanctification of time*. . . .
> The Sabbaths are our great cathedrals. . . . When we celebrate the Sabbath we adore precisely something we do not see. To name it queen, to call it bride is merely to allude to the fact that its spirit is a reality we meet rather than an empty span of time which we choose

to set aside for comfort or recuperation. . . . The Sabbath is the presence of God in the world, open to the soul of man. . . . What is the Sabbath? *Spirit in the form of time.*[25]

In the Sabbath, then, Moses transmitted to Israel and the world the highest degree of spiritual holiness, "the presence of God in the world, open to the soul of man."

More than anything else, it is this factor that distinguishes the Sabbath from the festivals. Unlike the intrinsic holiness of the Sabbath, the festivals as originally established derived their holiness from association with the Temple:

> These are the feasts of the Lord, which ye shall proclaim to be holy convocations, to offer an offering made by fire unto the Lord. (Lev. 23:37)

It is not the feast days themselves that contain holiness but the assemblies convened on these days; and these are "holy convocations," *mikra'ei kodesh*, because in them the holiness of the Temple is transmitted to the worshiper through the sacrificial offerings of which he partakes. God said that "at the door of the tabernacle . . . I will meet with the children of Israel, and the tabernacle shall be sanctified by my glory" (Ex. 29:42–43). These meetings are to take place at three specified times during the year, at the feasts of Passover, Shavuot, and Sukkot (Deut. 16:16). Rosh Hashana and Yom Kippur complete the list of the Mosaic holidays.

Of the five Mosaic holidays, only two seem to have been established to function independently of Temple worship—Passover and Yom Kippur. Passover was established prior to the Temple to memorialize an historical event, and it remains the oldest such holiday to be continuously observed anywhere in the world: "And this day shall be unto you for a memorial: and ye shall keep it a feast to the Lord throughout your generations . . . for ever" (Ex. 12:14). Yom Kippur, as first defined, seems to have been instituted so that it could survive the destruction of the Temple and carry on its power of ritual atonement. This can be seen more clearly in Kaplan's translation:

> On the 10th day of the 7th month you must fast [literally "afflict

your souls"] and not do any work. . . . This is because on this day
you shall have all your sins atoned, so that you will be cleansed. . . .
It is a Sabbath of Sabbaths to you, and . . . you must fast. This is a
law for all time. (Lev. 16:29–31)

Though the Temple absorbed the Passover sacrifice, it had originally been offered by family groups, "a lamb for an house" (Ex. 12:3),
and such home-based feasts can continue to memorialize the redemption from Egypt, as can the other commanded home rituals of clearing
the house of all leaven and eating matzoh for the seven days of the
festival. Similarly the command to afflict one's soul on Yom Kippur,
traditionally interpreted to mean fasting, seems to have been granted
a power of atonement independent of the simultaneous Temple ritual
involving the scapegoat.

Passover and Yom Kippur are also distinguished from the remaining Mosaic holidays because observance of them is necessary to maintain one's identification with the people of Israel:

For whosoever eateth leavened bread from the first day until the
seventh day, that soul shall be cut off from Israel. (Ex. 12:15)

And ye shall do no work in that same day: for it is a day of atonement, to make an atonement for you before the Lord your God. For
whatsoever soul it be that shall not be afflicted in that same day, he
shall be cut off from among his people. And whatsoever soul it be
that doeth any work in that same day, the same soul will I destroy
from among his people. (Lev. 23:28–30)

So that one's soul not be cut off from the formative historical experience of Israel, on the seven days of Passover one must "eat unleavened
bread . . . the bread of affliction . . . that thou mayest remember the day
when thou camest forth out of the land of Egypt all the days of thy life"
(Deut. 16:3). And to ensure that one's soul will be included in the final
perfection of Israel as "a kingdom of priests and an holy nation," one
must atone yearly for one's sins on Yom Kippur through the self-
affliction of fasting. Thus it is the sacrificial acts that afflict the spirit,
through dietary restriction and fasting, that could best survive the destruction of the physical Temple and maintain their sacramental power.

Similarly, those holidays at which Temple attendance was not commanded, Rosh Hashanah and Yom Kippur, have been able to assume a
preeminent position in the post-Temple era precisely for the reason
that they were not centered on the sacrificial feasts.

Not only will one be cut off from Israel for not fasting on Yom
Kippur but one must also observe it as a "sabbath of rest" (Lev. 23:32),
abstaining from all work, on pain of death. The Torah ordained seven
special days on which no work was to be done: the first and seventh
days of Passover, Shavuot, Rosh Hashanah, Yom Kippur, and the first
and eighth days of Sukkot. But the penalty of death applies only to
work on Yom Kippur, an extreme penalty that links this holiday most
closely to the Sabbath.

> Ye shall keep the sabbath therefore; for it is holy unto you: every
> one that defileth it shall surely be put to death: for whosoever doeth
> any work therein, that soul shall be cut off from among his people.
> Six days may work be done; but in the seventh is the sabbath of
> rest, holy to the Lord: whosoever doeth any work in the sabbath
> day, he shall surely be put to death. Wherefore the children of Is-
> rael shall keep the sabbath, to observe the sabbath throughout their
> generations, for a perpetual covenant. (Ex. 31:14–16)

Work on the Sabbath is the ultimate defilement of covenantal holiness that both cuts the soul off from Israel and is punishable with
death. To abstain from work on the Sabbath and on Yom Kippur, the
"Sabbath of Sabbaths," is, then, to "choose life" (Deut. 30:19), that
life filled with the Presence of God: "for he is thy life and the length
of thy days" (Deut. 30:20). It is this Presence that fills these holiest of
holidays, the Sabbath and Yom Kippur.

Though the remaining festivals can no longer be transmitters of
the specific holiness attached to the Temple sacrifices, they can, as
presently observed, provide a structure that facilitates identification
with the history and hopes of Israel. The Mosaic festivals fall into two
main groups devoted to memorializing the past and actualizing the
future. Extending from Passover, through the counting of the Omer,
to Shavuot, the festival identified with the giving of the Torah, the
spring festivals memorialize the Exodus from Egypt and bring the
present-day observer through the seven weeks of gathering Omers of

manna to that encounter at Mount Sinai at which the Covenant of Holiness through Torah can ever be newly made. The fall festivals, from Rosh Hashanah and Yom Kippur to Sukkot, begin with the announcement of a New Year through the sounding of the Shofar and bring the observer through a final period of ritual atonement to the Temple space of the Sukkah that is spiritually built on the mountain in Messianic Jerusalem. At the holy mountain in Sinai, the festival of the first fruits, Shavuot, is celebrated with a rededication to the covenant made that day for the salvation of the mortal Nefesh soul. At the holy mountain in Jerusalem, the festival of the latter fruits and of the vine, Sukkot, is celebrated in the Messianic Temple of Ruach consciousness. Significantly, the Mosaic Passover is a seven-day festival, its seven days not only memorializing the Exodus but also the Creation, whereas the eight days of Sukkot take us beyond creation, not to a past holiness within creation but forward to the wholly spiritualized realm of future perfection.

The festivals now function like the Sabbath to bring the soul into the world of Tikkun, but the spiritual development made possible through the festivals must now be dependent upon the strength of one's own spiritual discipline. The feast days of communion with God are no more. But the intrinsic holiness of the Sabbath is still intact. It is still the "sign" by which one can experience the divine power of sanctification: "Verily my sabbaths ye shall keep: for it is a sign between me and you throughout your generations . . . for a perpetual covenant. . . . And he gave unto Moses, . . . upon mount Sinai, two tables of testimony, tables of stone, written with the finger of God" (Ex. 31:13, 16, 18). Sabbath observance is the only ritual included in the Ten Commandments, the epitome of Torah spoken with the voice of God and written with His finger.

On Mount Sinai, God made a covenant with his redeemed people in which he promised that obedience to His voice would be rewarded with holiness and priestly empowerment. The Sinai Covenant involves only the quintessential Ten Commandments, and the instrument of its transformative holiness is the Sabbath.

CHAPTER 4

Prayer and the Moabite New Covenant of Love

To Love and Serve God

The Commandment

With this chapter we come to the highest level of covenant—the covenant enacted at Moab, which links the new commandment to love God with such a repetition of set words as defines the nature of liturgical prayer. In this first section, we shall attempt to understand the meaning of the central commandment of the new Moabite Covenant, particularly as revealed through the atonement experience. This will be shown to lead to the regular practice of liturgical prayer, which the next section will examine with respect not only to the nature and order of the prayer service but also to methods of performance that can enhance its mystical effectiveness. The concluding sections will offer a quasi-Lurianic explanation of both the purpose and effectiveness of prayer, and they will show how prayer can accomplish that divine unification through which the cosmos can be rectified and the Kingdom of God can be realized on Earth.

We begin with the commandment to "love the Lord thy God with all thine heart, and with all thy soul, and with all thy might" (Deut. 6:5). This commandment marks the first point at which love of God is enjoined upon man in the Torah, and perhaps in the history of religious thought and behavior. Whatever the pre-history of the Book of Deuteronomy may be, it was in 621 B.C.E. that the High Priest Hilkiah was credited with the discovery of the scroll of this book in the crumbling walls of the Temple. This discovery immediately had far reaching effects, causing the religious reforms of King Josiah and influencing the thought of Jeremiah. For it is in terms of a new covenant of the heart that both Josiah and Jeremiah express their response to this discovery.

Josiah, in his role as king, initiates a new communal covenant based on the essential involvement of the heart in all religious practice, a condition that shows his recognition that the essence of the new covenant with which Deuteronomy closes involves just such heart involvement:

> And the king stood by a pillar, and made a covenant before the Lord, to walk after the Lord, and to keep his commandments and his testimonies and his statutes with all their heart and all their soul, to perform the words of this covenant that was written in this book. And all the people stood to the covenant. (II Kings 23:3)

Hilkiah and others were sent to inquire of Huldah, the prophetess who "dwelt in Jerusalem in the college" (II Kings 22:14), regarding the divine wrath that Judah's idolatries would seem, from the words of Deuteronomy, to have merited. Her prophetic response was that Josiah would escape the curse God would bring on Jerusalem "because thine heart was tender, and thou hast humbled thyself before the Lord" (II Kings 22:19). As we shall see, these are essential conditions for realizing the intent of the central commandment of Deuteronomy to love God.

But before turning to the development of this concept in Deuteronomy, we should also view its further development in the prophetic understanding of Jeremiah, an understanding that seems to get to the core of its meaning:

> Circumcise yourselves to the Lord, and take away the foreskins of your heart, ye men of Judah and inhabitants of Jerusalem: lest my fury come forth like fire, and burn that none can quench it, because of the evil of your doings. . . . And I will give them an heart to know

me, that I am the Lord: and they shall be my people, and I will be their God: for they shall return unto me with their whole heart. . . . Then shall ye call upon me, and ye shall go and pray unto me, and I will hearken unto you. And ye shall seek me, and find me, when ye shall search for me with all your heart. . . . Behold, the days come, saith the Lord, that I will make a new covenant with the house of Israel, and with the house of Judah: Not according to the covenant that I made with their fathers in the day that I took them by the hand to bring them out of the land of Egypt; which my covenant they brake, although I was an husband unto them, saith the Lord: But this shall be the covenant that I will make with the house of Israel: After those days, saith the Lord, I will put my law in their inward parts, and write it in their hearts; and will be their God, and they shall be my people. (Jer. 4:4, 24:7, 29:12-13, 31:31–33)

The circumcision here required, as we shall soon see it is also in Deuteronomy, signifies a new covenant of the heart. And, as in Deuteronomy, this is an operation that can finally only be performed by God. But the precondition for such a change of heart is the prayerful search for God that springs out of the longing of the heart for the experience of divine communion, a longing that develops that tenderness of heart and humility of the self of which Huldah spoke. The result of such a consummation will be a heart not only made new through an opening metaphorically akin to circumcision but bearing within it the law of this new covenant, capable of discerning from its own feelings what is the Way of God and desiring to walk only on that path.

But Josiah and Jeremiah, as well as all who follow them on the path of the heart—both in Judaism and in the religions derived from it[1]—are only developing what is already contained whole in Deuteronomy, the understanding of the central role played by holy love in redeeming the soul from its material enslavement to a new life both divine and eternal as well as the understanding of what is required for its achievement. We can only arrive at such understanding, however, by recognizing the significance of the context in which it is placed, the final address of Moses to the Israelites before they are to enter the Promised Land, in the course of which the people do make this new covenant of the heart, the "gracious covenant" (Deut. 7:9),[2] through which alone they will be capable of perpetual survival in this land.

Moses begins his discourse by rehearsing the earlier covenant of the Ten Commandments made with the Israelites at Sinai, commandments through whose practice in the Promised Land they would continue to "fear the Lord thy God" (Deut. 6:2). That fear had been instilled in them through the terrifying mode of the divine delivery: "The Lord talked with you face to face in the mount out of the midst of the fire, I stood between the Lord and you at that time, to shew you the word of the Lord: for ye were afraid by reason of the fire, and went not up into the mount" (Deut. 5:4–5). But the new covenant he is to make with them and their descendants—"with him that standeth here with us this day before the Lord our God, and also with him that is not here with us this day" (Deut. 29:15)—is introduced with that new commandment that is to be its sign, the commandment that "thou shalt love the Lord thy God with all thy heart, and with all thy soul, and with all thy might" (Deut. 6:5) that contains the core meaning of the Sh'ma. We have seen in chapter 2 that the meaning we are to hearken to in the proclamation of the Sh'ma is not simply the identity of Israel's God and His unity but also the potential, ultimate, and necessary unification of the transcendent and immanent aspects of the divine both with and through Israel. It is to achieve this unification of what in later rabbinical and kabbalistic thought are referred to primarily by the names "Holy One, blessed be He," and "Shekhinah" that Israel is now required to "love the Lord thy God." But Israel is enjoined not only to feel such love of the divine; it must also repeat the words that are to instill this love at certain set times of the day. And the association suggests a necessary connection between the ability to feel such love and the practice of prayer that was later understood to be instituted here.

This association appears again in the passage now considered to be the "second paragraph" of the Sh'ma:

> And it shall come to pass, if ye shall hearken diligently unto my commandments which I command you this day, to love the Lord your God, and to serve him with all your heart, and with all your soul, that I will give you the rain of your land. . . . Therefore shall ye lay up these my words in your heart . . . speaking of them . . . when

thou liest down, and when thou risest up . . . that your days may be multiplied, and the days of your children, in the land which the Lord sware unto your fathers to give them, as the days of heaven upon the earth. (Deut. 11:13–21)

In this passage the commandments of the new covenant are reduced to the essential two, "to love the Lord your God, and to serve him with all your heart," and it is the reciting of these words that seems to signify the proper way of serving God with one's heart. Though earlier biblical texts associated service to God with the animal sacrifices offered by the Sanctuary priests, here it seems to refer to the practice of regular prayer that later came both to supplant the animal sacrifices when they could no longer be performed and to fulfill their original purpose. Indeed, as Rabbi Joseph B. Soloveitchik has noted:

The Talmud associates the precept of prayer with the verse, "to serve Him with all your heart" (Deut. 11:13). "What is service of the heart? It is prayer" (T. B., Ta'anit 2a). But what is meant by service of the heart? How does one fulfill this requirement? . . . Even those Sages who argued that "intention" was not a necessary component in the observance of the commandments admitted that conscious intent is a prerequisite for prayer, for its very fulfillment must come from the heart.[3]

Truly to pray to God and to love Him must come from such an opening of the heart as alone can fulfill the conditions of this new covenant and serve as its sign. To the old circumcision of the flesh and the requirements of the Sinai Covenant are now to be added the two higher characteristics of the new covenant with the new circumcision they require:

And now Israel, what doth the Lord thy God require of thee, but to fear the Lord thy God, to walk in all his ways, and to love him, and to serve the Lord thy God with all thy heart and with all thy soul. . . . Circumcise therefore the foreskin of your heart, and be no more stiffnecked. (Deut. 10:12, 16)

If the purpose of the Sinai Covenant can be said to be the rectification of the fallen Nefesh soul and initiation of the Ruach soul, the purpose of the new covenant at Moab is to complete this development with the perfection of the Ruach soul and the simultaneous initiation of the Neshamah soul. Before the people of Israel could be ready for this higher covenant, however, they had to wander for forty years in the wilderness, developing themselves through the holiness of Sabbath observance. Their animal functions had to be purged of their grossness as they partook of this holiness, so that through the sanctified and sensitized flesh man could experience an ecstasy recognized to be divine. The Nefesh soul can experience the divine either through the spiritualization of the sensual (associated with the Patriarchal Covenant whose sign is the circumcision of the flesh) or through the spiritualization of the temporal (primarily the observance of the Sabbath that is the sign of the Sinai Covenant). But the Ruach soul can experience the divine directly through the heart, especially when that heart is engaged in prayer. For the sign of this new covenantal power is an inner circumcision of the heart, an operation by which all that closes the heart in is removed to expose that hidden tenderness that Huldah could recognize in Josiah.

But even as Moses assembled all of Israel to take the "oath" (Deut. 29:13) of this new covenant, he knew that this "stiffnecked" people would not be able to perform the circumcision of the heart necessary for them to keep this covenant and so continue to receive the blessing that results from fulfilling it. Rather, he prophesies that they will first merit the curse, losing the Promised Land and becoming a scattered people, but that they will finally return to God and be redeemed from their captivity:

> And it shall come to pass, when all these things are come upon thee, the blessing and the curse, which I have set before thee, and thou call them to mind among all the nations, whither the Lord thy God hath driven thee. And shall return unto the Lord thy God, and shalt obey his voice according to all that I command thee this day, thou and thy children, with all thine heart, and with all thy soul; that then the Lord thy God will turn thy captivity, and have compassion upon thee, and will return and gather thee from all the nations whither the Lord thy God hath scattered thee. (Deut. 30:1–3)

The new covenant will only begin to be fulfilled when those who have "forsaken the covenant of the Lord" (Deut. 29:25) "return" to God and his ways. This "return" from a figurative condition of exile is, as Rabbi Soloveitchik has shown, the true meaning of "Teshuvah," commonly understood to mean "repentance."

> Every sinner is really in exile, banished to a remote corner of the heavens, "dispersed" among the nations . . . alienated and blown to and fro by each gust of wind.[4]

But to return from such spiritual alienation, the will is as inadequate to accomplish its own redemption as it was to prevent the intended blessing from turning into a curse. What is still required is the circumcision of the heart of which man has proven himself incapable. And this, we are told in what is probably the most important verse in the Bible, can come only from God:

> And the Lord thy God will circumcise thine heart, and the heart of thy seed, to love the Lord thy god with all thine heart, and with all thy soul, that thou mayest live. (Deut. 30:6)

This key verse has three clauses, all of greatest significance and all causally connected. The final clause, "that thou mayest live," grants the reward of life to the accomplishment of the two stipulated preconditions: the love of God consequent upon the divine circumcision of the heart. Elsewhere this reward is applied to fulfillment of the whole of the Moabite Covenant, thereby equating these preconditions with the whole of the new covenant, just as Sabbath observance had previously been equated with the whole of the Sinai Covenant. And the life promised here goes beyond earthly reckoning; it is a divine life—"for he is thy life, and the length of thy days" (Deut. 30:20), reckoned as "the days of heaven" (Deut. 11:21). But such redemption from the captivity of mortality is finally dependent upon one crucial factor—our ability to love God, and over this, we are told, we have no power because it can proceed only from the grace of God, from His secret disposition to perform the required circumcision of the heart that will permit it to experience the salvific love. This disposition cannot be forced since, as we have just been told, "the secret things belong unto the Lord our God" (Deut. 29:29). As we become psychologically ready to begin Teshuvah, we are suddenly confronted with our utter helplessness, with our complete dependence upon divine grace. No matter how many our good deeds and right intentions, such finite factors can never add up to the infinite.

In our present state of exile, we are brought to this confrontation every year on the Sabbath just before the High Holy Days in which this Torah portion of Nitzavim is read. And it seems clear that the rabbis who devised the yearly cycle of Torah readings intended the reading of Deuteronomy to coincide with these penitential holy days so that the final Day of Atonement, Yom Kippur, can function as it was intended. As Rabbi Soloveitchik explains in his translation of Leviticus 16:30:

> Yom Kippur—the Day of Atonement—has a double function. The first is *kapparah*—acquittal from sin or atonement. . . . The second aspect of Yom Kippur is *taharah* —catharsis or purification. As it is written: "For the virtue of this very day shall acquit you of sin, to cleanse you". . . . The Day of Atonement possesses a special power of purification not present in penitence which takes place on any other day of the year.[5]

Thus the reading of Deuteronomy that precedes Yom Kippur can serve to prepare the soul for the "special power of purification" through which it can achieve the highest form of atonement. This is the sure sense that it has experienced the circumcision of the heart that can bring it into the new covenant with God projected by Moses and Jeremiah. But the words of Deut. 30:6 can only serve in this way if the reader has been engaged in an intense search for their salvific meaning and their implications have spoken directly to the soul.

Early in Deuteronomy, Moses had already announced the initial failure of the covenant he was about to establish, with the consequent scattering of Israel from the Promised Land, as well as the later return from exile, saying: "But from thence ye will seek the Lord thy God; and thou shalt find Him, if thou search after Him with all thy heart and with all thy soul" (Deut. 4:29). In addition to its plain meaning, that the search for the path of return to God will be rewarded if it is undertaken with the deepest levels of the heart and soul, this verse

145

has additional resonances provided by the meaning of the words here translated as "seek" and "search." The latter is a form of the Hebrew root *d-r-sh* that, in addition to meaning "search," also can mean "to interpret." Thus one means of finding one's way back to God would be through study and proper interpretation of the Torah, an interpretation in which the intellect is not separated from the heart and soul but calls upon their deepest intuitions. Such interpretation can lead one to that recognition of one's utter dependence upon divine grace at which we arrived in our earlier analysis of Deuteronomy 30:6. This insight can in turn lead to the secondary implication of the word translated as "seek," a form of the Hebrew root *b-k-sh* that can also mean "to pray." Thus the passage can be understood to mean that when the exiled pray to God they shall find Him (or be answered) if they have correctly interpreted what they should pray for and yearn for it from the depths of their being. Not only does this suggest that Torah study and prayer are the means for finding one's way to God but also that effective prayer can only come from such study. For once one has recognized that salvation is only possible through love of God and that this is wholly dependent upon God's grace, the only recourse left to the heart yearning for redemption is prayer. If one has never previously been able to utter a true prayer—to pray with all one's heart and soul—this recognition can give rise to such a heartfelt prayer as Avinu Malkenu, the prayer attributed to the great talmudic Kabbalist, Rabbi Akiba:

> *Avinu Malkenu hanenu va'aneinu ki ein banu ma'asim aseh imanu tzedaka vachesed vehoshi'einu.* (Our Father, our King, be gracious to us and answer us, for we have no meritorious deeds; deal charitably and kindly with us and deliver us.)[6]

As Rosh Hashanah arrives we are thus prepared to prostrate ourselves during the Aleinu prayer, to try during the ritual of Tashlich to cast all our sins into the depths of the sea, and always to pray for the grace to overcome all obstacles to our love of God. And we discover that the liturgical prayers arranged so long ago give perfect voice to our own most pressing need, that they have been constructed precisely to facilitate the return from a condition of spiritual exile to the new covenant of the circumcised heart. But all our prayers during the

Days of Penitence come up against the solid obstruction of our inability to conceptualize the divine object of our intended love in any form that could inspire such love.

On the one hand, Teilhard de Chardin is right when he says that one cannot love the collective All of the philosophers but only a personal God:

> So long as it absorbs or appears to absorb the person, collectivity kills the love that is trying to come to birth. . . . As such collectivity is essentially unlovable. . . . But if the universe ahead of us assumes a face and a heart, and so to speak personifies itself, then in the atmosphere created by this focus the elemental attraction will immediately blossom. . . . For love to be possible there must be coexistence . . . the uncompromising affirmation of a personal God.[7]

But on the other hand, we are enjoined by the Second Commandment against the idolatrous imagining of any form such a personal God might take. Indeed, it is most significant that the sole context in which the human love of God is mentioned in the first four Books of Moses involves this prohibition of imaging:

> Thou shalt not make unto thee any graven image, or any likeness of any thing that is in heaven above, or that is in the earth beneath, or that is in the water under the earth: Thou shalt not bow down thyself to them, nor serve them: for I the Lord thy God am a jealous God, visiting the iniquity of the fathers upon the children unto the third and fourth generation of them that hate me; and showing mercy unto thousands of them that love me, and keep my commandments. (Ex. 20:4–6)

It would seem that the kind of contemplative exercises recommended in the classic works of popular morality to inspire such love,[8] the contemplation of the divine works of power or mercy, can only lead to a form of idolatrous worship, at best inspiring reverence rather than love or, if the latter be claimed, a species of nonsalvific sentiment.

It is with this total failure of the mind to illumine the path to the desired love, while longing for such love is ever increasing, that the Day of Atonement finally arrives. We come to the communal confession of sin knowing only one thing: we cannot achieve on our own the redemptive love that could purge us of all that has blocked our way to God. Our only hope is humbly to acknowledge that "we have no meritorious deeds" and to pray that God will "deal charitably and kindly with us and deliver us." And then the miraculous atonement sweeps through us, and we experience a love unlike and beyond all our preconceptions.

The Experience

Perhaps the most famous example of this classic pattern of return through the "virtue" of the Day of Atonement is that of the near apostate Franz Rosenzweig who, in 1913, had an experience so transformative that he became the preeminent philosopher of Judaism in our century. In his great work, *The Star of Redemption*, he speaks more authentically than any before him on the nature of the love relationship between man and God he had first experienced on that Yom Kippur when he discovered: "This God of love, he alone is God!"[9]

What Rosenzweig discovered on that fateful Yom Kippur is that the love we are supposed to experience with our whole heart, soul, and might, that love which becomes a revelation of the reality of God and the ground of our faith, is not our love for God but His love for us, that God is the lover and the soul the beloved:

> It is love which meets all the demands here made on the concept of the revealer, the love of the lover, not that of the beloved. Only the love of a lover is such a continually renewed self-sacrifice; it is only he who gives himself away in love. The beloved accepts the gift. That she accepts it is her return-gift, but in her acceptance she remains within herself and becomes a contented soul at peace with herself . . . the relationship between God and the soul ever remains the same. God never ceases to love, nor the soul to be loved. . . . And because the soul holds on to him, therefore God allows himself to be held by it. Thus the attribute of faithfulness endows the soul with the strength to live permanently in the love of God.[10]

Central to this redemptive experience is the overwhelming awareness that one is not the subject "but the object of love."[11] And it is because God's love is experienced not as "an attribute, but an event,"[12] that it can be experienced entirely without the conceptual images attached to idolatrous sentiment.

But Rosenzweig mistakes the nature of this encounter when he attributes only the emotion of peace to the "beloved soul."[13] For what is most distinctive about this experience is that this love is felt as the emotion of one's own heart while one is constantly made aware that one's heart is not its source, that it has arisen from no contemplation of divine perfections and has no object beyond the heart that feels it. It is not that a personal feeling of peace is absent from the total experience, but this response of the reflexive consciousness to the experience that has possessed the soul does not have the commanding power of the love throbbing in the heart. The relationship of these two emotions has been better understood by Abraham Isaac Kook, the late Chief Rabbi of Palestine before the founding of the present State of Israel, in describing the culminating experience of successful return or penitence: "After every consideration of penitence a man should be happier and more at peace with himself than he was before. This is certainly the case . . . if the disposition of divine love has begun to vibrate in him."[14]

The essence of this experience, then, is that one's heart has become a vessel for receiving the influx of divine love. But it can only become such a vessel through the workings of the holiness engendered in the soul through adherence to the Sinai Covenant, the sanctification transmitted through observance of the Sabbath and the commandments. As Rav Kook has said:

> The grace of God's love, a boon from on high, is destined to break out from its confinements, and the holiness of life will hew a path toward this delight, so as to enable it to appear in its full splendor and might.[15]

The mystical tradition has long associated the specific holiness of the Sabbath with the Shekhinah, and so, too, can the longing of holy beings for the final boon of divine love be identified with that of the Shekhinah, as Rav Kook has also shown:

> Every righteous person experiences great anguish because he does not feel sufficiently close to God, and his great thirst remains

149

unquenched. Because of this anguish all his organs are tense with endless longing, and he finds no peace in all the delights and pleasures of the world. This is in essence the anguish of the *Shekinah*, the anguish of the divine Presence, for all life in all the worlds is astir with longing that the supreme perfection of godliness be made manifest in them.[16]

For the heart to become the perfect receptacle of the divine love, it must make the Shekhinah become manifest within it, lifting the holy spark of her immanence in the soul until its pure longing for unification with the transcendent is freed from all the shells of material desire that had previously obscured and deflected it. Thus, in one of the major ethical treatises of the Kabbalah, the *Reshit Chokhmah* of Elijah de Vidas, a product of sixteenth-century Safed, the heart that expresses this longing of the soul is explicitly identified with the Shekhinah: "His soul should continuously yearn for the *Shekinah* whose name is 'heart.' That is what is meant by 'desire of the heart.'"[17] As de Vidas further explains:

"Cleaving" to God consists in a person's attaching himself with his soul to the *Shekhinah* and concentrating all his attention upon Her unification, as well as upon the separation from Her of all the evil shells. . . . We can awaken this love through our prayers and through our deeds, uniting the *Shekhinah* with the Holy One, blessed be He.[18]

In the experience of receiving an influx of supernal love, there is repeated on the emotional level, then, that same distinction between influx and vessel that, on the archetypal sexual level, characterizes the masculine and feminine Partzufim engaging in unification, Yichud. Traditional Kabbalists have not always been clear on this distinction since their own masculinity has often caused them to reverse the sex of their divine partner, as in de Vidas's typical statement: "It is proper that he feel passionate about carrying out the commandments since, through their performance, he makes love to the King's Daughter, that is, the *Shekhinah.* . . ."[19] But Rosenzweig is correct in his characterization throughout of the loving God as masculine and the beloved soul as feminine. The fact that God and the soul are traditionally given these genders in the folk imagination thus seems to be due less to the influence of cultural male supremacy than to the authentic experience of divine love as that given only to the truly receptive heart. In becoming truly receptive, therefore, the heart manifests itself as the divine Shekhinah, the perfect vessel that alone can properly mate with the Holy One, blessed be He. And so through the loving emotion of the divinely circumcised human heart, the Yichud of the Shekhinah and the Holy One, blessed be He, can take place that defines and accomplishes the Tikkun, or cosmic rectification, central to Lurianic thought.

This Tikkun has both an outer cosmic and an inner spiritual nature. On the inner or human level, the divine Yichud accomplishes the conception of a new or higher soul. The innate Nefesh soul develops the higher soul dimensions that permit its personality to survive the dissolution of physical vitality through a process of encounter and ever increasing commitment between the human and divine that defines the essence of covenant. As we have seen, the initial Sinai Covenant is concerned to develop the Ruach level of soul that can participate in the realization of a "holy nation." When one's mystical intention or Kavanah makes one mindful of the holy energy present in effective religious observance, particulary of the Sabbath, one experiences the growth of the Ruach soul, of the body of holiness that informs our physical frame when our actions initiate the divine Yichud. This is felt most powerfully when the candles ushering in the Sabbath are lit, and the Maariv prayers said. But to progress from the Ruach soul to the higher level of the Neshamah soul, it is necessary to enter into the new covenant of the circumcised heart that depends on the grace of God. And when the grace of this divine love pours into the heart, one experiences the formation of the new Neshamah soul body. This is qualitatively different from the Ruach soul body with which one was previously familiar. The lower Ruach level had a dense, smokelike quality that seemed to flow through one to connect the inner holiness with the holiness of the surrounding Sabbath in one continuum. The Neshamah soul body not only has a lighter, electric or flamelike quality but it is also definitely centered in the heart and radiates from it to fill and inform all of the physical body.

These differences reflect the differences between these soul levels, for where the Ruach experience is one of entering into the cosmic flow, the Neshamah experience is centered in that self which is above this flow, which has been perfected by participating in the experience of divine love. De Vidas's distinction between the final rewards of these three soul levels is relevant here:

> If he merits reward on the level of vital-soul [nefesh] alone, his resting place will be in the location where the vital-souls reside following death. And if he merits reward on the level of spirit [ruah], he will enjoy Paradise. If he merits reward on the level of super-soul [neshamah], he will be privileged to ascend to the upper realm of Paradise. Those who attain the grade of super-soul are called God's lovers. . . . And the love of one who attains the grade of super-soul will be continuous, preventing him from separating himself from the Creator on account of his great desire for Him.[20]

The characteristic of the new soul conceived through the Yichud of the Shekhinah and the Holy One, blessed be He, in the loving emotion of one's own heart, is its continuous desire to sustain this state of closeness to the divine. In this special sense the Neshamah souls are called "God's lovers"—not that they initially experience the love in their heart as deriving from themselves rather than from God but that they love and wish to perpetuate this experience. Thus de Vidas advises those who would have this experience of divine love to "clothe yourself with the love for that world where the super-souls reside. There they are bound up in the bond of eternal life, cleaving to their Maker."[21] So, too, Rav Kook tells us: "The soul is agitated by the intensity of the higher delight, and the love of this supernal delight enhances all the spiritual and the moral dispositions of the self."[22] It is "love for that world where the super-souls reside," the "love of this supernal delight," that the soul can claim as its own and that fulfills Jeremiah's prophecy of the new covenant: "After those days, saith the Lord, I will put my law in their inward parts, and write it in their hearts."

The heart in which the divine law is written represents the perfection of the Ruach soul. This happens together with the final salvific conception of the Neshamah soul that establishes the "bond of eternal life." And it is the development of this fledgling Neshamah soul, which is its own higher self, that the fully perfected Ruach soul loves. In the later section entitled "The Heart of the Matter," we will come to understand how such love of its own spiritual development can also be equated with the soul's love of God, but first we must recognize how the desire of the soul to perpetuate its experience of God's love serves to internalize the covenant, how, in the words of Rav Kook, "the love of this supernal delight enhances all the spiritual and the moral dispositions of the self." The conception of a new soul through the experience of divine love has long been acknowledged as the sign of such grace. As Rabbi Soloveitchik has shown:

> It is this repentance of liberation and redemption that the Talmud calls a "repentance from love" . . . with which Maimonides deals in Chapter 7 of the Laws of Repentance . . . for in it the sinner vanishes and is replaced by a new man who essentially has never sinned and is in no need of expiation, of cleansing, of purification. He is in a wholly liberated and redeemed state. . . . This is repentance which stems from the spontaneous eruption of the divine flame which possesses man's soul, "God's candle."[23]

The mark of the "wholly liberated and redeemed state" is the soul's experience of possession by the divine flame, and in its attempt to hold on to this experience and enhance its waning flame, the soul discovers the laws of the inner covenant.

What the soul newly born in divine love first discovers are the conditions that open the heart to the influx of this love and those that distract the consciousness from its joy and lead to the heart's contraction. It learns to sustain and return to the experience of divine love by cultivating the receptive mode. It also discovers that any form of outgoing energy, even talk and interaction with sympathetic people, will lead to the lessening or losing of the divine experience. It has long been recognized that this circumstance initially leads to a pursuit of solitude. As de Vidas writes:

> We may infer from this that the love of solitude is a primary means for attaining the love of God. For during the time that a person draws near to his fellowmen in love, it is impossible for him to cleave to God.[24]

Rosenzweig, too, has said, "In its bliss at being loved by God, the merely surrendered self has become dead to the world, nay to everything

153

except God altogether."[25] In its solitude, the soul learns that the proper receptive mode can be achieved most immediately and simply through rest. This is the same condition that serves to transmit the Sabbath holiness. It may also be achieved by any other method of meditative relaxation that allows the self to be centered in its inner stillness. But the soul also learns that there are some activities that do not interfere with the heart's receptivity to divine love, and such activities have, in fact, been long recommended as means of achieving a state of receptivity. These are, first, the study of the Torah and of any texts dealing with the relationship of the soul to God that one would be drawn to in attempting to understand this experience. The second activity that enhances the flame of divine love in the heart is attending communal religious services, where the power of the Minyan and the Torah scrolls to make the divine seem palpably present can be experienced as perhaps never before and counteracts any negative effects of the expenditure of energy, transforming it, rather, into a yet more effortless experience of divine communion.

But sooner or later, depending upon the nature and regularity of one's religious practice, one discovers the easiest and most efficient means of achieving the highest state of that Devekut (cleaving) through which divine love can become manifest in the heart, and it proves to be the very practice instituted together with the commandment to love God—regular liturgical prayer. For once one has uttered the one true prayer of the soul for its salvation and has experienced the redemptive influx of the divine love in the emotion of one's own newly opened heart, one not only becomes capable of prayer but discovers its true nature, that prayer is the only means of opening the heart to God and the soul to its own infinite nature and that it also establishes a direct channel for the influx of the divine love that comes in response.

Meditation can do much to sensitize the soul to the presence of higher energies and to develop a certain power of mastery over those energies, but only prayer can open the heart and, through the purification of the soul, ensure that the effect of those energies will be redemptive rather than destructive to the soul. For that is precisely what prayer is and does: it opens the heart to the recognition of its finite limitations and to that hope against hope that it can somehow make contact with a force beyond itself that can give it assurance of its salvation from mortality. To pray means to open one's heart to the possibility of communicating with the infinite, and when this is truly done, it proves miraculously effective. The very words that utter the cry for salvation serve to conduct the answering influx of divine redemptive energy, uniting the finite and the infinite in a mystic embrace.

By vacating the soul of the ego, the humility of prayer transforms it into the receptacle of grace that can be said to manifest the Shekhinah. Just as it was initially in response to prayer that the heart experienced a divine love in which the transcendent and the immanent were united, so such a Yichud of divine influx and receptacle—of the Holy One, blessed be He, and the Shekhinah—can be said to take place in every subsequent instance of mystical prayer. The belief that prayer can accomplish such a Tikkun is deeply rooted in the Lurianic Kabbalah, and it is clearly stated in the first chapter of the *Etz Chayyim* of Chaim Vital, in relation to the aftermath of the Shevirah (the breaking of the vessels) and the return of most of the light on high:

> And despite all this, there still remained some holy sparks in the vessels. . . . And this is what remains for us to rectify through prayer. . . . Just as the souls of the righteous raise the female waters for the purpose of uniting the Male and Female, in the same way the Male and Female can raise the female waters, for the purpose of uniting Abba and Imma, from the same gleanings that fell down from above . . . and this is . . . the mystery of the unification of "Hear, O Israel."[26]

The view that in the prayers of the righteous a unification of male and female Partzufim (divine personalities) takes place that helps to rectify the shattered cosmos has continued to play a vital role in the later tradition of Hasidism. Martin Buber recognized this in his definition, through quotation, of the thought of the Baal Shem Tov:

> Only the prayer that takes place for the sake of the Shekina truly lives. "Through his need and his want he knows the want of the Shekina, and he prays that the want of the Shekina will be satisfied and that through him, the praying man, the unification of God with His Shekina will take place". . . . He does not think about the satisfaction of his needs. . . . Rather he does all for the sake of the want of the Shekina, and all will be resolved of itself, and his own suffering

too will be stilled out of the stilling of the higher roots. For all, above and below, is one unity." "I am prayer," speaks the Shekina. A tzaddik said, "Men think they pray before God, but it is not so, for prayer itself is divinity". . . . "He makes his . . . soul the throne of the light of God's glory, and the light streams round about him, and he sits in the midst of the light and trembles and rejoices."[27]

The prayer that "truly lives" is done for its own sake, to experience the divinity within it. This experience resolves all human problems and transforms the soul of the praying individual into the site of "the unification of God with His Shekina," a unification whose ecstasy he shares. Two key hasidic concepts that Buber describes are those of Hitlahavut, which he defines as "'burning,' the ardor of ecstasy,"[28] and which more literally suggests a flame or knife blade that burns or stabs inwardly, and Avodah, meaning service in the primary sense of prayer. Of these he says: "Hitlahavut is as far from avoda as fulfillment is from longing. And yet hitlahavut streams out of avoda as the finding of God from the seeking of God."[29] For a person whose heart has been opened to the flame of divine love, prayer too has been transformed and becomes the principal means of attaining that state of Hitlahavut that was the object of his first true prayer, when his need for divine communion was first coupled with a true humility before the sovereignty of God. Such an intention and humility— Kavanah and Shiflut—are the remaining two key concepts that for Buber comprise the essence of Hasidism. Of Kavanah he says:

> Kavana is the mystery of a soul directed to a goal. . . . But there are no *goals*, only *the goal*. There is only one goal that does not lie . . . into which all ways flow. . .: redemption. . . . Just that is kavana: the mystery of the soul that is directed to redeem the world. . . . "When a man stands in prayer and desires to join himself to eternity . . . it is his own powers that he must redeem."[30]

In the later discussion of the perfection of the Neshamah soul, we shall see that this results from just such a directed effort to redeem the world. But we are not yet at that point. We are still at its commencement in the perfection of the Ruach soul, and this involves the Kavanah of the redemption of the self through prayer.

The hasidic Tzaddikim differ from the Lurianic in their understanding of the appropriate Kavanah for prayer. Although they accept the cosmology of Isaac Luria, the Ari, they reject his enormously complicated system of Kavanot, a second level of mental attention to the kabbalistic meanings imputed to various stages and words of the prayers that can turn the act of prayer into a form of mental acrobatics. This is made most explicit by Rabbi Nachman of Bratslav, as recounted by his disciples:

> Rabbi Nachman had told many of his disciples to study the kabbalistic writings of the Ari. But even these individuals were advised not to follow the kabbalistic devotions found in these works.
>
> Rabbi Nachman said that perfect prayer consists of [keeping in mind] the plain meaning of the words. . . . Devotion is concentrating on the meaning of the words, and listening to them very carefully.
>
> Another time Rabbi Nachman spoke of prayer, saying that true devotion is the binding of thought and word.
>
> If you listen carefully to your own words, strength will enter your prayers by itself. All your powers anticipate the time when they will be drawn into words of holiness. When you focus your mind on your prayers, this strength rushes to enter the words . . . simply say the words. In most cases, God will then touch your heart with a flame, and it will be aroused to pray with feeling.[31]

It is the spontaneity of the feelings aroused through the simple act of prayer that the Baal Shem Tov preached:

> You can pray very quickly at times. This is because the love of God is burning in your heart very strongly. The words then leave your mouth of their own accord when you pray silently.
>
> When you attach yourself on high, you can be worthy of being lifted still further by the very same prayer. Our sages thus teach us, "When one comes to purify himself, he is helped from on high."
>
> Through prayer, you can attach your thoughts on high. From the power of such prayer, you can reach even higher levels. Then, even when you are not praying you can be attached to the spiritual.[32]

Prayer is spontaneous and ever more powerful once it has become the vehicle for the burning of that love through which the divine Yichud is consummated: "I heard from my master [the Baal Shem Tov] . . . that when you pray, your main intent should be to unify the Divine Presence with its Master."[33] "You attach yourself on high" and are thus "lifted still further by the very same prayer" when that prayer is simply for the experience of the divine love that opens and fills the heart with its burning. And this "burning" has the same purifying effect as the sacrificial fires of the Temple, consuming the animal ego and yielding a new sublime state of the soul that can remain permanently "attached to the spiritual." Thus the principal disciple of this founder of Hasidism, Dov Baer, the Maggid of Mezhirech, showed that it was only such egoless praying that could provide the proper Kavanah necessary to accomplish the highest purpose of prayer:

> Think yourself as nothing, and totally forget yourself when you pray. Only have in mind that you are praying for the Divine Presence.
>
> You can then enter the Universe of Thought, a state that is beyond time. . . . But in order to enter the Universe of Thought where all is the same, you must relinquish your ego, and forget all your troubles.
>
> Furthermore, if you consider yourself as "something," and ask for your own needs, God cannot clothe Himself in you. God is infinite, and no vessel can hold Him at all, except when a person makes himself like Nothing.[34]

The "Universe of Thought" can be identified with that of the Neshamah soul, the dimension of the mental Sefirot. God can only "clothe Himself in you," in response to the egoless prayer for the divine Presence, and when this Neshamah soul is thus generated, it takes the impress not only of one's personality but also of one's body. This final implication of mystical prayer will be further developed in the third section of this chapter. But first we must conclude the present discussion of the experiential aspect of the love of God to which we are commanded in Deuteronomy.

Once it is discovered that the redemptive experience of divine love can be attained whenever one engages in the ritual of prayer, a change comes over the newly redeemed soul. No longer need such an individual devote all his or her consciousness to the subtle changes in

the degree of such attachment to the divine, ever concerned to perpetuate that state through those means that lead to ever greater seclusion from the world. Knowing that this experience is available whenever one prays allows for a regularization of the spiritual life that permits one to go once more about one's business, though this business will also have undergone a radical change and become ever more directed to the work of hastening the coming of the Messianic Kingdom. Where previously the experience of Devekut had streamed through one whenever the consciousness was turned away from the world, now as one engages in regular, liturgical prayer with this new effectiveness of Kavanah, Devekut tends to become more confined to the actual periods of Davening, with the moments of spontaneous communion becoming more rare. But where before any lessening of the experience of abiding in the divine love had caused anxiety because of the very uncontrolled nature of its spontaneity, the confidence one now has that it can always be reached in prayer enables one to accept its limitation to these periods without fear of permanent loss and with the sense that one's will remains "attached to the spiritual." With this new commitment of the will to the practice of regular prayer, which may be considered the ritual sign of the new covenant, one's attitude toward this *mitzvah* changes from obligation to desire. Rabbi Nachman had said, "All your powers anticipate the time when they will be drawn into words of holiness." And it is true that anyone who regularly experiences the divine burning during prayer is drawn to its performance as to a romantic tryst. His or her senses go into an anticipatory state of aroused excitement as the projected time of prayer approaches. This arousal tends to hasten its commencement so that the initial state of altered consciousness may be perfected and the ready vessel filled by the perfecting divine influx.

It is also true that the established liturgy is composed of "words of holiness" that have a power far beyond that normally possessed by personal prayer, for they carry within them an abiding resonance of all the times they have been repeated through the centuries. As a group gathered together to pray or meditate produces an energy that facilitates and deepens the prayers of each of its members, so any ritual that has been passed down through time gains a similar power to enhance the devotions of those who have maintained its unbroken tradition, however these spatial and temporal effects may be explained.

It is not without cause that we tend to revere anything to which a long past has become attached. The practice or object has survived because it was cared for, and those who thus cared to preserve it found it precious because it produced a response in them that made them wish to become a link in its chain of preservation, a response compounded both of some original power and the added power it had accumulated through the very fact of being thus reverently passed down. So whether the power of traditional liturgy is explained on natural psychological or supernatural spiritual grounds, the fact remains that it has this double power—an original power based on the discernment of the priests and sages who composed it, which gave it the right expressions to bring the praying soul into the proper relationship of dependence that could produce the needed receptivity to the divine grace, and the added power of a tradition to focus the form to be taken by this experience. And it is not only the repetitions by others but also by oneself that increases its power to produce the desired effect, carving ever deeper ridges in the consciousness through which the remembered effects can serve to stimulate their recurrence, as a steepened channel can better conduct a flow. In this connection, Buber has also pointed out: "Repetition, the power which weakens and discolors so much in human life, is powerless before ecstasy, which catches fire again and again from precisely the most regular, most uniform events."[35]

Now that our discussion has arrived at the point where experience of the love of God and the regular practice of liturgical prayer can be seen to merge, it will be necessary to expand upon the form such devotions should take to increase their capacity to yield the proper effects of mystical prayer.

The Prayer Service

This section will be primarily concerned with the order of the service and a method of its delivery suited particularly to the practice of private "Davening," the Anglicized term for Hebrew liturgical prayer. A major reason that private prayers have always been preferred by some is that the mechanical nature of much public prayer interferes with its effectiveness for those who are capable of experiencing its ecstasy. Such feelings were expressed by the sixteenth-century legal authority

David Ibn Abi Zimri in a famous responsum much cited by the Hasidim: "Were I not afraid I would go so far as to say that it is better for a man to recite his prayers in private than to pray together with people with whom he cannot get on."[36] And so also did the Baal Shem Tov once explain his refusal to enter a particular house of prayer:

> I cannot enter there. . . . The house is full to the brim of teaching and prayer. . . . During the day the people speak here words without true devotion, without love and compassion, words that have no wings. They remain . . . like decaying leaves until the decay has packed the house to overflowing and there is no longer room for me in there.[37]

While any form of communal prayer, by the very fact of its being, produces a certain degree of facilitation of this activity, for those whom prayer truly overcomes this facilitation may be less than the distraction it offers. These individuals will naturally turn to private devotions.

But there are even more compelling reasons for private prayers, at least for the daily morning service, having to do with the establishment of a private rhythm for the delivery of some of the key portions of the service as well as for the service as a whole. It is primarily a question of timing that motivates many ardent souls to prefer private devotions. This is both because private prayer will enable them to proceed at their own pace, selecting and lingering over the passages that have become most meaningful to them, and because they are not forced to cut the experience off at its formal conclusion. The Mishnah (Ber. 5:1) refers to the practice of the early Hasidim, who would spend an hour preparing themselves for prayer. And as we saw in chapter 2, the kabbalistic *Sha'ar ha-Kavanah* extended this to a three-hour practice: one hour preparing for prayer, one hour of prayer, and one hour to allow for the full effects of the prayer.[38] The hours before and after the hour of mystical prayer would most likely be spent in forms of meditation, a more directed form preceding the formal prayer service and a more spontaneous, free-floating form after its conclusion.[39]

There are many today who could profit from the reinstitution of all or part of the practice of these early Hasidim, particularly the final meditative period attributed to the early Hasidim in the *Sha'ar ha-Kavanah*. Similar periods of quiet meditation have been incorporated into the Catholic Mass and the Hindu Arati service, and it could be adopted in more modern forms of Jewish communal Davening. But if not communally, it is certainly appropriate for private Davening. Once prayer has become high and effortless, it is no longer necessary to preface it with the practice of directed meditation. But if prayer has not yet been opened up through the circumcision of the heart, then a kabbalistic meditation like the one developed in the second chapter would be appropriate for developing the sensitivity of the soul to the point where it does become capable of effective prayer. If this particular meditation is used as a preface to prayer, however, it would be necessary to defer the performance of the words of the Sh'ma until the regular prayer service, when it could be performed with the same breathing and melody earlier developed for this meditative practice. But in this case, one would have to retain the softly uttered line inserted in the liturgy between Deuteronomy 6:4 and 6:5 and defer the singing of *vehayah* to its traditional place at the beginning of the second paragraph of the Sh'ma. The twelve full breaths with which the essential Sh'ma can thus be melodically performed would then become as powerful a technique for heightening the effect of mystical prayer as they are for initiating the altered consciousness of meditation. In the following study of the liturgy, we will first consider the larger structure of the service, paying particular attention to the order of certain stressed vowel sounds that can facilitate the emotional progress through the course of the morning service for those engaged in prayer. And we will then pay special attention to four important prayers: from the introductory phase only Ana Bekhoach, and from the mandated portion, the Kedushah, the Sh'ma with its immediately surrounding blessings, and the first sentence of the Amidah.

Between the liturgical Kedushah and the Sh'ma, the first of which is meant to arouse awe and the second love of God, comes the prayer that God should "unite our hearts to love and fear Your Name," a prayer appearing in the second benediction before the Sh'ma, Ahavah Rabbah, to be discussed later. The importance of both of these devotional emotions to the highest purposes of such service was recognized, then, from what we will see to have been the very foundation of the liturgy. It is the successive development of these two emotions that is the keynote of the two Mosaic Covenants, the Sinai Covenant directed toward developing reverential fear as the Moabite Covenant is directed toward engendering love. Through such fear, the individual is taught the very limits that can truly define his individuality. Through respecting the rights of his God, parents, and neighbors, the aim of the Ten Commandments, he discovers his own dignity, the bounds that permit his exercise of free will. Were the value of his own individuality not thus first inculcated, his development of love for God would prove destructive to the true purpose of covenant, resulting in a merger with the divine that would annihilate all human personality. But we are warned never, even in the height of love, to lose our fear of God, and this because we have very good reason for such fear; it is the protector of that very personality which is our great offering to the divine, not as a sacrifice but as a garment. Thus as our love serves to bind us to God, our fear serves to preserve our particularity, and this in the same manner as particles are bound and yet distinguishable within the atom, the same laws operating along the entire scale of creation. Such an understanding of the true purpose of retained fear of God within even the height of mystical prayer can be found in the works of two hasidic thinkers, Dov Baer, the Maggid of Mezhirich, and Israel of Koznitz, the Maggid of Koznitz, as cited in the excellent study of hasidic prayer by Louis Jacobs:

> R. Dov Baer draws certain conclusions. . . . Where there is only joy, where man enjoys God without any sense of remoteness from Him, the act of contemplation is superficial. Hence R. Dov Baer advises his followers to rise at midnight to weep for their sins, which create a barrier between the soul and God. . . . The Maggid of Koznitz writes that a man must fear God as well as love Him, otherwise the great love a man has for God would lure his soul away from his body and he would die in longing during his prayers.[40]

If man is to achieve the ultimate purpose of the Tikkun, the development of divine personality, he must maintain the "barrier between the soul and God" that will prevent the total loss of the self in the experience of the divine love, which makes this experience not a simple unification but Devekut, communion.

The authors of the prayer service recognized the importance of achieving and retaining individuality in the telling references to the first grammatical person within the service, particularly in the introductory sections preceding the Bar'khu. Though the standard kabbalistic division of the service is into four ascending stages and one concluding stage of descent, I would suggest a simplified three-fold structure of the service: an ascending introductory stage, the plateau of Devekut from the Bar'khu through the Amidah, and a descending concluding stage. In the first stage, the most essential elements are four carefully constructed and ordered prayers: Mah Tovu ("How goodly"), Adon Olam ("Master of the Universe"), Ana Bekhoach ("Please, by the power"), and Ashray ("Happy," a line from Psalm 84 followed by the whole of Psalm 145). If these alone are said, or preferably sung to the various melodies that have become associated with them, they provide an introductory précis of the whole structure and meaning of prayer.

Mah Tovu, beginning with the biblical line, "How goodly are thy tents, O Jacob, and thy tabernacles, O Israel" (Num. 24:5), is a forty-two-word prayer that, in this short compass, makes eleven references to the first person, *ani*. The "ee" sound that characterizes this grammatical person resounds throughout this introductory prayer. It might be noted that the Lubavitcher Siddur, *Tehillat Hashem*, is defective in the number of the words of this opening prayer of the morning service, an example of the type of changes some Hasidim made in the Prayer Book of which another Hasid, Chaim Lazar Spira of Munkacs, complained:

> I cannot discover the reason why some Zaddikim and some Hasidim changed a good deal of the Prayer Book. This applies also to some of our teachers and elders who preceded us, may their merits shield us, who added much in the prayer of the Eighteen Benedictions and took no care with regard to the number of words.[41]

Spira understood that both the original prayers and their ordering were carefully wrought by those who appreciated the mystic significance of number. Accordingly, the most authentic and powerful prayers are those which exhibit such esoteric principles of internal structure. The effectiveness of prayer would be greatly enhanced if the introductory and concluding phases of the service were stripped of all or most of the later additions and reduced to their purest essences.

Just as Mah Tovu clearly introduces the person entering the sacred space of prayer, so is this personal self acknowledged in the next significant prayer, Adon Olam. This is a ten-line prayer, whose first six lines are devoted exclusively to the glory of God while its last four introduce the person of the praying individual in its relationship to a caring God. Significantly, this is the same numerical division as that of the Sefirot into the divine upper six and human lower four, which was earlier noted as one of the traditional ways of understanding the Sefirot.

The third prayer I would include in the minimum introductory phase is a prayer whose context gives it a significance equal to that of the Sh'ma and the Amidah. This is the forty-two-word prayer Ana Bekhoach, previously discussed in chapter 2 with reference to the forty-two-letter name of God it contains, which would seem to have been designated as the model for prayer in view of its placement directly after the paragraph describing the Temple sacrifices. This placement suggests that prayer had been divinely accepted in substitution for the animal sacrifices rendered impossible by the destruction of the Temple. Ana Bekhoach may thus be considered a model of such prayer as could serve as a true substitute for the redemptive sacrifices of the Temple, and what is most significant about this model is that its formal multiplication of six words by seven lines indicates that the purpose of prayer is precisely to produce a generative unification of that which such numbers signify—the six days of worldly creation with the seventh of otherworldly power, the finite with the infinite, the immanent Shekhinah with the transcendent Holy One, blessed be He. Introduced by a description of the order of the Temple sacrifices, Ana Bekhoach is thus a prayer for the grace of unification with the divine in which the wholly personal element has become sacrificed in the fires of communal devotion.

But the first person returns in the final introductory prayer of Ashray, the only portion of the introductory section to be required by tradition. This prayer is largely devoted to the extraordinary Psalm 145, an alphabetic acrostic in which each line begins with another letter of the alphabet with the single exception of the letter *nun*.[42] Placed in the service shortly before the stage of Devekut, it defines the meaning of such prayer as was modeled by Ana Bekhoach and is to be fulfilled by the Sh'ma and the Amidah: "The Lord is nigh unto all them that call upon him, to all that call upon him in truth" (Psalm

145:18). The function of true prayer is to draw down the Presence of God. Moreover, in one of the few references in the Psalms to love of God, such loving communion is seen as preserving the individual: "The Lord preserveth all them that love him" (145:20). And this Psalm begins and ends with first person references. Within the context of the service, this would seem to imply a reaffirmation of the self after it has been purified by the fires of sacrificial devotion marked by Ana Bekhoach. The reverent self who first entered the tent of meeting in Mah Tovu, and has been purified of its dross in Ana Bekhoach, re-emerges triumphant as a happy individual dwelling in the house of the Lord: "Happy are those who dwell in Your House; they will yet praise You forever."[43] This purified individuality is necessary for the following central stage, the higher "I-Thou" state of Devekut, to use Buber's terminology.

As we enter the two mandatory main sections of the service, the dominant person shifts from the first to the second. In the Sh'ma it is God who is addressing the one who prays as Thou and in the Amidah it is the praying individual who now addresses the Thou to God, completing the dialogue of Devekut with the heart sound of "ah" of the second person singular, *atah*. The progression of sounds in the Hebrew personal pronouns is of particular importance for an understanding both of the order and effectiveness of prayer since the final sounds of these pronouns resonate different portions of the body; the "ee" of *ani* ("I") is a constricted head sound while the "ah" of *atah* ("thou") is an open chest sound. But the rabbis would not allow the soul to become lost even in the highest ecstasy of the Amidah, surrounding its direct address to God with reminders of its enduring individuality. Thus the original prayer composed by the Great Assembly five centuries before the common era was later surrounded by prayer formulae referring to the first person, the introductory "My Lord, open my lips, and my mouth shall declare Your praise," and the concluding, "May the words of my mouth and the meditation of my heart be acceptable before You, Lord, My Strength and my Redeemer." These personal references seem to form a shell of individuality around the influx of the divine Presence that has otherwise absorbed the self during this prayer, thus preserving that self for the role it must play during the final stage of the descent.

This third stage is marked by the shift to the dominant sound of the first person plural, the "oo" sound of *anachnu* ("we"). Though the final Alaynu prayer is the traditionally required portion of this section that must be said, equally important is Avinu Malkanu, whose thirteen words contain six such "oo" sounds filled with a special power to resonate and open the bowels of compassion. For in the descent from Devekut with the divine, the soul reaches out with new purpose to community, not with the heart's opening to the divine love but with the constriction of the gut as it experiences the pain of humanity, that pain of which the abdominal "oo" sound is the expression. It should be noted that the thirteen words of the original prayer attributed to Rabbi Akiba were probably intended to allude to the thirteen attributes of divine mercy since it is for the grace of such unmerited mercy that Avinu Malkanu so powerfully appeals. Again the Lubavitcher Siddur errs in adding words to this prayer without regard for the significance of the number of its words, thirteen, to its meaning. Though this Siddur is the best aid to mystical prayer, it is important that it be used judiciously and in conjunction with other Siddurim that preserve more traditional versions of some of the prayers. It should also be noted that precisely because of the desperation of its plea, tradition bars use of Avinu Malkanu on the Sabbath. On the Sabbath, then, the "oo" sound of the communal "we" has to be carried primarily by the remaining two passages I would recommend as the minimal form of the concluding section, Ein Kalohaynu and the final Alaynu, with their popular melodies. But on weekdays, Avinu Malkanu, chanted with proper Kavanah, can be the most powerful means of completing the purpose of prayer with the opening of the bowels of compassion, drawing the influx down from the heart, where it has abided since the Sh'ma and the Amidah, to the resonant chamber of the abdomen. It seems clear that the earliest composers of the liturgy were aware of much of the resonances of various bodily centers to the intoned vowels[44] and sought to maximize the power of certain sounds and the significance of certain numbers in their orchestration of the subtle dimension of the service.

I will later have some concluding remarks on the nature of the "Descent of the Influx," as the final stage of the service is traditionally called, but I should now summarize the structure of the service that has just been suggested. This would surround the central portion, from the Bar'khu introduction to the Sh'ma through the Amidah, with an introductory ascending phase composed of four passages—Mah Tovu, Adon Olam, Ana Bekhoach, and Ashray—and a concluding descending phase composed of three passages—Avinu Malkanu, Ein Kalohaynu, and Alaynu. Again the numbers of these supplementary passages is significant. Together they comprise the sabbatical number of completion and apart they define the qualitative difference between these two phases. The four of the ascending phase can be associated with Earth, from which one is ascending, and the three of the descending phase with the spiritual and heavenly, from which one is descending after the central experience of Devekut. Having defined the broad structure of the service, I will now give greater attention to four most important prayers.

Of the introductory passages, that with the greatest power is the ancient prayer Ana Bekhoach, beginning, "Please, with the power, the greatness, of Your right hand, untie what is bound up." As we have seen, this prayer has precisely forty-two words, a point of similarity with the opening portion of the Amidah and also with the prayer that introduces the service, Mah Tovu. But the forty-two words of Ana Bekhoach are even more significant as a number than those of these other prayers since they form an acrostic, each word of which begins with a letter of the "name of forty-two letters."[45] Thus Ana Bekhoach may be said to contain and communicate the force of this divine Name. Of all the passages from the introductory readings, it is Ana Bekhoach that best establishes the proper relationship of the one praying to the object of this prayer. For the kindness (Chesed, associated with the "right hand") implored from this great power is the untying of "what is bound up"—the redemption of the soul with the Shekhinah within it. As the third line also shows, this redemption can be understood to be the product of the unification that can be affected by such prayer: "O please, Mighty One, guard as the apple of the eye all those who seek Your unification." Because this esoteric meaning had to be concealed in a word that could also be taken as signifying no more than the divine unity, the prayer ends: "Our appeals accept and hear our cries, You who know all the world of our secret hopes." In view of the mystical significance of this prayer, I am including my own translation and a musical setting of Ana Bekhoach, adapted from traditional cantorial melodies, for use in performing this prayer. I hope that this setting, combined with the music I composed for the Sh'ma and that later to be given for the Kedushah, will contribute to a revitalization of the prayer service for those seeking to renew the covenant. In musical notation on the following page, I have correlated the music with the phrasing of the Hebrew, and some adjustments will have to be made for the English translations.

In the seven lines of six words composing Ana Bekhoach, we can see a further significance of the number forty-two, one that appears to be alluded to in the closing sentence of the first paragraph of the *Zohar*: "And as the ideal covenant was formed through forty-two copulations, so the engraven ineffable name is formed of the forty-two letters of the work of creation."[46] These "forty-two copulations" seem to be primarily related to the unification of the sixth and seventh days of creation. But as we saw in chapter 2, they can also be related to the unification of the sixth and seventh Sefirot, Tiferet and Netzach, which can be further identified with the Neshamah and Ruach hearts. Ana Bekhoach can thus be taken to signify the unification of the double heart—not in its traditional understanding as containing the good and evil inclination but as combining the hearts of the higher levels of the soul[47]—and it suggests that the goal of prayer is a unification not only *through* but also *of* the heart. Surrounding the slowed delivery of the essential two-line Sh'ma by such delivery of those Hebrew prayers containing the significant number of forty-two words—Mah Tovu, Ana Bekhoach, and the opening blessing of the Amidah—can enormously increase their mutual power to effect that state of Devekut esoterically signified by the multiplication of six by seven.

But a further epitome of the forty-two words of ideal prayer can be constructed by combining the sixteen words of the essential Sh'ma (Deut. 6:4–5) with the two most important thirteen-word prayers that precede and follow it, the Kedushah and Avinu Malkanu. I would suggest that such a three-part formula could be used to perform the Sh'ma upon retiring, the last with its famous melody. Melodic performance of these most important thirteen word passages should also be encouraged in the daily morning prayers, a practice that we will see can enable the central vowel of each to be particularly resonated, the

Figure 4. Ana Bekhoach. Musical Setting and Translation by Leonora Leet.

"o" of the Kedushah, the "ah" of the Sh'ma, and the "oo" of the Avinu Malkanu. Whether or not the remaining portions of the service are recited in Hebrew or English, it would be most helpful that these and the other cited forty-two-word prayers be recited or sung in Hebrew and with the slowed delivery that can so enhance their effectiveness, this being most imperative for the most sacred words of the liturgy, the Kedushah and the Sh'ma.

The prayer service proper begins with the Bar'khu, and it should be recognized that all that immediately follows it serves as an introduction and setting to the Kedushah. Though the material between the Bar'khu and the Kedushah ostensibly involves only the blessing of the Creator of the heavenly lights, the compilers of the service seem to have been aware of the esoteric understanding of the identification of these heavenly bodies with the angels and used it to enrich the cosmic setting for the Kedushah. Aryeh Kaplan has shown much evidence of this traditional identification:

> As the commentaries explain, God's Providence works through the angels, but these angels, in turn, work through the stars and planets. As some authorities put it, the angels are, in a sense, like souls to the stars. Thus, for example, some sources speak of the stars as having intelligence, but the commentaries note that this is actually speaking of the angels that are associated with them . . . and this also means that the stars and planets are the "bodies" of these angels. . . . There is therefore a one-to-one relationship between the stars and angels. . . . Each named angel is integrated by the star that serves as its body.[48]

The identification of the stars with angels is important in this context because it is the angels who are traditionally understood to sing the heavenly Kedushah. The singing of the Kedushah is, in fact, the chief activity of the angelic hosts in the Merkabah literature of Throne visions. As Hugo Odeberg has pointed out: "The significance of the celestial *Qedussa* is indicated by the stress laid on its performance. . . . It is the symbol of, and, at the same time, the actual realization of the Kingdom of Heaven, in the celestial spheres."[49] Thus in the human singing of the celestial Kedushah in the prayer service, man can ideally experience himself as one with the angels singing before the heavenly Throne.

The Kedushah appears in three forms in the service, the first in the benediction before the Sh'ma, the second in the Amidah, and the third just before the closing Aleinu. As scholarly opinion is still divided as to which of these was the original site,[50] I shall accept the arguments of those who claim its original location was before the Sh'ma, and for the reason just given of its meaningful association of the heavenly choir with the stars. As a liturgical formula, the Kedushah is most interesting, particularly with the response of the Ophanim and Chayot to the Seraphim that, like the phrase inserted between the first two verses of the Sh'ma—"Blessed be the name of his glorious kingdom forever and ever"—is an early compilation containing esoteric meaning. As will shortly be considered more fully, the blessing added to the Sh'ma may be understood to contain significant references both to the concept of "Name" and to the Shekhinah, the latter kabbalistically identified with the Sefirah Malkhut, which means "kingdom." This suggests that the knowing would have understood the Sh'ma not to signify a unity but rather a unification. In the Kedushah, Isaiah's theophany—"Holy, holy, holy is the Lord of hosts; the whole earth is full of His glory" (Isaiah 6:3)—is followed by a response from Ezekiel 3:12, "Blessed is the glory of the Lord from its place," "Glory" also being an esoteric signifier of the Shekhinah.

The whole is a significant formula because of the many repetitions of the same "o" sound. The exact number depends on whether the unaccented "o" in Adonai should be counted. But since "Adonai" is read here as a substitution for the biblical Tetragrammaton, it is unlikely that it would have appeared in Isaiah's original formulation. The "o" in *khol* should also not be emphsized since it is a short "o" closer to "awe." Since the remaining number of "o"s is a more significant number, I would suggest that the formula be understood to contain exactly ten "o" sounds. There are seven "o" sounds in the words that the Seraphim address to the lower angelic orders, which may be associated with the seven Sefirot of creation, and three in the words that the Ophanim and Chayot address to the higher sphere of the Seraphim, which can similarly be associated with the supernal triad of Sefirot. With this introduction, we can now turn to the actual Hebrew words. In the Kedushah proper these are: "Kadosh, kadosh, kadosh Adonai tzevahot. Melo khol ha-ahretz kevodo." To which is responded:

"Baruch kavod Adonai mimekomo." To facilitate the lengthening of these "o" sounds in delivery, I would like to offer a melody of my own composition, each phrase of which should be given a full breath:

Figure 5. The Kedushah. Music by Leonora Leet.

The nine words of Isaiah's theophany distinguish between the divine figure seated upon the Throne and His earthy "glory," while the four words of response from Ezekiel reinforce the understanding that the "place" of the "glory," later or already identified with a distinct divine Presence (Shekhinah) in the creation, is below that of the transcendent Lord, on the level of the Earth or its symbol, the Throne. As in the line inserted after the first verse of the Sh'ma, the purpose of this compilation appears to have always been both to allude to the esoteric belief in the distinction between the transcendent and immanent aspects of the divine—later identified with the Holy One, blessed be He, and His Shekhinah—and to accomplish their Yichud through the act of prayer. The identification of the Shekhinah with the Throne and its involvement in this unification is made explicit in a quote from the *Zohar* included in the Lubavitcher Siddur:

> The mystery of Shabbat: she *[malchut]* is on Shabbat united within the mystery of Oneness so that the [supernal] mystery of Oneness may rest upon her. [This takes place during] the Maariv Prayer of Shabbat eve, for then the holy Throne of Glory merges into the mystery of Oneness, and is ready for the holy transcendent King to rest upon it.[51]

The Kedushah embodies the awesome state of mystical vision, a spiritual state whose emotional quality would seem to be clearly associated with the sound of these words. For it is possible to recognize an association between the affective content of the "o" sound and the emotion of awe that the words of the Kedushah both convey and are meant to inspire. Such an association is reinforced by the Hebraic linguistic practice of giving the dot signifying the "o" sound a unique place *above* the Hebrew letters, as if to suggest that with this vowel sound we are meant to look up. But in all linguistic groups, the "o" sound is expressive of the primitive emotional response of awe and wonder. This response represents a necessary religious stage prior to the response of love, one that we have seen should coexist with love even in the highest of spiritual states. Given the quality of the "o" sound and its insistent repetition in the Kedushah, the mode of delivery that seems to be suggested is one in which each of these "o"s is drawn out to complete a full breath, a method that requires it to be intoned or sung. The melody I have written for this purpose was recently given and that I composed for the Sh'ma can be found in the second chapter. But whether or not these melodies are used, it is important to recognize the special use of repeated vowel sounds in these biblical passages, passages that have come to occupy a central position in the liturgy.

Following soon after the awe-inspiring "o" sounds of the Kedushah are the "ah" sounds shown in chapter 2 to complete the five phrases in the second verse of the Sh'ma (Deut. 6:5). Again this is a sound expressive of a primitive emotion, that of the fulfilled heart, and this emotion is also what this verse is meant to arouse, wholehearted love

175

of God. If the Kedushah and Sh'ma are intoned or sung with long drawn-out phrases that emphasize these affective vowels, the body will become a resonant receiver of the emotional content of prayer conveyed through the power of such emotionally charged verbal-melodic sounds. A mode of intoned or melodic delivery involving such deep breathing will lift prayer into a heightened experience of the heart opened and fulfilled by the very act of hearing enjoined upon it at the opening of the Sh'ma. For the Sh'ma is not only the first but, properly done, still the most powerful means of achieving the true end of prayer, divine love, and it has the greatest esoteric significance.

The *Zohar*, in a passage quoted earlier in chapter 2, makes clear that the unity proclaimed in the Sh'ma is really a unification, Yichud: "This is the mystery of Unification (*Yichud*). . . . the mystery of 'Hear O Israel, God is our Lord, God is One.' . . . The mystery is that the two are united as one." In the *Zohar* this unification is understood in terms of the sexual metaphor involving the transcendent masculine and immanent feminine aspects of the divine, aspects referred to by the talmudic names of the Holy One, blessed be He, and the Shekhinah. In the Sh'ma what corresponds to the divine immanence is YHVH Elohaynu, the form of the godhead with which we are personally associated, the Lord *our* God, while the unqualified Tetragrammaton corresponds to the divine transcendence. Such an understanding of divine immanence appeared already in the biblical references to the Shekhinah as the divine Presence. But in the gender differentiations of the *Zohar*, the divine immanence of the Shekhinah was further identified with the feminine, the divine transcendence with the masculinity of the Holy One, blessed by he, and the whole Sh'ma understood to proclaim their unification. Thus, what the Kedushah distinguishes, the Sh'ma reunites:

Hear, [O] Israel, YHVH Elohaynu [and] YHVH [are] one.

As earlier suggested, the line inserted right after this verse in the liturgy—"Blessed be the name of his glorious kingdom forever and ever"—is suggestive of such esoteric meaning, of the unification of the unspecified Lord with that more particularized divine form, "our God," which could be signified by the term for the "Name," *shem*, in the added blessing. This suggestion is supported by Zechariah's famous prophecy (14:9) of such unification, which appears at the close of the final Aleinu prayer in all the services: "On that day the Lord shall be One and His Name One."[52] This indicates that in the days of the Second Temple the term for the Name was already understood to represent a divine hypostasis differentiated from that signified by the Tetragrammaton, a difference at least of greater specificity. Thus the liturgical addition of this softly voiced blessing after the first verse of the Sh'ma would have early indicated to the knowing that the Sh'ma signified a divine unification rather then a simple unity. But there was a still deeper level of unification signified in the Sh'ma, one deriving from the understanding of the mystical community of Israel as the divine son, an understanding going back to the biblical statement, "Thus saith the Lord, Israel is my son, even my firstborn" (Ex. 4:22). As we shall see more fully in the next section, the purpose of prayer is twofold, to bring about the divine Yichud and also to redeem the soul of the praying individual, a process by which he may be said to become the twice-born son of the very masculine and feminine divine aspects he is unifying through his prayer and one with them in divinity. I suggest that this is the final meaning of the Sh'ma, a meaning that may be expressed as follows:

Hear: Israel, YHVH Elohaynu, [and] YHVH [are] one.

This ultimate meaning and purpose of prayer can now be seen to have already been contained in the original core of the liturgy, the Sh'ma, and it informs the blessings surrounding it.

The Sh'ma, with the benedictions coming just before and after it, forms the core of the oldest of Hebrew liturgies, and it is clearly the contribution of the priests of the Second Temple.[53] As Ismar Elbogen has shown with reference to the central Mishnaic verses on this earliest of prayer services:

The first definitely attested example of daily public worship comes from the Temple itself. The priests on duty, "men of the watch," interrupted the offering of sacrifices every morning in order to go [to] the Chamber of Hewn Stone, there to devote a short while to prayer. (M. Tam. 5:1)[54]

The order of this first attested liturgy is given in this crucial verse of the Mishnah, Tamid 5:1:

> The officer said to them, "Recite ye a Benediction!" They recited a Benediction, and recited the Ten Commandments, the *Shema*, and the *And it shall come to pass if ye shall hearken*, and the *And the Lord spake unto Moses*. They pronounced three Benedictions with the people: "True and sure," and "Abodah," and the Priestly Blessing; and on the Sabbath they pronounced a further Benediction for the outgoing Course of priests.[55]

From this we can see that the three paragraphs of the Sh'ma had already become a unit and that this had been further unified with the benedictions coming just before and after it. The identity of the benediction immediately following it is certain, since the Mishnah gives its still current name, "True and sure." That coming just before it is undoubtedly Ahavah Rabbah, "With abounding love," as this issue seems to be have been resolved in the Talmud (BT Ber. 11b). The remaining two daily blessings were the Avodah, now following the Amidah and the Priestly Blessing.

With the omission of the Ten Commandments,[56] the priestly liturgy already contains all three paragraphs of the Sh'ma with its framing blessings. The present first blessing on creation, which relates the stars to the heavenly choir singing the Kedushah, "is apparently no older than the geonic period, having originated in the circles of the Merkava mystics."[57] Excluding, then, this first benediction of the present service, in the remaining core of the priestly liturgy we can already see something of the interpretation of the Sh'ma developed or revealed in the Kabbalah, that the Sh'ma is meant to convey a unification rather than a unity, an interpretation I have extended to include the third party of Israel, which is to achieve the divine unification implied by the first verse of the Sh'ma through the love commanded in its second verse. Such an interpretation appears to be implied in the surrounding blessings.

Ahavah Rabbah begins with God's abounding love and asks:

> for the sake of Your great Name and for the sake of our forefathers who trusted in You and whom You taught the laws that bring eter-

nal life. . . . grant our heart understanding to comprehend and to discern, to perceive, to learn and to teach, to observe, to practice and to fulfill all the teachings of Your Torah with love. . . . may we rejoice and exult in Your salvation. . . . Blessed are You Lord, who chooses His people Israel with love.[58]

In this benediction on the revelation of Torah, we have a prayer for the heart understanding of the message and mechanism of eternal salvation hidden in the Torah. But the clues are already all there for the discerning in the essential association of the Name and divine love with such salvation. This association contains the deepest core of the priestly doctrine of salvation, that such salvation will not be due to a Messianic redeemer, the prophetic doctrine, but to the workings of divine love in the receptive human heart, a salvific process that also involves and is needed to perfect the Name, that aspect of divinity which is later, and perhaps already, associated with the divine Presence, as that is or will be associated with a divine feminine aspect.

Although the full doctrine is already suggested in Ahavah Rabbah, it is further reinforced by a comparison of just the surrounding blessings themselves. We have seen that the blessing coming before the Sh'ma is concerned with the grace of divine love—"Blessed are you Lord, who chooses His people Israel with love"—and that immediately following it is concerned with deliverance: "Blessed are You Lord, who delivered Israel." If these two are conflated, we again have the suggestion that the deliverance to be achieved will be accomplished not *because* of God's love but *through* it. When we now turn to the Amidah, we will see that such conflation of deliverance with divine love is also its secret message. Though the Amidah was not part of the priestly liturgy as defined in Mishnah Tamid 5:1, it was the product of the Great Assembly that had been founded by the priest Ezra and so would have contained priestly members as well as reflecting priestly understanding.[59] Such a priestly understanding of salvation as was just seen to inform the Sh'ma and its surrounding blessings can also be clearly seen in the opening of the Amidah.

In the first blessing of the Amidah we are still centrally concerned with the same conceptual content as that of the Sh'ma and its surrounding blessings, the redemption to be wrought by love. The first sentence of the Amidah can be translated as follows:

Blessed are you, Lord our God and God of our fathers, God of
Abraham, God of Isaac, and God of Jacob, great, mighty, and awesome God, the highest God, who is full of good kindnesses [chasedim],
possessor of all things, who remembers the kindness [chaseday] of
the Patriarchs, and brings a redeemer to their children's children,
for the sake of His Name, with love [be-ahavah].

This may be interpreted as meaning that the God we acknowledge as
the source of all blessing is also He who, like us, has a special relationship to our ancestral fathers, that this most powerful God of all that
exists is also full of the same quality of Chesed that equally permeated
the Patriarchs, and that probably by reason of this similarity he remembers His covenantal bond to the Patriarchs to the end that their
descendants may be redeemed, for the sake of His Name, with love.
The final two points require special consideration.

In the Lubavitcher Siddur, the esoteric meaning of the Name, especially as the Zechariah 14:9 reference came to be understood, is made
most explicit in a passage from the Zohar that appears just before the
earlier Zoharic quotation from this text included in the Sabbath service:

The Holy One, blessed be He, who is One above, does not take His
seat upon His Throne of Glory until she enters into the mystery of
oneness, similar to His to be oneness corresponding to Oneness.
This, as we have stated, is the esoteric meaning of the words: "The
Lord is One, and His Name is One."

From this it becomes clear that the esoteric meaning of "His Name" is
the Partzuf (divine personality) of the Shekhinah and that all divine
action "for the sake of His Name" involves the unification of the Holy
One, blessed be He, with His Shekhinah, the referent of "she" in the
text. As we have seen throughout this section, this unification is to be
accomplished through the prayers of the righteous that bring about
this mystical unification by means of the love thus generated in their
hearts. In other words, the "redeemer" that God brings to the descendants of the Patriarchs is the very force of the divine love that enters
the hearts of the righteous during their prayers to effect both the unification of the Lord with His Name and the present redemption of

these righteous souls, such souls as form that true Community of Israel esoterically understood to be included in the threefold divine unification proclaimed in the Sh'ma. Both the essential Sh'ma and the opening blessing of the Amidah may be said, then, to convey the same message of redemption through divine love that the proper delivery of their Hebrew words can begin to effect. In this connection, we can conclude this analysis of the prayer service with a consideration of how the placement of the essential Sh'ma in the order of the service can be related to the importance of full breathing.

As understood by the Kabbalists, the morning Shacharit service is divided into the four ascending steps of introductory readings, verses of praise, the Sh'ma and its surrounding blessings, and the Amidah, steps that are related both to an ascent through the four worlds and through the levels of the soul. It is the association of the Sh'ma with the Neshamah soul that presently concerns us and this because of the suggestive relationship Aryeh Kaplan has drawn between this soul level and the breath:

> *Neshamah* is associated with breath. . . . *(neshimah)*. . . . The highest level of the soul is thus the *neshamah*, which is, as it were, the "breath of God." This is the "vessel" that holds the spiritual nature that God wishes to give us. . . .
>
> Therefore, in the third section of the service, a person has a *neshamah* experience, in which he feels an intimacy with God, as if God were breathing on him, as it were. This is the level of divine love and unity.[60]

Repetition of the Sh'ma with proper Kavanah can bring one to "the level of divine love and unity" because this is what the two essential verses of the Sh'ma define, the divine unification that Israel can effect and share when the regular, prayerful repetition of the words of this goal has opened the heart of the praying individual so that it can become the proper vessel for receiving the redemptive influx of divine love.

A crucial aspect of this "*neshamah* experience" is connected with experiencing the divine breath, not so much "as if God were breathing *on* him" but as though God were *breathing* him. At the point that the heart begins to experience the divine influx of love, the lungs also seem to be possessed by a volition not their own, which extends or stops the breath in a manner not understood by the personal consciousness but whose effect is to heighten the heart experience of "burning," just as a bellows fans the flame of a fire. In the strange rhythm of this breathing, one can truly be said to experience the Ruach Elohim Chaim, the "breath of the living God," and this expression, which was identified in chapter 2 as the essential "mantra" of the meditative technique hidden in the *Sefer Yetzirah*, can also be used at times or throughout the final period of relaxation that it is here suggested should follow the more active phases of prayer.

We have now arrived at the "Descent of the Influx" phase of the service, that which draws the Shefa from the heart area to the lower torso, and it has a few stages. It may be said to begin with the repeated act of bowing during the Amidah, the silent standing prayer, and to develop with great intensity during Avinu Malkanu. But the full power of this final descent of the Shefa can best be received if the act of prayer is not abruptly terminated with the close of verbal recitation but extended to include a final period of relaxation. And it is further suggested that the time given to this preferably prone relaxation period should approximate that given to the recitation of the prayer service. For it is in this period, when the recital of verbal passages that partially determined the rate of breathing is over, that the altered rhythm of the breath becomes most pronounced, spontaneously inflaming the heart with a love whose burning radiates out to fill the whole body with the divine breath. It is almost as though the breath were the male member and the heart the female, the expressive emotion of the heart responding to the rhythm of the breath as though it were being made love to by the force directing this rhythm, as though this force inflating and compressing the lungs had a lover's sensitivity to just what was needed to initiate and heighten the heart's capacity for feeling. And if the radiant energy that seems to fill the body can be identified with the developing Neshamah soul body, then it would further seem that this Tzelem was conceived through this Yechud of divine breath and feeling that has utilized one's own lungs and heart for its consummation, this ecstatic experience serving further to spiritualize all of the bodily organs so that the body may provide the proper vessel for the higher soul now beginning to inform it.

Support for such a practice of relaxation following prayer comes not only from the early Hasidim but also from that eighteenth-century revival that is still with us. Jacobs reports of Menahem Mendel of Kotzk that "so lost was he in prayer that it used to take him some time afterwards before he became aware of his surroundings."[61] And another recent study of modern hasidic prayer is also suggestive of such a final nonverbal form of the prayer-state:

> There are two types of prayer-state generally described in Hasidic sources. *Qatnut*, the "lower" or ordinary state in which one generally begins his prayers, is opposed to *gadlut*, the "greater" or expanded state of mystical consciousness. . . . While the simple devotions of the *qatnut* state are highly valued, the true goal of the worshiper is to enter that world where "he may come to transcend time." . . . Verbal prayer gives way to abstract contemplation, to a liberation of the worshiper's mind from all content other than his attachment to God. First all of one's energies are concentrated on the word as spoken with fullness; now the word itself is released, and nothing remains with the worshiper but the fullness of heart that, paradoxically, also marks him as an empty vessel, ready to receive the light from above.[62]

The final purpose of prayer, that union of the Shekhinah immanent within the soul with the transcendent energy of the Holy One, blessed be He, drawn down by the appeal of such a vessel, a union that also accomplishes the conception of a new and higher soul, is, then, best attained in the Gadlut "state of mystical consciousness" following upon verbal prayer. And when regular private prayers are allowed to complete themselves in a period of floating meditation, the time that is spent is amply repaid by the enormous increase in alertness and vital energy to which this practice leads, new resources needed to accomplish the special work in the world for which these new souls have been graced. To understand the fullest meaning of these newly conceived souls and how they are able to accomplish this work, it is to Lurianic cosmology that we must finally turn, and this not only to explain the nature, order, and sounds of prayer but the miracle of its effectiveness.

The Heart of the Matter

The interrelated commandments to love and to serve God are the commandments of the new covenant designed to bring Israel to a Messianic state of society far beyond that first entrance into the spiritually civilizing force of divine covenant first entered into at Sinai. These commandments were previously explained in terms of the Lurianic concepts of Shevirah and Tikkun. But there is a preceding cosmological concept without which the meaning of the Tikkun cannot be fully comprehended. This is the Lurianic concept of Tzimtzum, the divine "contraction" and withdrawal of the infinite light that left a spherical primordial space for a finite creation.

The most important aspect of this doctrine for our purposes is the idea that the primordial space, called Tehiru, from which the light of Ein Sof was retracted, is still understood to contain a residue of this light, called Reshimu. This residual light—"the remnants of the light of *Ein-Sof* that remained behind even after the *zimzum*, like the drops of oil that remain in a vessel after it has been emptied"[63]—mingles with the roots of Din, or Gevurah, which had become concentrated in that area of the infinite from which the divine retraction is to take place and which this Tzimtzum is partially designed to eliminate from the divine nature. In the second act of creation, "there descends from the primordial, space-encompassing *Ein-Sof* a yod . . . which contains . . . the power of formation and organization.[64] As Gershom Scholem summarizes his presentation of the authentic Lurianic doctrine: "Thus both the subject and the object of the process of creation have their origin in God but were differentiated from each other in the *zimzum*."[65]

The nature of the progressive stages of creation may perhaps be better understood in terms of Israel Sarug's development of the action involving Din prior to the Tzimtzum:

> In the beginning *Ein-Sof* took pleasure in its own autarkic self-sufficiency, and this "pleasure" produced a kind of "shaking.". . . As a result of this "shaking," "primordial points" were "engraved" in the power of Din, thus becoming the first forms to leave their markings in the essence of *Ein-Sof*. The contours of this "engraving" were those of the primordial space, that was to come into being as the end-product of the process. As the light of *Ein-Sof* outside this

"engraving" acted upon points within it, the latter were activated from their potential state and the primordial Torah, the ideal world woven in the substance of *Ein-Sof* itself, came into being . . . the hidden law of the whole of creation that is inscribed within the "engraving" of *Ein-Sof* is henceforward active and expresses itself throughout all subsequent processes through the power invested in this one intruding *yod*. Made manifest in the vacated space are both the residue *(reshimu)* of the remaining light of its essence and some of the light of *Ein-Sof* itself, which acts as the soul that sustains all.[66]

It is from the very pleasure that infinite consciousness begins to take in itself that this consciousness is aroused to give some primordial form to the conscious source of this pleasure through which its essence can be expressed. In Sarug's somewhat erotically described construction, Din loses the negative connotation it had in Luria's thought. It is no longer the divine attribute of judgmental constriction that needed to be purged from the divine essence: instead it is seen as providing the formative capacity necessary for the unfolding of creation. From the initial forms engraved by the power of Din in the essence of Ein Sof, there emerge the contours of the primordial space, this being Sarug's explanation of the Tzimtzum. Most importantly, it is in these forms taken by the Reshimu remaining in this primordial space that the primordial Torah of creation is engraved. Thus "all subsequent processes" through which the "one intruding *yod*," derived secondarily from "the light of *Ein-Sof* itself," expands outward from the central point of primordial space to which it had gravitated will have to accommodate its unfolding to "the hidden law of the whole of creation that is inscribed within the 'engravings' of *Ein-Sof*," that is, within the residual light that defines the Torah for each stage of creation.

It has been necessary to wend our way through the obscurity in which the concept of the Tzimtzum is traditionally expressed because this concept seems to contain a hidden clue to the meaning of the Tikkun, in terms of our present concern, the way in which the purpose of this Tikkun, the ultimate purpose of creation, is to be accomplished through human fulfillment of the commandment to love and serve God, a key to the salvation to be accomplished through love.

We must now give further attention to two important aspects of Lurianic cosmology. The first is Sarug's understanding that embedded in the Reshimu is a hidden Torah defining the conditions permitting all the subsequent processes of creation. The second is the idea that each such stage is part of the process of Tikkun whose cosmic purpose is the rectification of the shattered form of the original emanation. The Tikkun has two complementary aspects, an inner aspect involving the salvific evolution of the human soul and an outer aspect involving the cosmic destiny of the divine. These two aspects may also be related to the Lurianic concept of the inner and the surrounding lights. The inner light represents the divine immanence in the human soul and the surrounding light the divine transcendence. These two varieties of the divine light can be further related to the original Lurianic distinction between the residual light within the Tehiru, which is to become the surrounding light, and the Yod-point, which contains the inner light or holy spark that is to inform all elements of creation. It is to *inform* all created elements quite literally insofar as it is this inner light that is endowed with what Scholem called "the power of formation and organization." But this Yod-point of light is to expand from a central cosmic point through a primordial space already filled with the surrounding light of the Reshimu, a light engraved with the universal laws of cosmic expansion.[67] This distinction is of particular importance in explaining the central premise of Lurianic cosmology, that the Tikkun is to be equated with the Yichud of the Holy One, blessed be He, and His Shekhinah. The identification of the Shekhinah with the holy spark within the human soul suggests that what is being drawn forth by the soul's longing, is none other than the transcendent form of the divine light that constitutes the Reshimu.

As we have previously seen, one result of this Yichud is the conception of the Neshamah soul of the person in whose heart this divine unification has come to fruition. Now if the divine substance of the transcendent Reshimu may be understood to be uniting with the divine substance immanent in this person, then the Neshamah soul conceived through this unification of divine universal substance and divine personal substance is precisely what gives personal form to the divine transcendence. But since the substance of the surrounding light is inscribed with what, from one perspective, can be considered the

Torah of all modes of cosmic expansion, the newly conceived soul
generated by this union of universal and personal divine substance
will be endowed with the very quality we earlier saw to be the final
result of the new covenant of love, consummated through prayer, that
will characterize the prophesied Kingdom: "After those days, saith
the Lord, I will put my law in their inward parts, and write it in their
hearts" (Jer. 31:33). In the Neshamah soul the personal has been inscribed with the divine law and the transcendent given personal form.
The final implication is that the being to whom we have, in Buber's
terms, addressed the genuine Thou of our prayers, our personal God,
is what, in one of its aspects, is only now becoming personalized as our
higher self. Thus *the ultimate nature and purpose of the Tikkun is the
personalization of the divine as the higher Neshamah souls of those perfected humans whom the process of Tikkun has in this manner lifted to
divine personality.*[68] This is not to say that a living person can be considered a divine personality but that his Neshamah soul, already in-
habiting the World to Come, is one of the many personal forms whose
achievement by the divine has been understood throughout the
Lurianic tradition to constitute the purpose of creation.

The major Lurianic spokesman, Chaim Vital, has shown in *Sha'arei
Kedushah* that effective devotions can produce a new kind of angel
drawn from the "substantial light" of the Holy Spirit. This angel was
called a Maggid and is, in effect, an expression of the individual's own
higher soul:

Man's own soul, if it is much purified, appears to him and guides
him on all his ways. . . . This influx and substantial light [which as
a result of the contemplative exercise is infused into the mystic's
soul] is what is called "thought" (*mahashabah*). Understand this well,
for it is no vain thing. If this were not so [that imaginative meditation produces these results], then the whole kabbalistic doctrine
concerning the right "intentions" and devotions at prayer
(*kawwanoth*) and concerning [the mystical significance of] man's
good and evil thoughts were as good as nothing. You will now understand why prophecy is not only possible *but necessary*; it is as if a
man held fast to the end of the bent down branch of a tree: when he
shakes it [his bit of branch] with sufficient strength, then of *necessity* the whole tree is shaken with it . . . for this drawing down of the

influx (*hamshakhath ha-mahashabah*) certainly never comes about by itself but [is effected] solely by the *kawwanoth and yihudim*. . . . From these a new angel is created and this angel then reveals himself to him. This is the matter of the *angels that are called maggidim* which is mentioned in some books. . . . And now let us explain the subject of prophecy and the Holy spirit. . . . It is impossible that anything that comes out of man's mouth should be in vain and there is nothing that is completely ineffective. . . . Consequently, when a man leads a righteous and pious life, studies the Law, and prays with devotion, then angels and holy spirits are created from the sounds which he utters . . . and these angels are the mystery of maggidim.[69]

As Vital shows, the "whole kabbalistic doctrine concerning the right 'intentions' and devotions at prayer," the doctrine that such devotions are "necessary" for the dual purposes of perfecting one's own higher soul and "the whole tree" of the divine Sefirot, is dependent on the esoteric truth that such spiritual exercises do have the effect of drawing down an influx of "substantial light" for the purpose of endowing it with the individual form of one's own higher and guiding personality.

Before considering the equally explicit expression given to this doctrine by the major twentieth-century Jewish philosophers who represent a conscious continuation of the Lurianic tradition, it might be useful to consider the way in which the cosmology of another important contemporary thinker, Teilhard de Chardin, both approaches and yet falls short of expressing this doctrine. It was Teilhard who coined the phrase "The Personalizing Universe,"[70] which best expresses the thrust both of his own and of Lurianic cosmology. In Teilhard's evolutionary thought, the cosmic development is toward ever more self-reflective consciousness, the characteristic of what he has named the "noosphere," the sphere or dimension of what the Greeks called "noos" and we "mind." It is man who first crosses the threshold of reflection that leads, in turn, to the process of "noogenesis," the creation of the sphere of mind over and above that of the thinking individual. But the ultimate step of cosmic evolution for Teilhard is the convergence in the noosphere, at the "Omega Point," of the individual reflective centers with the "Hyper-Personal" center in which all the personal centers are united without loss of their particularity:

In the perspective of a noogenesis, time and space become truly humanised—or rather super-humanised. Far from being mutually exclusive, the Universal and Personal (that is to say, the 'centred') grow in the same direction and culminate simultaneously in each other. . . . The Future Universal could not be anything else but the Hyper-Personal—at the Omega Point. . . . what is the work of works for man if not to establish, in and by each one of us, an absolutely original centre in which the universe reflects itself in a unique and inimitable way? . . . each particular consciousness remaining conscious of itself at the end of the operation, and even (this must absolutely be understood) each particular consciousness becoming still more itself and thus more clearly distinct from others the closer it gets to them in Omega. . . . finally to make all things double back upon *someone*.[71]

The problem with Teilhard's theology, and it resulted in his trouble with the Church, is that it is not only the personal form of God, the hyper-personal "someone" produced at the culminating point of noogenesis, that seems to be the product of human psychical development, but the very existence of God. As Julian Huxley has noted: "He seems to equate this future hyperpersonal psychosocial organization with an emergent Divinity."[72]

In kabbalistic evolutionary thought, however, this danger is avoided through the Lurianic concept of the Reshimu. For the Reshimu is that preexistent divine cosmic force that both establishes the conditions for human psychical development—the Torah for each of its stages—and aids this development at critical points through descents of its grace, adding such Chesed to the Gevurah delimiting the terms of this progress by giving the evolving soul a foretaste of the next stage to which it can develop. Rabbi Isaac of Kamarna speaks of just such a concept when talking of the "free sample" that the Baal Shem Tov used to explain the process of spiritual development:

The "free sample" is the Light that a person feels when he first begins to draw close [to God]. Through the taste of this Light, he can subjugate all evil, and return everything to the ultimate Good. This is [a "free sample"] given to the individual so that he should know the taste of serving God. A mark *(reshimu)* of this remains after [this Light] is withdrawn, in order that he should know what to seek.[73]

But we have now to consider the most important aspect of the Reshimu, its own transition from divine ground of being to personal form through just this spiritual evolution of man, which is also the reason that its energy has thus been activated to draw and channel such human development.

It is this awareness of the divine involvement in its own personalization that distinguishes the evolutionary thought of Rav Kook from that of Teilhard. Noting that "the doctrine of evolution that is presently gaining acceptance in the world has a greater affinity with the secret teachings of the Cabbalah than all other philosophies,"[74] he explains:

> However life breaks down into particularization, it continues to draw light from the original divine light, and it needs to return to the higher realm, together with the essence of our souls. Then we shall not ascend devoid of riches and we shall not fail because of feebleness, for we shall not return naked to the higher realm. We shall have with us our multicolored robes we acquired as a result of the proliferation of all life. . . . The primary role of penitence, which at once sheds light on the darkened zone, is for the person to return to himself, to the root of his soul. Then he will at once return to God, to the Soul of all souls . . . to be illuminated by the light of life. This is the mystical meaning of the light of the Messiah, the manifestation of the soul of the universe, by whose illumination the world will return to the source of its being. . . . Evolution sheds light on all the ways of God. All existence evolves and ascends. . . . Existence is destined to reach a point when the whole will assimilate the good in all its constituted particulars.[75]

For Rav Kook the process of return seems to relate the particular soul with two different levels of general soul, the Messianic "soul of the universe," which illuminates the path of return to that source of being it shares with the particular evolving souls, and the "Soul of all souls," which is that divine source and the final whole in which "the good in all its constituted particulars" will be both assimilated and retained with all its "multicolored robes." The lower levels of this general soul, in which the individual souls are unified without losing their particularity, may be further identified with both an individual's own Neshamah soul and a more collective form of divine personality, particularly that of Ze'ir Anpin. This Partzuf, also equated with the Holy One, blessed be He, can be associated with Rav Kook's "soul of the universe," as this can further be associated with the Reshimu, here the "light of life." It also appears to have a certain horizontal relationship with the individual Neshamah souls who communicate its collective will to the lower dimension of the Ruach souls. Thus the individual Neshamah soul relates to the Ruach soul as part of the personalized collective unity of the Holy One, blessed be He; but as regards its own consciousness, it retains its individual form while also engaging in Devekut with the unlimited divinity of Ein Sof, Rav Kook's "soul of all souls."

This personalizing of the divine level that can be identified with the Holy One, blessed be He, is explained most explicitly by the two major Jewish philosophers of our century, Franz Rosenzweig and Martin Buber, and, given the dates of their works, it is hard to determine whether they developed their understanding of Lurianic cosmology independently or through the influence of one upon the other, and if the latter, whether in one or both directions. For while Buber's *I and Thou* was published two years after Rosenzweig's *The Star of Redemption*, in 1923, his *The Legend of the Baal-Shem*, containing many of his later ideas, was published much earlier, in 1907. And the question of modern influence is similarly open regarding Rav Kook, whose *The Lights of Penitence* was published two years after *I and Thou* and four years after *The Star of Redemption*, in 1925. Clearly these ideas were much more "in the air" during the early 1920s than they are at present, but a review of their appearance in these works will show that they represent the most sophisticated form of Jewish theology yet to appear.

In his division of cosmic evolution into the three phases of "proto-cosmos," equated with creation, of "cosmos," equated with revelation, and of "hyper-cosmos," equated with redemption, Rosenzweig comes close to Teilhard's somewhat later formulation, though the hyper-cosmic form of Rosenzweig's God is not solely the product of human development but involves its interaction with man:

He is Redeemer in a much graver sense than he is Creator or Revealer. For he is not only the one who redeems, but also the one who is redeemed. In the redemption of the world by man, of man by means of the world, God redeems himself. Man and world disappear in the redemption, but God perfects himself. Only in redemption, God becomes the One and All which, from the first, human reason in its freshness has everywhere sought and everywhere asserted, and yet nowhere found because it simply was nowhere to be found yet, for it did not exist yet. . . . The Jew . . . fulfills the endless customs and precepts "for the sake of uniting the holy God and his Shekhina." To confess God's unity—the Jew calls it: to unify God. For this unity is as it becomes, it is Becoming Unity. And this Becoming is enjoined on the soul and hands of man. Jewish man and Jewish law—nothing less than the process of redemption, embracing God, world, and man, transpires between the two. The fulfilling of the commandment is inaugurated and stamped as an act which brings redemption nearer, with a formula in which the individual elements, such as they are absorbed into this last One, once more resound individually. . . . In the innermost sanctum of the divine truth, where man might expect all the world and himself to dwindle into likeness of that which he is to catch sight of there, he thus catches sight of none other than a countenance like his own. The Star of Redemption is become countenance which glances to me and out of which I glance.[76]

Rosenzweig understands that the task "enjoined on the soul and hands of man"—to effect the Lurianic unification of "the holy God and his Shekhina"—results in a true "becoming" of the divine, a "Becoming Unity" in which God is redeemed as well as man and in which man finds his own individuality both preserved and perfected as the divine countenance—the divine face that is his own. In this last assertion, Rosenzweig appears to be echoing a kabbalistic tradition that when one achieves the highest vision of the man on the Throne, his face will be one's own. Thus Abraham Abulafia, the great kabbalistic master of meditation, writes: "When an individual completely enters the mystery of prophecy, he suddenly sees his own image standing before him. . . . It is thus written, 'Over the form of the Throne there was a form like an image of a Man' (Ezek. 1:26)."[77] It is in such a traditional conception that the identification of the Neshamah soul with the level of divine personality becomes most clear and we can understand the Neshamah soul most precisely as the personalization of God.

Buber seems to be speaking about Rosenzweig's "Becoming Unity" when he says:

> What turgid and presumptuous talk that is about the "God who becomes"; but we know unshakably in our hearts that there is a becoming of the God that is. The world is not divine sport, it is divine destiny. . . . This is known by him, too, who offers up his little will to God and meets Him in the grand will. "Thy will be done," he says, and says no more; but truth adds for him "through me whom Thou needest."[78]

Also like Rosenzweig, he defines the great meeting of God and man—what he calls the I-Thou relationship and Rosenzweig the relationship of love—as identical with revelation:

> What is the eternal, primal phenomenon, present here and now, of that which we term revelation? It is the phenomenon that a man does not pass, from the moment of the supreme meeting, the same being as he entered into it. . . . The reality is that we receive what we did not hitherto have, and receive it in such a way that we know it has been given to us. . . . Man receives, and he receives not a specific "content" but a Presence, a Presence as power. . . . First, there is the whole fullness of real mutual action, of the being raised and bound up in relation: the man can give no account at all of how the binding in relation is brought about, nor does it in any way lighten his life—it makes life heavier, but heavy with meaning. Secondly, there is the inexpressible confirmation of meaning. Meaning is assured. . . . It has become present to us and in its presentness has proclaimed itself to us as salvation. . . . But the revelation does not pour itself into the world through him who receives it as through a funnel; it comes to him and seizes his whole elemental being in all its particular nature, and fuses with it. The man, too, who is the "mouth" of the revelation, is . . . an organ, which sounds according

to its own laws; and to sound means to *modify.* . . . The revelation that then makes its appearance seizes in the totality of its constitution the whole elemental stuff that is thus prepared, melts it down, and produces in it a form that is a new form of God in the world. Thus . . . ever new provinces of the world and the spirit are raised to form, summoned to divine form. Ever new spheres become regions of a theophany. It is not man's own power that works here, nor is it God's pure effective passage, but it is a mixture of the divine and the human . . . we shape eternally the form of God.[79]

For Buber, man's highest role is to give to the "whole elemental stuff" the personal form through which he becomes fused with the divine. Thus is there realized, from this "relational life of salvation . . . a human cosmos with bounds and form, grasped with the spirit out of the universal stuff of the aeon."[80] In this last phrase, as in the one quoted in the previous sentence, Buber seems to be referring most directly to the Lurianic concept of the Reshimu, the "elemental stuff" of the universe that is graduated through all the stages or aeons of the human or personalized cosmos-to-be. This elemental stuff establishes that the "form of God" which "we shape eternally" will not simply be a form of Teilhardian "noogenesis," wholly derivable from man. Rather, it will be a true fusion of the divine universal substance with the personal form earned by man through the prior process of cosmic evolution, a fusion that represents the culminating achievement of that evolution and the purpose of the whole cosmic process. Finally, like Rosenzweig, Buber understands this personalizing of God to result from the new being that emerges when man becomes capable of receiving the divine Presence into his life "as power."

Buber derived this understanding of the fundamental Lurianic message that he first transmitted to the modern world from his study of the Hasidim. And of all the Hasidim it was probably the Mezhirecher Maggid who most clearly showed the purpose of creation to be God's desire, quoted earlier, to "clothe Himself in you." He understands this process of divine personalization to be the esoteric meaning of the traditional relationship of Israel to the creation:

It is known that when God willed to create all universes, He did so because of Israel. . . . Thus, for example, a person might have a thought to build a house in which to live. He then builds this house and lives in it.[81]

It is for the development of the righteous man or Tzaddik that the universe came into being, so that God might have a personal form in which to dwell.

But this is that intermediate form of transcendence that was identified both with the Holy One, blessed be He, and the Reshimu. Kaplan has shown of the former:

> I have explained that the word "blessed" when applied to God refers to His immanence. However, we must also understand what the word "holy" means when applied to God . . . when we say that God is "holy," we are saying that He is separated from the mundane to the greatest extent imaginable. Therefore, when . . . we speak of God as "the Holy One, blessed be He," we are saying that he is "the transcendent One, Who is immanent" . . . the term "Holy One, blessed be He" therefore bridges the gap between God's transcendence and His immanence. It is as if God was very far away but was stretching out His hand to enable us to grasp it. This is represented by the *vav* of the Tetragrammaton.[82]

Earlier we saw that such a descent of redemptive power seemed to be the form of divine Chesed exemplified by the Tikkun or return aspect of the cosmic process. Similarly, its Tzimtzum aspect can be said to define the Torah-informed Reshimu and seems expressive of the divine aspect of Din or Gevurah. But between these two attributes comes Tiferet, the Sefirah that is to harmonize their polarity and with which the *vav* is most closely identified. Not only is Tiferet to be identified most closely with the Holy One, blessed be He, as lover of the Shekhinah and, therefore, as the divine element most involved in the salvific opening of the human heart, but the association here being made of this element with the Reshimu also seems to be suggested by the very meaning of this name as Kaplan has expounded it. For if Ein Sof is to be identified with the infinite light surrounding the cosmic sphere of the Tzimtzum, and the Shekhinah with the inner light that exists within the forms of the creation, then the Holy One, blessed be He, can only be associated with that intermediate transcendence identified with the surrounding residual light within the circle of the Tzimtzum. It is the movement of this Tiferet-identified median aspect of the Reshimu into the human heart, in response to the magnetic attraction of that human longing which most perfectly manifests the yearning of the Shekhinah, that seems to produce the human and cosmic reversal from Gevurah to Chesed that marks the redemptive process.

Perhaps the clearest statement of the way in which man's holy intentions can draw down and become identified with this supernal light was made not by a Hasid but a talmudic scholar, Chaim of Volozhin, the most famous pupil of the Vilna Gaon, who summarized the essence of the Kabbalah for his own students in his work *Nefesh ha-Chayyim* (The Soul of Life):

> When a pure human mind conceives the idea of performing a meritorious deed, the thought immediately produces an impression in the root of that man's soul above, building and planting countless Upper Worlds and Forces. . . . Thus, by the very thought, Man arouses and draws upon himself the Surrounding Light of Supernal Holiness, which assists him in carrying to completion that contemplated good deed. After the deed is performed, the Holiness and Light retire to the root of that man's soul, and that is his reward in the World to Come: it is Man's own handiwork. . . . The real truth is . . . that the World to Come is actually identical with Man's own deeds; it is that portion which he expanded, added and prepared by his own efforts.[83]

In Chaim of Volozhin's understanding of the Kabbalah, the "Surrounding Light," once drawn down by the devotions of the lower soul, retires "to the root of that man's soul," and becomes henceforth identified with what seems to be his own Neshamah soul. It is such personalizing of the divine transcendence by his own higher soul that man's devout thoughts and prayers can effect and that becomes "his reward in the World to Come," one "expanded, added and prepared by his own efforts."

This understanding of the personalized form of the divine as one's higher self can give new meaning to such a standard liturgical formula as "the God of Abraham, the God of Isaac, and the God of Jacob." We can understand the word *Elohei,* here translated as "the God of," as signifying the Godhead or God-self of each of the Patriarchs. Such an understanding seems to underlie a passage in the difficult fourteenth-century kabbalistic text the *Sefer ha-Temunah:*

> Awesome and wonderful is the name of the God of hosts, in which are combined His powers and the hosts in which He is garmented. And that is the upper will, the divine will in all of them. And all of them are called Elohim Chayyim [the Living God], becoming one name, and the Elohut [state of being divine] one Elohut, one God . . . but the three supernal attributes . . . have one will for all of them. Therefore, it is said of these Elohut: "Elohei Avraham, Elohei Yitzchak, Velohei [and the God of] Ya'akov."[84]

Another hasidic master, in describing the unification to be accomplished in prayer, also seems to interpret "Eloheikha" (your God) in this way: "The Presence within you, *your* God, is joined together with 'the Lord'—its eternal source."[85] In both cases, the highly developed soul is understood to constitute the personal expression of a collective Godhead. A most esoteric tradition would thus seem to suggest that in prayer the living individual can both emulate and achieve such a God-self as those of the Patriarchs he addresses. It is not only the five standard Partzufim of Lurianic cosmology that can be considered personalities of the divine but also the Patriarchs identified with the Sefirot of Chesed, Gevurah, and Tiferet. Nor is it just these Patriarchs but the highest development of all souls that can justly be called divine personalities. Louis Jacobs comes to a similar conclusion in defining the nature and purpose of hasidic prayer:

> Hasidic prayer is, then, an exercise in assisting the divine unification and participating in it, sharing the joy and delight which attend unification as all worlds and all souls become attached to God. . . . The essential idea here is that at a high stage of authentic contemplation the divine in man's soul meets God, as it were. The divine meets the divine.[86]

In their concept of the goals of prayer, the Hasidim tirelessly repeat their open revelation of the secret core of the Kabbalah, which is the belief that by participating in the divine union that only he can accomplish, man can achieve his own divinization.

Having seen the way in which Lurianic cosmology can relate the purpose and efficacy of prayer to an understanding of cosmic structure and history, we are now in a better position to appreciate the final implication of such prayer as can realize the love of God, to comprehend what precisely makes the divine opening of the heart salvific for man as well as the cosmos. What this is depends upon the premise that has been developed throughout this section, namely, that the conception of the Neshamah soul that results from this opening involves a direct influx of divine substance. What is more, this substance is one in which the law is embedded, thus fulfilling Jeremiah's prophecy for the new covenant: "After those days, saith the Lord, I will put my law in their inward parts, and write it in their hearts" (Jer. 31:33). And if the conception of the Neshamah soul involves such a new influx of divine substance, then the resultant soul will have the Law written in its heart and, as the kabbalistic tradition has always assumed and implied, will truly partake of the divine. Its threefold union of the inner and surrounding lights with that new identity and form that these lights will henceforth assume in the soul newly conceived by them will give to the human soul a divine nature, most importantly including the attribute of eternal survival, just as it gives to the ultimately divine cosmic substance a personal form, the divine thus becoming personalized as one's higher self. Only in such personalizing of the divine consciousness can man truly recognize the divine as constituting the whole cosmos. As said in Deuteronomy 4:39 and repeated in the Aleinu prayer: "Know this day and take unto your heart that the Lord is God; in the heavens above and upon the earth below there is nothing else."[87] He can know that there is "none apart from You, our King—in the life of the World to Come"[88] because he has already become, in the words of a major kabbalistic text, "a son of the world to come."[89]

The God whose love we can truly begin to return, through the attraction and desire we begin to feel for those states that nourish the development of this higher soul, will thus be a God who wears our own face. And as we begin to identify our personal consciousness more and more with that of the Neshamah soul, we will begin to love the God we can then recognize as our own highest self as well as the God we can recognize in the personalized forms of other equally developed Neshamah souls. Where the Ruach soul experiences the divine love as something received from a wholly other source, the Neshamah soul can truly adopt this burning love in the heart as its own. And by experiencing itself as its source, the Neshamah soul can direct it outwardly to those neighbors and strangers through whose similar spiritual development the Kingdom of God will finally be realized. Thus it is only in this ultimate process of redeeming the world that the soul also finally becomes capable of obeying the deepest intent of that commandment through whose fulfillment God, man, and the world are to be redeemed: "And thou shalt love the Lord thy God with all thine heart, and with all thy soul, and with all thy might." Having analyzed the process by which the divinely conceived Neshamah souls can truly be called the sons of the World to Come, we can now further explore the way in which these souls serve to hasten the coming of that world.

The Kingdom

The three modern interpreters of the mystical message of Judaism—Buber, Rosenzweig, and Kook—who we earlier saw to support this view of personal salvation, are all also agreed that such redemption is only the prelude to the further service of such souls: the effort to redeem the world by which their own souls are perfected. In *I and Thou*, Buber explained:

> Meeting with God does not come to man in order that he may concern himself with God, but in order that he may confirm that there is meaning in the world. All revelation is summons and sending. . . . God remains present to you when you have been sent forth; he who goes on a mission has always God before him: the truer the fulfillment the stronger and more constant His nearness.[90]

The work of the Neshamah soul is the redemption of the world, and through this work the Neshamah soul can both grow to its full power and be an ever more sustained presence in the individual conscious-ness. In his much earlier work, *The Legend of the Baal-Shem*, Buber had explained the type of Kavanah that can transform prayer into the holy burning of its fulfillment as "the mystery of the soul that is directed to redeem the world." We can now further understand why this purpose must involve such a purified individuality as can personalize the divine and thereby effectively direct its holy power:

> Uniqueness is the essential good of man that is given to him to unfold. And just this is the meaning of the return, that his unique-ness may become ever purer and more complete. . . . Only in his own way and not in any other can the one who strives perfect him-self. . . . The individual redeems the fallen worlds. And yet the individual is not a whole, but a part. And the purer and more per-fect he is, so much the more intimately does he know that he is a part and so much the more actively there stirs in him the commu-nity of existence. . . . [He lives] devoted to the multitude and col-lected in his uniqueness, fulfilling on the rocky summits of solitude the bond with the infinite and in the valley of life the bond with the earthly.[91]

The Neshamah soul recognizes itself as a part of a whole that has a double nature—both that higher infinite form of the divine in which it is united on a supernal level with all other Neshamah souls and the earthly community which the Neshamah souls already form and are working to extend to all of existence as the realized Kingdom.

Once one recognizes oneself as part of this larger whole, one also realizes that one cannot divorce one's personal salvation from that of the whole. The imperfection of any part undermines the salvation of the whole and thus of oneself. It is this recognition that ultimately motivates great souls to devote themselves to the redemption of the meanest of souls, as Rav Kook has shown:

> Great souls cannot dissociate themselves from the most universal concerns. . . . When the knowledge of God is suffused by a great love, when it is pervaded by its true illumination, according to the capacity of each soul to receive it, there radiates from its absolute

light a love for the world, for all worlds, for all creatures, on all levels of their being. . . . They feel and they know that the nearness of God, for which they yearn, can only lead them to joining themselves with *all* and for the sake of *all.* . . . They want that every particular shall be preserved and developed, and that the collective whole shall be united and abounding in peace.[92]

Rosenzweig also recognized that it is only through such love of the "neighbor" as can bring the Kingdom into being that man can finally fulfill the commandment to love God:

> Man can express himself in the act of love only after he has first become a soul awakened by God. It is only in being loved by God that the soul can make of its act of love more than a mere act, can make of it, that is, the fulfillment of a—commandment to love. . . . The love for God is to express itself in love for one's neighbor. It is for this reason that love of neighbor can and must be commanded. . . . The bond of the consummate and redemptive bonding of man and the world is to begin with the neighbor and ever more only the neighbor, the well-nigh nighest. . . . The cultic prayer stakes everything on the one plea for the advent of the kingdom; all other pleas, though otherwise nearer at hand, are only incidentally prayed together with and for the sake of this one plea. It shows love that the eternal is the nighest and thus releases the irresistable force of the love of neighbor upon it; thereby it compels the redemptive advent of the eternal into time.[93]

Rosenzweig sees that if the Kingdom is to result from love of one's neighbor it is because it is only through such love that one can express the love for God that is more crucially commanded. But it would seem that if "the love for God is to express itself in love for one's neighbor" then this can only arise if one can *see* God in that neighbor; and as the previous analysis should have shown, one can only thus see God in one's neighbor if both are fully realized Neshamah souls, something not likely to occur with respect to the neighbor who happens to be "nighest."

It was, in fact, Jesus who first coupled love of God and of the neighbor as expressing the essence of the Law (Matt. 23:36–40). But though these two commandments may be said to represent the highest levels of the two Mosaic Covenants, it is significant that they do appear in these separate covenants. The commandment "thou shalt love thy neighbor as thyself" (Lev. 19:18) appears at the central point in the Torah and this has been taken to signify its great importance. But to love one's neighbor as oneself need not be taken to imply the necessarily prior relationship of love between man and God, as Rosenzweig would have it, since it can also be an expression of the enlightened self-interest that is more consistent with the tenor of the Sinai Covenant. Love of one's neighbor only needs to be commanded to the extent that it is not the spontaneous expression of a divinely opened heart, to the extent that one's self-love is selfish. A Nefesh soul can be raised to the lowest level of community by learning that its own self-interest is involved in the welfare of its society, that, for instance, to pollute it for personal profit is equally dangerous to the self. By learning that it is a part of a larger whole, the Nefesh soul can become elevated through the very extension of its self-love to the Ruach level at which a new covenant of love becomes possible.

In Deuteronomy the commandment to love God is made the prerequisite for attaining the Promised Land. This, as has been indicated throughout this chapter, involves more than a normal state of consciousness; ultimately it requires the state of consciousness of the Neshamah soul. In that state it becomes spontaneously possible to love one's neighbor as oneself if both the self and the neighbor have been recognized to be divine. Such a neighbor is not, however, he or she who may be "nighest," but he or she for whom one can feel a spiritual affinity. The Sabbath morning service makes reference to holy societies (chavurata kadishata) of masters and sages that had existed both in Israel and Babylon, and in sixteenth-century Safed there were similar holy brotherhoods. Today we are witnessing a small revival of the Havurah movement, one which, though it may contain fewer saints, yet shows the special feature of such voluntary societies, the creation of a network of light that can illuminate the darkened path to spiritual development in periods of transition, strengthening the personal soul growth whose effects will radiate out to aid the redemption of others.

At the level of the new covenant, then, it is not necessary to command the love of the neighbor. It is another form of love that is commanded to complement the love we are to develop for God, a form of love involving an imitation of divine love. In a major section involving the love of God, we are told that God

> loveth the stranger, in giving him food and raiment. Love ye there-fore the stranger: for ye were strangers in the land of Egypt. (Deut. 10:18–19)

To realize the Kingdom, it is not love of the neighbor but of the stranger that needs to be encouraged, in accordance with the divine example and in response to our own memory of such a condition. The differ-ence between the idolatrous nations and Israel can be reduced to the ultimate measure of their distance from God, those further removed being strangers to the divine Presence and those close to it being its neighbors, as it is written: "For what nation is there so great, who hath God so nigh unto them, as the Lord our God is in all things that we call upon him for?" (Deut. 4:7). We can call neighbors those people with whom we can form the community of a congregation whose members each have daily experiences of the nearness of God in prayer.

Thus the real distinction is that between the secular and the sa-cred, between the vision that denies the existence of the divine and the vision that sees it permeating all things. The modern Jew, who can grant to each of the major religions its own path to the same salvation, can bring this understanding to the recitation of the final Aleinu prayer:

> It is incumbent upon us to praise the Master of all things . . . that He has not made us like the nations of the world . . . for they bow to vanity and nothingness. But we bend the knee, bow down, and of-fer praise before the supreme King of kings. . . . He is our God; there is none else.[94]

The commandment to love the stranger means that it is not enough to rest content with the promise of personal salvation nourished by knowledge and experience of the divine, as the following paragraph of the Aleinu prayer implies: "And therefore we hope to You, Lord our God, that we may speedily behold the splendor of Your might, to banish idolatry from the earth—and . . . to perfect the world under the sovereignty of the Almighty." It is also incumbent upon us to contribute to the great work of banishing idolatry from the Earth by helping to uplift those who are strangers to the divine glory filling this Earth, to uplift them through an effective sharing of our own experience of divine truth.

This mission to the stranger is necessary if the Kingdom is to extend beyond the isolated societies of the holy to embrace the whole world. But it need not be understand to be dedicated to the conversion of those of other faiths and nations, for the stranger, who is also within our gates, and to whom the message should be primarily directed, can as easily be a member of one's own family. Indeed, the central historical prophecy of Deuteronomy is that the people of Israel, who were once few and strangers in Canaan and then grew to greater numbers while strangers in Egypt, will once again be dispersed from the land they failed to keep to become strangers in many lands. It is from this estranged position that the crucial act of Teshuvah, return, will take place. But as we have seen, this return is impossible without the further influence of divine compassion:

> And it shall come to pass, when . . . thou shalt . . . return unto the Lord thy God . . . with all thine heart, and with all thy soul; that then the Lord thy God will turn thy captivity, and have compassion upon thee, and will return and gather thee from all the nations, whither the Lord thy God hath scattered thee. . . . And the Lord thy God will circumcise thine heart. (Deut. 30:1–6)

The divine compassion, *rachamim* rather than *ahavah* (love), which was directed toward us in our initial phase of Teshuvah, is now required of us in our efforts to redeem the stranger. It is because we cannot truly love what is beneath us but only what is on or above our level, that we can love the divine image only to the extent that we can recognize it in ourselves or our neighbor. But between this understanding of the neighbor and of the stranger there is also the difference in the form of divinity they represent. The neighbor, as an imputed Neshamah soul, represents a personalization of the divine transcendence whereas the stranger contains only the unredeemed spark of the divine immanence. Such a distinction seems to be implied in the similar discrimination made by de Vidas between "whether we are called 'children' by virtue of possessing souls deriving from the divine world of 'Emanation,' or 'servants' when we possess souls which derive from the Shekhinah."[95] It is because of that holy spark of the Shekhinah that we care about the spiritual destiny of the stranger. For however distressing the behavior of a thwarted soul may be to our peace, it is far more distressing to that soul and arouses our compassion.

Those who experience the bliss of divine love wish they could uplift such an unredeemed soul by communicating to it something of their own experience. And through acts motivated by such loving compassion, they may succeed in conveying a "free sample" of a higher state similar to that divinely given them in the circumcision of their hearts. This free sample may have the same effect of opening the heart to the possibility of spiritual enlargement, thus initiating its development from the Nefesh to the Ruach state. For the Neshamah soul has the divine power to bestow such evidences of grace as can initiate the process of spiritual growth, the process of return. It is through the power to organize and effect such works of spiritual reclamation that the Neshamah soul normally displays the great power that marks the highest possible level of the soul that can be manifested while still on Earth. And it is only such a dedication of this power to the redemption of the whole world that can also serve to perfect its instrument. Where the Ruach soul can only pray to "behold the splendor of Your might," the Neshamah soul can demonstrate it. But to arrive at such a divine manifestation of power, the soul must pass through the Ruach level of true receptivity to the divine love. It is the only way and it ensures that in the soul's final development of divine personality the uses of power will be harmonized with the dictates of love.

Meditation alone cannot effect this, for though it can generate considerable power directed to achieving both understanding and change, it provides no mechanism for opening the heart. The initial movement into Ruach consciousness can only come from some evidential experience of a higher energy coming from beyond the personal will and perceived as a palpable Presence, such as that provided by the Sabbath. Only the evidential experience of supernatural energies, energies that it is the purpose of organized religion to conserve and transmit, can stimulate the desire for the closer and more sustained presence of these energies that may finally result in the act of prayer. For as Rosenzweig has said, "Prayer is the last thing achieved in revelation. . . . To be able to pray."[96] But should a higher soul that has been completed through the opening of the heart consequent on true prayer desire to meditate for those ends for which it can provide a special focus, all will now seem to be processed through the heart's burning. The morning Amidah prayer ends, "May the words of my mouth and the meditation of my heart be acceptable before You, Lord, my Strength and my Redeemer."[97] But only a higher soul can achieve the true meditation of the heart learned in prayer, the words of the mouth uniquely fusing with the heart in this highest form of meditation that releases its full power of transformation, the power to transform this world into the divine Kingdom.

We have seen that the love of God capable of effecting this transformation can only be realized by those Neshamah souls who can recognize God in themselves and in other equally developed souls that can be called their spiritual neighbors. But what the previous section has also shown is that God can only be so recognized if we can accept the divine opening of the heart as achieving the conception of a higher soul *composed of divine substance*. This is the ultimate implication of Lurianic cosmology.

This discussion of the commandments to love and serve God is a fitting conclusion to the attempt that has here been made to develop an understanding of Jewish mystical cosmology and practice suitable to the Aquarian Age now before us. For it reveals the final purpose in which they are joined, that through the androgynous sons of the World to Come—the offspring of the divine transcendence and divine immanence that were united in the love-filled heart opened in prayer—the commandments to love both God and the stranger can be fulfilled, which can rectify the cosmos and realize the Kingdom of God on Earth.

The Biblical Power Word Vehayah

Introduction to the Biblical Uses of Vehayah

Chapter 2 introduced a new understanding of the Hebrew word *vehayah*, normally translated "and it shall come to pass," not only indicating that it was widely used throughout the Bible as a special tool of spiritual empowerment but also suggesting its incorporation into the kabbalistic meditation offered there. Because of the potential importance of this recovered meaning both for biblical studies and contemporary practice, it is necessary to provide a more comprehensive treatment of the biblical uses of this term.

This appendix will accordingly attempt to prove that use of *vehayah* as a power word to channel the manifesting power of God was the most widespread spiritual practice in the whole of the Bible. In this groundbreaking study of the Hebrew text, I will demonstrate that the word *vehayah* is not simply a signifier of future causality; rather that this reversed form of the letters of the Tetragrammaton (not Yod-Hey-Vuv-Hey but Vuv-Hey-Yod-Hey) is consistently used to *influence* what "shall come to pass." Going back to Cain and forward to the last of the prophets, the contexts where it is used provide a special perspective through which the nature of magical-miraculous manifestation in the full range of its powers is exposed and the Bible revealed as a precise guide to the spiritual dimension of reality. Such a lexical study will also complement the similar study of the biblical references to the Shofar in chapter 1, which should chart a new direction for the investigation of biblical language and provide a powerful key to unlock the innermost secrets of the Bible.

This study of magical practice in the Bible can also expand our understanding of what may well have been an important part of Hebraic priestly training—the use of such spiritual-magical techniques as have always been associated with ancient priesthoods. The most famous example is that imputed to the temple priests of ancient Egypt in the *Aesclepius* portion of the *Corpus Hermeticum*, a pseudepigraphal work now thought to be a product of the Hellenistic period and to reflect Jewish influence.[1] The alleged ability of these priests was their power to make the statues of their gods talk by ritually drawing down spirit into them. As Aesclepius is told: "They are animated statues full of *sensus* and *spiritus* who can accomplish many things, foretelling the future, giving ills to men and curing them."[2] A similar tradition of the ability of the adept to give life and prophetic powers to a formed figure, here through the use of divine names, has been associated since talmudic times with the use of the *Sefer Yetzirah*,[3] the first extant text of the Kabbalah, which is dated as early as the third century C.E. and which has been understood to attribute to the patriarch Abraham the ability to make what was known as a *golem*. We will later also see an example of a serpent statue made by Moses and endowed by him with curative powers (Num. 21:8–9), an empowerment through what appears to be use of the reversed Tetragrammaton, *vehayah*, as a power word. That reversing the letters of the Tetragrammaton was understood to be the most basic of magical practices can be seen in such a more modern example as that of Marlowe's *Doctor Faustus*, as this conjurer begins his incantations:

> *Within this circle is Jehova's name*
> *Forward and backward anagrammatised. . . .*
> *Then fear not, Faustus, to be resolute*
> *And try the utmost magic can perform.*[4]

The various biblical categories of *vehayah* usage range from the empowerment of prayer and sacrifice to all the levels of spiritual mastery, of which the highest is prophecy, the ability not simply to foretell but to determine the future. Such a study should not only make a contribution to biblical studies but reclaim this potent spiritual tool from the natural oblivion or forced suppression to which it has been subject. Since there is no written or oral law condemning its use as a power word, the time may now be ripe to tap its power once more. Nor should the revival of this tool be feared since it will be shown to contain a Providential dimension that ensures that its irreverent use will prove self-defeating.

Such use of a power word to focus the operations of spiritual energy in accordance with the human will is the simplest and most direct form of the meditative technique outlined in chapter 2. In this appendix the biblical meaning of *vehayah* will be established through a comprehensive survey of its use in a broad range of biblical contexts, in the process opening a new window on the spiritual teachings of the Bible. Though little attention has previously been given to the word *vehayah*, analysis of its biblical usage will reveal the ways in which man has learned to interact with a spiritual dimension of reality in fulfillment both of this higher will and of his own spiritual development. The following analysis demonstrates in particular that this reversed form of the Tetragrammaton was knowingly used by biblical masters as a special vehicle for controlling the manifesting power of God, as well as being an expression used by God to depict this manifesting power. This primary definition of *vehayah* as the manifesting form of divine power introduced the earlier treatment of this most potent of biblical power words in chapter 2. As shown there the power of the word *vehayah* to bring the divine unity into manifestation can be supported by a most significant passage in which it is juxtaposed to the Tetragrammaton, the crowning epiphany of Moses:

> And he said, I will make all my goodness pass before thee, and I will proclaim the name of the Lord [YHVH] before thee. . . . And it shall come to pass [VHYH], while my glory passeth by, that I will put thee in a cleft of the rock, and will cover thee with my hand while I pass by: And I will take away mine hand, and thou shalt see my back

parts: but my face shall not be seen. (Ex. 33:19–23)[5]

The "face" (*panim*) can be understood to refer to the nonmanifest essence of the divine, the "back parts" (*achorim*) to the manifesting form of the divine in the process of time, in what "shall come to pass" (*vehayah*). Thus the form of the name that Moses sees through "a cleft in the rock" would seem to be not YHVH but VHYH, not the forward but the reversed backward arrangement of the divine letters, that through which all the glory of the creative power can pass. In most passages where it is used, *vehayah* should not be translated but, as here, taken as a noun denoting some relationship to the divine power of manifestation.

Let us now survey the major biblical appearances of *vehayah* beginning with the first:

> And a river went out of Eden to water the garden; and from thence
> it was parted, and became [VHYH] into four heads. (Gen. 2:10)

Understanding *vehayah* as a noun, we can equate it with the river issuing from Eden that becomes parted into four heads (streams). The word for river, *nahar*, derives from the root *nahor*, meaning to "flow, stream, shine, or beam," suggesting that the river *vehayah* is the stream of light issuing from the original creation, Eden. We are told that this river was divided into four heads upon leaving the Garden, and as we shall see, there are four main headings under which the biblical uses of *vehayah* can be classified.

The First Level of Usage: Prayer

An example of the first classification of usage appears in the very next reference:

> And Cain said unto the Lord, My punishment is greater than I can
> bear. Behold, thou hast driven me out this day from the face of the
> earth; and from thy face shall I be hid; and I shall be a fugitive and
> a vagabond in the earth; and it shall come to pass [VHYH], that every
> one that findeth me shall slay me. And the Lord said unto him,
> Therefore whosoever slayeth Cain, vengeance shall be taken on

him sevenfold. And the Lord set a mark upon Cain, lest any finding
him should kill him. (Gen. 4:13–15)

The first use of *vehayah*, on the human side, is in the empowerment of
prayer. Here the murderer Cain, without any plea of mitigating circumstances or promise either of change or reciprocity, prays to God
for a reversal of the decree or probable consequence that "every one
that findeth me shall slay me," initiating his prayer with the power
word *vehayah*, which can here be translated: "Please, God, let it not
come to pass." And so powerful is appeal to God under the term *vehayah*
that it is answered with sevenfold protection.

Pleas from one person to another can also be strengthened by
resorting to *vehayah*, which appears to bring a divine power to bear on
the side of whoever pleads. Thus Abraham beseeches Sarah:

Therefore it shall come to pass [VHYH], when the Egyptians shall see
thee, that they shall say, This is his wife: and they will kill me, but
they will save thee alive. Say, I pray thee, thou art my sister; that it
may be well with me for thy sake. (Gen. 12:12–13)

Abraham prays to Sarah to protect him from inevitable destruction,
using *vehayah* in exactly the same manner as had Cain. And not only
does she accede to his wishes, but divine protection is also elicited:
"And the Lord plagued Pharaoh and his house with great plagues because of Sarai Abram's wife" (Gen. 12:17). Similarly, Judah implores
Joseph to reverse his decree for Benjamin's imprisonment so that his
father Jacob will not die of grief: "It shall come to pass [VHYH], when
he seeth that the lad is not with us, that he will die. . . . Now therefore, I pray thee, let thy servant abide instead of the lad a bondman to
my lord" (Gen. 44:31, 33). This *vehayah* prayer so moves Joseph that
he not only grants the appeal and finally reveals himself to his brothers but he comes to a state of final enlightenment in which he understands that the true purpose of his superiority is not to make others
bow down to him but to enable him to deliver those weaker than
himself: "And God sent me before you to preserve you a posterity in
the earth, and to save your lives by a great deliverance" (Gen. 45:7).

That the power of *vehayah* could evoke such an insight is evidence that the divine Presence has been drawn by its employment

into the exchange. For it is precisely through acts of "great deliverance" that we may discern the divine exercise of this first category of *vehayah* power. As the human expression of this level of *vehayah* power is in prayer, so its divine expression is in the grace that ensures redemption. When Abraham and Judah plead in this manner to another human, they place that human in the position of divine surrogate and the divine then works through that surrogate to provide protection and deliverance in answer to what amounts to a prayer.

Later examples of *vehayah* used in personal appeals to other individuals are David's appeal to Saul and Abigail's appeal to David. In the former case, David had refrained from killing Saul when he had the power to do so, even though Saul was in pursuit of David, and was trying to kill him. Now he bows to the ground before the freed Saul and appeals:

> The Lord therefore be judge, and judge between me and thee, and see, and plead my cause, and deliver me out of thine hand. And it came to pass [VHYH], when David had made an end of speaking these words unto Saul, that Saul said, Is this thy voice, my son David? And Saul lifted up his voice, and wept. (I Sam. 24:15–16)

Again it seems more appropriate to leave *vehayah* untranslated and to understand it as the power word with which David concludes his plea to the Lord that He plead his cause with Saul, thereby ensuring his deliverance. Its effectiveness is immediately shown as Saul's heart is pierced by divine compassion and he recognizes his true relationship to David.

The same appeal, to make peace rather than pursue vengeance, is made to David by Abigail as she bows herself to the ground and says:

> Upon me, my lord, upon me let this iniquity be. . . . Let not my lord, I pray thee, regard this man of Belial, even Nabal. . . . And it shall come to pass [VHYH], when the Lord shall have done to my lord according to all the good that he hath spoken concerning thee, and shall have appointed thee ruler over Israel; That this shall be no grief unto thee, nor offence of heart unto my lord, either that thou hast shed blood causeless, or that my lord hath avenged himself: but when the Lord shall have dealt well with my lord, then remem-

ber thine handmaid. And David said to Abigail, Blessed be the Lord
God of Israel, which sent thee this day to meet me: And blessed be
thy advice, and blessed be thou, which hast kept me this day from
coming to shed blood, and from avenging myself with mine own
hand. (I Sam. 25:24–25, 30–33)

To the power of prayer, Abigail adds two higher powers of *vehayah*—
sacrifice and prophecy—which we shall consider later. She offers herself to appease his vengeance while at the same time prophetically
lifting his spirit above the immediate impulse to revenge through the
revelation of the surety of his future success that she prefaces with the
power word *vehayah*. So effective is this *vehayah* prophetic appeal that
it lifts David to that higher self that can not only forgo personal vengeance but also prophetically discern the workings of Providence in
bringing Abigail to meet him that day. For such Providential direction of Abigail's mission is, indeed, indicated by the text: "And it was
so [VHYH], as she rode on the ass, that she came down by the covert of
the hill, and, behold, David, and his men came down against her; and
she met them" (I Sam 25:20). Here *vehayah* seems to indicate that
events are divinely guided in accordance with plans for the immediate or final redemption of individuals or humankind. Such unsolic-
ited expressions of the divine will through history constitute God's
exercise of the first degree of *vehayah* power.

The Second Level of Usage: Covenant

The prayers and responses associated with the first level of *vehayah*
power are not based on mutually recognized covenants. What distinguishes the second level of this power is precisely this, that it involves
the power of covenant. The first example of prayer invoking this added
power of covenant occurs when Jacob, frightened by the approach of
Esau, divides his company into two bands and says:

If Esau come to the one company, and smite it, then [VHYH] the
other company which is left shall escape. And Jacob said, O God of
my father Abraham, and God of my father Isaac, the Lord which
saidst unto me, Return unto thy country, and to thy kindred, and I
will deal well with thee: I am not worthy of the least of all the

mercies, and of all the truth, which thou hast shewed unto thy servant; for with my staff I passed over this Jordan; and now I am become two bands. Deliver me, I pray thee, from the hand of my brother. (Gen. 32:8–11)

Jacob invokes the power of *vehayah* to save at least one of the two bands into which he has divided all he has gained through divine favor. But he adds to this hope for deliverance a further prayer claiming divine protection on the basis of the personal covenant he had made with the God of his fathers at Bethel. He recognizes, however, that he must rest his hope for deliverance not on his worth but on the freely given divine covenant.

Not only can *vehayah* prayers be made on the basis of past covenants but as part of present and particular covenants, as in the case of Hannah:

And she vowed a vow, and said, O Lord of hosts, if thou wilt indeed . . . give unto thine handmaid a man child, then I will give him unto the Lord all the days of his life, and there shall no razor come upon his head. And it came to pass [VHYH], as she continued praying before the Lord, that Eli marked her mouth. Now Hannah, she spake in her heart; only her lips moved, but her voice was not heard: therefore Eli . . . said unto her, How long wilt thou be drunken? . . . And Hannah answered . . . I have drunk neither wine nor strong drink, but have poured out my soul before the Lord. (I Sam. 1:11–15)

Having made her vow, Hannah seems to have continued praying the heartfelt word *vehayah*, doing so with such intensity of soul that she appeared to be drunk. That Hannah was a great prophet is shown not only in the extraordinary prayer or psalm of praise that she composes after the birth of her son Samuel (I Sam. 2:1–10) but also in her knowledge of the use of the power word *vehayah* in prayer and of what may be a technique of silently resonating its sound through her heart to amplify its power—"she spake in her heart."

In addition to sealing covenants between individuals and God, *vehayah* also seems to be the generally accepted means of ensuring the binding character of covenants made between individuals. Thus Laban says to Jacob: "Now therefore come thou, let us make a covenant, I and thou; and let it be [VHYH] for a witness between me and thee. . . . God is witness betwixt me and thee" (Gen. 31:44, 50). Here it seems clear that *vehayah* is invoked as a witness of the covenant between Laban and Jacob and that the passage would be better translated, "and let *vehayah* be a witness between me and thee." Such witness, moreover, implies the Presence of God to watch over and ensure the faithful observance of this *vehayah*-bound covenant.

Other examples of the use of *vehayah* to seal covenants among people involve Rahab and Bathsheba. In the former case, the harlot Rahab asks the spies she has protected to swear "by the Lord" (Jos. 2:12) to reciprocate this protection upon the victory of Israel: "And it shall be [VHYH], when the Lord hath given us the land, that we will deal kindly and truly with thee" (Jos. 2:12). And in the latter case, Bathsheba invokes the power of *vehayah* to remind David of his vow "by the Lord thy God" to appoint their son Solomon as his successor (I Kings 1:17–21). Again "by the Lord" and *vehayah* appear to be identical. Both cases show that God can be so called upon if an impending event is about to violate a covenant to which He was witness.

God is, then, either a direct participant or witness to all covenants sealed with the power of *vehayah*. Perhaps the most spectacular of such covenants is the vow sworn to by Jephthah:

> And Jephthah vowed a vow unto the Lord, and said. If thou shalt without fail deliver the children of Ammon into my hands, Then it shall be [VHYH], that whatsoever cometh forth of the doors of my house to meet me, when I return in peace from the children of Ammon, shall surely be the Lord's, and I will offer it up for a burnt offering. (Jud. 11:30–31)

The tragedy of Jephthah is that he misuses spiritual power in the pursuit of his own personal glory. He gathers "vain men" (Jud. 11:3) around him and his concern is always: "Shall I be your head?" (Jud. 11:9). This does not prevent him from being an instrument of the divine purpose to conquer Ammon but it ensures that his personal victory will also prove self-defeating when his only child comes out to greet him. But Jephthah's daughter accepts her sacrificial role in recognition of the binding character of his *vehayah* oath and the fact that God has fulfilled his side of the bargain: "Do to me according to that which hath proceeded out of thy mouth; forasmuch as the Lord hath taken vengeance for thee of thine enemies" (Jud. 11:36). As in Hannah's personal covenant, divine favor is to be purchased with personal sacrifice, a feature of the higher uses of *vehayah* power that will later be considered.

Whether the use of a *vehayah* oath can protect an individual in the case of proven false witness is not absolutely determined. In the case of the Gibeonites, who falsely proved they had come from a far country by the condition of their bread—"behold [VHYH], it is dry, and it is mouldy" (Jos. 9:12), it does afford protection: "We have sworn unto them by the Lord God of Israel: now therefore we may not touch them" (Jos. 9:19). But it does not protect those whose perjury is uncovered through the famous test of Shibboleth:

> And it was so [VHYH], that when those Ephraimites which were escaped said, Let me go over; that the men of Gilead said unto him, Art thou an Ephraimite? If he said Nay; Then said they unto him, Say now Shibboleth: and he said Sibboleth: for he could not frame to pronounce it right. Then they took him, and slew him. . . . (Jud. 12:5–6)

It obviously helps to have a good lie detector when someone suspicious requests admittance with the password of *vehayah*!

Not only is the protective power of *vehayah* invoked among individuals but between individuals and God. Indeed, it seems to have acquired a talismanic status for both general and specific protective purposes. Both of these uses may be seen in connection with the second and third sons of Judah. Although Shelah's birth is mentioned immediately after the births of his older brothers Er and Onan, it seems quite clear that Shelah was born much after them, since he was a child when they were of marriageable age (Gen. 38:11). If he was born after the death of one or both of her older sons, then we may see in the position of the word *vehayah* after the name of Shelah an attempt by his mother Shuah to protect him at birth from the divine punishment that had overtaken her older sons: "And she yet again conceived, and bare a son; and called his name Shelah: [VHYH] and he was at Chezib, when she bare him" (Gen. 38:5). The word *Chezib*, which appears to be used as a place-name, literally means "ceased bearing," with the implication that Shuah was at a state past childbearing, or at menopause, when she bore him. His birth must have seemed miraculous to her, as was the birth of Isaac to Sarah, and whether or not she had prayed for such a child in the manner of Hannah, she may have similarly devoted him to the Lord with the word *vehayah*. Or she may have simply named him while invoking the talismanic power of *vehayah*. And it does seem to have kept him from a levirate marriage to Tamar after the death of Onan (Gen. 38:14) and to have preserved his life.

Not so fortunate was Onan's use of *vehayah* to protect himself while disobeying the procreative commandment of marriage:

> And Onan knew that the seed should not be his; and it came to pass [VHYH], when he went in unto his brother's wife, that he spilled it on the ground, lest that he should give seed to his brother. And the thing which he did displeased the Lord: wherefore he slew him also. (Gen. 38:9–10)

Onan seems to have committed his famous sin with *vehayah* on his lips, but it does not serve to protect him against God's displeasure at this willful crossing of divine intention, the general commandment to "Be fruitful, and multiply" (Gen. 1:28), and the specific Providence related to the child to be born of Tamar.

For Peretz, one of the twins born to Tamar and Judah, is to be the ancestor of David, and thus of the Messiah. Though all three of Shuah's sons failed to impregnate Tamar, her own zeal to bear a child of Judah's line led her to impersonate a harlot and so mate with Judah himself. So too Ruth the Moabite, who would not leave her mother-in-law, Naomi, after the death of her Hebrew husband, is bidden by Naomi to play the part of a harlot with her kinsman Boaz. She lays at his feet and he swears by *vehayah* to legitimize their union: "Tarry this night, and it shall be [VHYH] in the morning, that . . . then will I do the part of a kinsman to thee, as the Lord liveth" (Ruth, 3:13). Their child Obed, the grandfather of David, is brought to Naomi with the words: "And he shall be [VHYH] unto thee a restorer of thy life" (Ruth 4:15). It is, then, through what appears on the surface to be harlotry, that Israel is to give birth to a redeemer, a restorer of life. As the prophet Hosea said: "Though thou, Israel, play the harlot. . . . I will ransom

them from the power of the grave; I will redeem them from death"
(Hos. 4:15, 13:14). The occurrence of *vehayah* in texts associated with
the children of Tamar and Ruth suggests the possibility of an oversee-
ing Providence working itself out through what seem to be uncon-
nected employments of *vehayah*.

The point of departure for this discussion of Messianic Providence
was the talismanic use of *vehayah* by Shuah and Onan, which seemed
to work when applied to the innocent Shelah but not when used by the
guilty Onan. Another example of the inefficacy of *vehayah* occurs when
Sisera, the enemy of God, invokes it in an appeal to Jael for protection:
"It shall be [VHYH], when any man doth enquire of thee, and say, Is
there any man here? that thou shalt say, No" (Jud. 4:20). She nonetheless "smote the nail into his temples" (Jud. 4:21) and is celebrated for
this in Deborah's great song as "blessed above women" (Jud. 5:24).

There is, then, a factor of Providential justice operating within
that power called *vehayah* that can cut off its protective power or turn
its power against the user who wrongfully attempts to exploit it for
personal or vicious ends. In the deepest sense, therefore, all uses of
vehayah can be said to entail some form of covenant, some recognition that its power is not to be invoked under false pretenses but within
the restrictions of the Third and Ninth Commandments, those prohibiting taking the name of the Lord in vain and false witness.

We have thus far been considering the concept of covenant in
connection with prayer and individual agreements or vows, but its
major significance is, of course, in the great, historical covenants God
makes and renews with the favored representatives of mankind and
with Israel. And here too we find the most significant of such covenants to be bound through the power of *vehayah*. The first of these
covenants was made with Noah, and in it there appears the second
use in the Torah of the word *vehayah* after the initial occurrence defining it as having four categories. Remarkably, this second instance
falls within the second of its categories. God announces to Noah, "With
thee will I establish my covenant" (Gen. 6:18), instructs him on the
construction of the ark and the animals to be brought into it, and
says: "And take thou unto thee of all food that is eaten, and thou shalt
gather it to thee: and it shall be [VHYH] for food for thee, and for them"
(Gen. 6:21).

Vehayah would seem here to have a double meaning. In this instance and elsewhere in the Torah, God binds himself through the power of *vehayah* to provide food for those with whom he has made a covenant. This is, in fact, the essence of the successive covenants He makes, culminating in the opening to the second paragraph of the Sh'ma with its promise that obedience to the commandments would bring the rain necessary for the production of food: "And it shall come to pass [VHYH], if ye shall hearken diligently unto my commandments. . . . That I will give you the rain of your land in his due season . . . that thou mayest eat and be full" (Deut. 11:13–15). Here, as earlier at Sinai, God swears by *vehayah* to provide food for those who observe his law. In the case of the Manna, this oath is more specific: God will provide for the Sabbath: "Behold, I will rain bread from heaven for you. . . . And it shall come to pass [VHYH], that on the sixth day . . . it shall be twice as much as they gather daily" (Ex. 16:4–5). Thus God bestows on man both food and Sabbath; man has only to gather it in. Noah, too, is told to "gather" in his food, but he is told as well that *vehayah* is what properly sustains both man and beast. Noah's Ark can be considered the first Ark of the Covenant and those whom it redeems from the certain death of the flood are filled with the spiritual food of faith in the sustaining power of God, faith in his word, *vehayah*.

Vehayah appears as well in the covenants with Abraham and Jacob. It is used twice with Abraham to ordain two separate acts of consecration.

> As for me, behold, my covenant is with thee, and . . . thy name shall be [VHYH] Abraham; for a father of many nations have I made thee. . . . And ye shall circumcise the flesh of your foreskin; and it shall be [VHYH] a token of the covenant betwixt me and you. (Gen. 17:4–5, 11)

To be a bearer of the covenantal promise, Abraham must be transformed both internally and externally through the power of *vehayah*. First his name is changed by the addition of the letter *hey*, which also appears in both *vehayah* and the Tetragrammaton. The covenant that is to descend through many nations is established through the invisible token of a new spiritual name and the visible token of circumcision, and both become carriers of the covenant through a ritual charging with the power of *vehayah*.

But a covenant involves two partners. When God appeared to Abraham, he said: "Walk before me, and be thou perfect. And I will make my covenant between me and thee, and will multiply thee exceedingly" (Gen. 17:1–2). After Abraham had been uplifted through the empowerment of covenant, he challenged God's justice regarding Sodom and Gomorrah:

> That be far from thee to do after this manner, to slay the righteous with the wicked: and [VHYH] that the righteous should be as the wicked, that be far from thee: Shall not the Judge of all the earth do right? (Gen. 18:25)

Here Abraham appears to use *vehayah* both to protect himself from God's anger and to influence Him to alter his stated purpose; it could be better translated as "God preserve me and forbid." Abraham is as concerned as God that his covenantal partner be perfect. He comes to the covenant as a free man who demands that his God be just. But God's justice was never at issue. He knew there was just one righteous man in the cities of the plain and had made provision for his safety. Nevertheless, God allows Abraham to confront the appearance of divine injustice so that he can work through it to a profounder basis for his faith. The redemption from slavery that is to preface the national covenant at Sinai was structured to produce just such free men as Abraham here demonstrates himself to be, for only the free can make a true covenant.

The reciprocal use of *vehayah* is again shown in God's covenant with Jacob. God appears to Jacob in a dream, standing above the ladder. Introducing Himself as the God of his fathers, He vows:

> The land whereon thou liest, to thee will I give it, and to thy seed; And thy seed shall be [VHYH] as the dust of the earth . . . and in thee and in thy seed shall all the families of the earth be blessed. And, behold, I am with thee, and will keep thee in all places whither thou goest, and will bring thee again into this land; for I will not leave thee, until I have done that which I have spoken to thee of. (Gen. 28:13–15)

To the original Abrahamic vow of multiplicity and the Promised Land,

God now adds the promises of protection wherever he may go and of final deliverance back to the place filled with the Presence of the Lord: "Surely the Lord is in this place" (Gen. 28:16). In response to God's vow, Jacob now makes a formal covenant stipulating the responsibilities of both partners:

> And Jacob vowed a vow, saying, If God will be with me, and will keep me in this way that I go, and will give me bread to eat, and raiment to put on, So that I come again to my father's house in peace; then shall [VHYH] the Lord be my God: And this stone, which I have set for a pillar, shall be God's house: and of all that thou shalt give me I will surely give the tenth unto thee. (Gen. 28:20–22)

God had first promised to multiply his progeny in a renewal of his earlier promises to Abraham and then to provide him with particular protection. It is this latter promise of protection and guidance through the spirit, of sustenance and final redemption, which Jacob makes the basis of his personal covenant with God. Jacob is essentially asking God to empower him through His Presence, and in return vows that his God shall be VHYH YHVH. The words translated "then shall the Lord be my God" are, in the Hebrew, VHYH YHVH *li l'Elohim*, which literally mean: VHYH YHVH for me for [a] God. Jacob, then, is making a covenant of power with the manifesting aspect of the divine—a covenant that will give him spiritual mastery. And we shall later see him exemplifying the power of such a master in his manipulation of the cattle through the use of *vehayah*.

The divine Presence, with the power to "keep me in this way that I go," will later be granted ritually to all members of the covenant in the fringes to be worn on their garments. For these fringes will be charged with the power of *vehayah*: "And it shall be [VHYH] unto you for a fringe, that ye may look upon it, and remember all the commandments of the Lord, and do them" (Num. 15:39). The power of *vehayah* will also be put into specific commandments connected with God's promise of redemption, which is an essential feature of the divine covenant. Thus of all the laws of the original Sinai Covenant pledged to in Exodus 24:7, only one is given the extra protection of sure recourse to God through *vehayah*:

If thou at all take thy neighbour's raiment to pledge, thou shalt deliver it unto him by that the sun goeth down: For that is his covering only, it is his raiment for his skin: wherein shall he sleep? and it shall come to pass [VHYH], when he crieth unto me, that I will hear; for I am gracious. (Ex. 22:26–27)

The power of *vehayah* to guarantee redemption is later extended to the institution of the Jubilee, the year of redemption, and in particular to the redemption of land (Lev. 25:28) and slaves (Lev. 25:50). Since the right of redemption from slavery in the Jubilee year is guaranteed by the protective power of *vehayah*, it can only be annulled through recourse to this power: "And it shall be [VHYH], if he say unto thee, I will not go away from thee . . . Then thou shalt take an aul, and thrust it through his ear unto the door, and he shall be [VHYH] thy servant for ever" (Deut. 15:16–17). Apparently the slave must swear with *vehayah* to renounce his right of redemption in the Jubilee and the master must bind him to perpetual service with the power of *vehayah*.

Another difficulty with the Jubilee was that as the seventh year approached, in which all loans, not simply the pledges of clothing, could be redeemed without repayment, people became reluctant to lend to the needy. To prevent such a negative consequence of the Jubilee, God made it a sin, punishable by *vehayah*, not to be charitable at this time (Deut. 15:9). A final sign of God's graciousness is His establishment, with the power of *vehayah*, of sanctuary cities to which murderers may flee to safety (Deut. 19:3, 10), thereby continuing that deliverance of murderers from human revenge begun with Cain. Thus we see how the covenantal promise of redemption becomes incorporated into the Law, whose very language guarantees that all manner of redemption shall be specifically under the protective power of *vehayah*.

The Third Level of Usage: Sacrifice

The third level or head of *vehayah* power is the power of sacrifice. This first appears in connection with the third biblical use of *vehayah* following the initial definition of its four "heads":

> And Noah builded an altar unto the Lord . . . and offered burnt
> offerings on the altar. And the Lord smelled a sweet savour; and the
> Lord said in his heart, I will not again curse the ground any more for
> man's sake. . . . And it shall come to pass [VHYH], when I bring a
> cloud over the earth, that the bow shall be seen in the cloud: And
> I will remember my covenant . . . and the waters shall no more
> become a flood to destroy all flesh. (Gen. 8:20–21, 9:14–15)

Here we see that sacrificial offerings to God can be rewarded with
divine favor, in this particular instance with a *vehayah*-bound covenant never again to cause general destruction through flood waters.

This sequence of actual or vowed sacrifice followed by a favorable
response, which we saw earlier in our discussion of prayer, constitutes
vehayah's third degree of power. For to the naked power of a prayer
like that uttered by Cain, the petitioner can first add the power of
covenant and then further strengthen it by offering a sacrifice. Thus
Hannah not only prayed for a son but made a private covenant that
she would repay the divine gift of this son by devoting him wholly to
the service of God. In this way she vowed a personal sacrifice of all
she would be given. Similarly, the power of covenant can be further
strengthened by offering a sacrifice, as when Jacob vowed to sacrifice
a tenth of all that God would give him.

In the case of both Noah and Jacob sacrifice becomes the human
response to a divine covenant ensuring redemption, and it is the promise of such redemption that primarily governs the ritual practice of
sacrifice. The most significant association of sacrifice and redemption
occurs at Passover, the account of which contains the greatest concentration of *vehayah* references in the Bible: Exodus 12:6, 13, 14, 25,
26, 48; 13:5, 9, 11, 14, 16. The sacrifice of the paschal lamb ensures a
double redemption, from both life and death in Egypt:

> And it shall come to pass [VHYH], when ye be come to the land
> which the Lord will give you, according as he hath promised, that
> ye shall keep this service. And it shall come to pass [VHYH], when
> your children shall say unto you, What mean ye by this service?
> That ye shall say, It is the sacrifice of the Lord's passover, who passed
> over the houses of the children of Israel in Egypt, when he smote

the Egyptians, and delivered our houses. (Ex. 12:25–27)

As the blood of the original sacrifice preserved Israel in Egypt, so the memorial feast of Passover shall serve as a perpetual reminder of the redemptive power of God.

The children of Israel were brought out of the house of bondage that they might freely make a national covenant with the God of their redemption, and a major feature of this covenant was the establishment of a sanctuary for offering sacrifices and of a hereditary priesthood to perform the sacrificial rituals. This priesthood was to descend from Aaron, who had been given a direct transmission of *vehayah* power: "And he shall be thy spokesman unto the people: and he shall be [VHYH], even he shall be to thee instead of a mouth" (Ex. 4:16). Thus it is the priest rather than the prophet who is empowered to be the final spokesman of God to the whole people. But because the spiritual development of the priest is not as high as that of the prophet, he must be specially protected in his contact with the holiness of the Temple.

This protection is afforded him by the holy garments, particularly the robe and the miter, both of which are charged with the protective power of *vehayah*. This protective power is placed primarily in the ornaments on the hem of the robe of the ephod: "And it shall be [VHYH] upon Aaron to minister: and his sound shall be heard when he goeth in unto the holy place before the Lord, and when he cometh out, that he die not" (Ex. 28:31–32, 34–35). With *vehayah* upon him as he attends to his ministry, he is surrounded as much by its power as by the robe that contains it. This *vehayah*-charged robe becomes the sacred armor that preserves his life in the fire of the divine Presence.

As the robe of the ephod affords protection, so the miter gives the power to make atonement for the people, the most important of all priestly functions:

And thou shalt make a plate of pure gold, and grave upon it like the engravings of a signet, HOLINESS TO THE LORD. And thou shalt put it on a blue lace, that it may be [VHYH] upon the miter; upon the forefront of the miter it shall be. And it shall be [VHYH] upon Aaron's forehead, that Aaron may bear the iniquity of the holy things, which the children of Israel shall hallow in all their holy gifts; and it shall be always upon his forehead, that they may be accepted before the Lord. (Ex. 28:36–38)

It is not only the plate engraved with the consecrating words "Holiness to the Lord" that is upon the miter but also the power of *vehayah*. And so crowned, the priest becomes empowered to atone for any iniquity or uncleanliness in the people's offerings. Thus the priest not only offers the people's sacrifices but renders them acceptable to God through the holiness of his office, thereby doubly atoning for the people.

The power of *vehayah* to bring multiplicity into unity can be seen most clearly with regard to the Sanctuary, the sacred center of ritual sacrifice:

And thou shalt make fifty taches of gold, and couple the curtains together with the taches: and it shall be [VHYH] one tabernacle. . . . And thou shalt make fifty taches of brass, and put the taches into the loops, and couple the tent together, that it may be [VHYH] one. (Ex. 26:6, 11)

Not only does *vehayah* serve to unify the various constituents of the Sanctuary but to sanctify them, in particular to confer holiness on the altar and all that shall touch it: "Seven days thou shalt make an atonement for the altar, and sanctify it; and it shall be [VHYH] an altar most holy: whatsoever toucheth the altar shall be holy" (Ex. 29:37).

It is *vehayah*, then, which sanctifies both priest and altar that they may transmit its holy power to the sacrificial offerings that bring atonement. God also guarantees the support of the Temple and its priests through the power of *vehayah*. In particular, in the wave and heave offerings ordained as the priest's portion (Ex. 29:26, 28) and the atonement money appointed for support of the Temple (Ex. 30:16). In addition, the priesthood is also guaranteed the sacrifice offered by individuals in support of their personal vows to God or the monetary value thereof. We have earlier seen how vows were both bound by the power of *vehayah* and strengthened by the offer of sacrifice; so it is not surprising to see this power introduced into the disposition of sacrifices made in association with such vows. The only surprise is the extent of these *vehayah* references, particularly in Leviticus 27: 3, 4, 5, 6, 7, 15, 16, 21. All of the references to Temple sacrifices, and there are others besides those cited that invoke *vehayah*, are summed up in one culminating reference introduced by *vehayah*:

> Then there shall be [VHYH] a place which the Lord your God shall choose to cause his name to dwell there; thither shall ye bring all that I command you; your burnt offerings, and your sacrifices, your tithes, and the heave offering of your hand, and all your choice vows which ye vow unto the Lord: And ye shall rejoice before the Lord your God. . . . (Deut. 12:11–12)

Vehayah both ordains and constitutes a dwelling place for the Name of God, a space in which sacrifice and rejoicing become one.

We approach here an understanding of the true meaning of sacrifice and the reason why it is a necessary bridge between the initiation of covenant and its end. In its simplest terms, any covenant involves sacrifice—the sacrifice of the freedom to act contrary to one's vow. Such freedom is freely sacrificed, however, because the individual hopes to gain a return greater than that which was given up. All covenants are entered into for mutual profit or some form of gratification, and they involve some necessary cost. In the case of the Sinai Covenant, the cost for Israel is obedience to the covenant, most particularly to the Ten Commandments, and the reward promised for such obedience is the transformation of Israel into "a kingdom of priests, and an holy nation." The Lord only knows what benefit He shall receive from such a "peculiar treasure." But he who observes the Sabbath and refrains from even coveting the rights of his God, his parents, and his neighbors, is sacrificing the ego demands of his lower nature for the higher experience of communion, and his reward will be empowerment and holiness, the two endowments that together produce the spiritual master.

Earlier I suggested that the ultimate function of ritual sacrifice is to make that atonement which will ensure redemption. It is such a state, redeemed from all the iniquities of the Fall through the sacrificial purification of the physical, that constitutes the fourth and highest level of *vehayah* power, that of the spiritual master or Tzaddik. The nature of Temple sacrifice accomplishes this spiritual process in both symbolic and actual terms. The animal nature of man, with all its sins, is offered up on the altar in the form of an actual animal sacrifice, and the fire transforms its material grossness into a purified and sweet smelling energetic essence that rises to the heavens. Sacrifices can either be wholly consumed on the altar as a "burnt offering, for a sweet savour before the Lord" (Ex. 29:25), or transformed by ritual fire into a holy meal of communion with God, family, and congregation, a source of rejoicing and holy empowerment. The latter were not only symbolic but, when performed by a sanctified priesthood in a sanctified Temple, actual sources of atonement and redemption: the divine holiness, drawn down into the sacrificial animal by the ritual ministrations of the attending priests, having been ingested with the food. But though such instruments of redemption no longer exist, they can still serve as a model of the functional nature of sacrifice.

Even when such sacrifice was at its height, there was always an understanding of its personal nature, as in Abigail's self-sacrificing offer and the willingness of Jephthah's daughter to be a sacrificial victim, and when actual animal sacrifices were made they entailed a personal sacrifice of private wealth. Something of the self is sacrificed, then, in all forms of sacrifice, animal or other, and what is sacrificed is precisely the animal for the spiritual nature. The Sinai Covenant offers holiness at the price of spiritual discipline, the sacrifice of immediate animal gratification. It redeems man from the bondage of animal instincts and frees the true will of the spiritual master.

The Fourth Level of Usage: Master Power

The power of the Tzaddik is the final unfolding of *vehayah* power and was there from the beginning. Each of the higher powers of *vehayah* are enfolded within the next lower level and implicit within it. The power of prayer implicitly involves the covenantal understanding that it can only safely ask for that which is consistent with the divine will. The power of covenant depends upon the sacrifice of the freedom to act counter to it. So, too, the sacrifice of chaotic freedom contains the secret of true willpower, the master power of manifestation. It is just because each use of *vehayah* entails all of its higher powers that prayer can be effective and can lead to the manifestation of what is needed.

But the spiritual master is he who can raise the laws of manifestation to a science, who can use his will efficiently to influence and alter the lower laws of nature, who knows precisely how to utilize the highest power of *vehayah*.

Since the first three levels of *vehayah* power were progressively unfolded in the first three occurrences of this word after that which defined it as having four categories, it would be nice to be able to find its fourth level in the very next reference, and perhaps we can. This fifth biblical reference (that is, the fourth after the initial four-headed definition) introduces Abraham's plea to Sarah that she save his life in Egypt by claiming to be his sister (Gen. 12:12). It appears in the section containing the words "the souls that they had gotten in Haran" (Gen. 12:5) on which the *Sefer Yetzirah* bases the tradition of Abraham's magical powers, interpreting the souls as Abraham's creations—Golems. And it follows shortly upon the statement that Abraham "called upon the name of the Lord" (Gen. 12:8). If we can infer that the name he called upon was *vehayah* and that he might have created souls through its use, then we may be able to discern in his reported *vehayah* usage the sign of a master, that he was prophetically able to divine the Egyptians' future response to Sarah and himself and knew how to influence her in such a way that the Lord's protection would also be elicited.

Whether or not the first five references to *vehayah* in Genesis may be said to encode so neatly both the definition of its four "heads" and then the ordered examples of its levels of power, the first clear use of the fourth level of *vehayah* power is by Abraham's servant Eliezer. Entrusted with the task of finding the proper wife for Isaac, Eliezer uses *vehayah* to set up a sign of the providential direction of events in his prayer to God:

> And let it come to pass [VHYH], that the damsel to whom I shall say, Let down thy pitcher, I pray thee, that I may drink; and she shall say, Drink, and I will give thy camels drink also: let the same be she that thou hast appointed for thy servant Isaac; and thereby shall I know that thou hast shewed kindness upon my master. (Gen. 24:14)

Eliezer has used *vehayah* to program a precise event for God to manifest and is successful, as he later reports, due to his use of *vehayah*

(Gen. 24:43). He exemplifies the second level of spiritual mastery, which might be called the Master of Synchronicity.[6]

Isaac uses the power of *vehayah* only once, to counter the power of the blessing stolen by Jacob under false pretenses. When Esau cries to his father, "Hast thou but one blessing, my father? bless me, even me also, O my father" (Gen. 27:38), Isaac is moved to use *vehayah* to redeem Esau, his favorite son, from the servitude to which he had just inadvertently doomed him in the stolen blessing: "and it shall come to pass [VHYH] when thou shalt have the dominion, that thou shalt break his yoke from off thy neck" (Gen. 27:40). Jacob will also use the power of *vehayah* to give special force to the blessing of his favorite son Joseph: "And Israel said unto Joseph, Behold, I die: but God shall be [VHYH] with you and bring you again unto the land of your fathers" (Gen. 48:21). The Patriarchal blessings, with the power to determine the destiny of progeny, clearly demonstrate a master power. The belief has persisted to the present day that parents are endowed with the power to bless their children. This may explain the need for children to honor their parents, as formulated in the Fifth Commandment: "Honour thy father and thy mother: that thy days may be long upon the land which the Lord thy God giveth thee" (Ex. 20:12). Honoring one's parents may ensure the blessings of long life in the Promised Land because of this parental capacity to transmit the divine power of blessing to favored children. But the power of such a blessing seems to depend on the spiritual level of the parent. In the case of Isaac and Jacob, it becomes one with divine Providence.

It will be remembered that Jacob made a covenant of power with God, and he uses the power of manifestation most spectacularly in his manipulation of the cattle. Both the selection and breeding of the cattle is placed under the control of *vehayah*.

> I will pass through all thy flock to day, removing from thence all the speckled and spotted cattle, and all the brown cattle among the sheep, and the spotted and speckled among the goats: and *of such* shall be [VHYH] my hire. (Gen. 30:32)

> And it came to pass [VHYH], whensoever the stronger cattle did conceive, that Jacob laid the rods before the eyes of the cattle in the gutters, that they might conceive among the rods. But when the

cattle were feeble, he put *them* not in [VHYH]: so the feebler were Laban's, and the stronger Jacob's. And the man increased exceedingly, and had much cattle, and maidservants, and menservants, and camels, and asses. (Gen. 30:41–43)

The words in italics are added to the biblical text and reveal the lack of understanding of the true meaning of *vehayah* by the translators of the King James Version. In the first instance, Jacob does not say that his hire shall be the spotted cattle but that he will derive his hire from *vehayah*, and he then knowingly sets about using its power. Having first selected all the cattle with any trace of white or brown, he takes rods of various woods and peels them so they reveal white strips within the remaining brown bark (Gen. 30:35–38). These rods work to produce spotted cattle from all the cattle mating in front of them (Gen. 30:39) when they are specifically charged with *vehayah*. Thus to his initial flock of spotted cattle, Jacob adds the spotted young of the stronger cattle within both his own and Laban's flocks. He personally supervises the mating of these stronger cattle, laying the rods before their eyes and directing the *vehayah* power to flow through the rods and into each conception. Genesis 30:41 would be better translated: "And then transmitting the manifesting power of *vehayah*, whensoever the stronger cattle did conceive, Jacob laid the rods. . . ." Similarly Genesis 30:42 should read: "But when the cattle were feeble, he did not put *vehayah* in[to the rods]." Through the selective use of such *vehayah*-charged rods, Jacob is able to direct the divine power of manifestation into producing an enormous increase of his personal fortune. He magically transforms a small flock into a source of great wealth. He may be said to represent the third degree of master power, the power of what might be called the Master of Transformation.

His son Joseph also uses *vehayah* to achieve great power and wealth but he uses it with the lowest or first degree of master power, the power of what passes for ordinary insight. Having wisely interpreted Pharaoh's dreams, he structures the remedy for Egypt's plight in a way that would make him virtual ruler of the land:

Now therefore let Pharaoh look out a man discreet and wise, and set him over the land of Egypt . . . and let him . . . take up the fifth part of the land of Egypt in the seven plenteous years. . . . And that food shall be [VHYH] for store to the land against the seven years of famine . . . that the land perish not. (Gen. 41:33–36)

By means of the channeling power of *vehayah*, Joseph directs God's covenantal promise of food so that it can produce both the salvation of Egypt and his own consequent elevation. Since his exalted position is wholly dependent upon Pharaoh, he uses *vehayah* to strengthen and enrich Pharaoh, reducing the people to serfdom on what had formerly been their own lands and making the high taxation perpetual law through the binding power of *vehayah*:

Then Joseph said unto the people, Behold, I have bought you this day and your land for Pharaoh: lo, here is seed. . . . And it shall come to pass [VHYH] in the increase, that ye shall give the fifth part unto Pharaoh. . . . And Joseph made it a law over the land of Egypt unto this day, that Pharaoh should have the fifth part. (Gen. 47:23–26)

Joseph uses *vehayah* on one other occasion, and that is to protect his family in their interview with Pharaoh and to ensure their success, a use that may seem to justify his other uses of it to gain and retain his potent position in Egypt:

And it shall come to pass [VHYH], when Pharaoh shall call you, and shall say, What is your occupation? That ye shall say, Thy servants' trade hath been about cattle . . . that ye may dwell in the land of Goshen; for every shepherd is an abomination unto the Egyptians. (Gen. 46:33–34)

Despite the fact that the Hebrews' shepherding is an abomination to the Egyptians, they are assured a dwelling place in Goshen because of Joseph's power, a power gained by and including the knowing use of *vehayah*.

The magical use of *vehayah* to obtain the worldly blessings of wealth and position has a Providential dimension built into it that ensures that any impropriety in its use will be self-defeating until it results in a transformative and saving insight. Thus Joseph is saved from the tormenting inner conflict between his vindictiveness and love for his brothers by Judah's *vehayah* prayer to him. And, when Jacob finds both Esau and Laban approaching him from opposite directions with anger at what they felt was the unfair advantage he had taken of them, he is moved to a *vehayah* prayer that prepares for the transformation of his nature and the change of his name to Israel. Not only does this Providential dimension ensure that its punishments will be correctional but that all manifestations of *vehayah* power will serve a higher purpose. The spiritual mastery of Jacob and Joseph acts first to extend Israel's might and then to grant them a temporary haven and heritage in Egypt.

As *vehayah* was instrumental in bringing Israel into Egypt, so is it instrumental in the Exodus from Egypt, and it achieves its most miraculous effects in the hands, quite literally, of Moses. This greatest of biblical masters will surpass his predecessors in his command of the full range of *vehayah* power, but he begins at the highest level of Patriarchal magic—exemplified by Jacob in his use of the rods—in which he is personally instructed by God.

The use of a rod to focus the divine power of manifestation is shown most spectacularly by God as He teaches Moses directly how to transform his rod into a serpent and back again into a rod (Ex. 4:2–4). He then demonstrates a second transformative power, making Moses' hand leprous and healthy again (Ex. 4:6–7). Finally, God charges Moses with the power of *vehayah* to command progressively greater belief in these signs as well as to produce a third most convincing sign, thus enabling Moses to use this compelling power at his own direction:

> And it shall come to pass [VHYH], if they will not believe thee, neither hearken to the voice of the first sign, that they will believe the voice of the latter sign. And it shall come to pass [VHYH], if they will not believe also these two signs, neither hearken unto they voice, that . . . the water which thou takest out of the river shall become blood upon the dry land. (Ex. 4:8–9)

Here again *vehayah* would be better translated in association with the sources of belief rather than just as an indicator of the future: "They will [surely] believe." The rod, the blood, and *vehayah* are again associated in the Plague of Blood (Ex. 7:19), the rod and *vehayah* in the Plague of Lice (Ex. 8:12), and just *vehayah* in the Plague of Boils

(Ex. 9:9). In all these instances, however, it is God who is using *vehayah* in his instructions to Moses, and Moses is as much the instrument of the divine will as is the rod. In all the miracles of the Exodus from Egypt, there is no evidence for Moses' personal use of *vehayah*. Moses' miraculous power, including his ability to talk face-to-face with God and live, is so great that it seems as though he does not need to descend to the use of a power word to bring his will into manifestation.

But there is one extraordinary instance where he does appear to use *vehayah* directly—in the battle with Amalek led by Joshua:

> And it came to pass [VHYH], when Moses held up his hand, that Israel prevailed: and when he let down his hand Amalek prevailed. But Moses' hands were heavy; and they took a stone, and put it under him, and he sat thereon; and Aaron and Hur stayed up his hands, the one on the one side and the other on the other side; and his hands were steady until the going down of the sun. And Joshua discomfited Amalek and his people with the edge of the sword. (Ex. 17:11–13)

Here Moses seems to be consciously directing the power of *vehayah* through his outstretched hands, which he is using in the same manner as rods. That such an instrument of power direction is necessary is shown by the lengths to which his companions go to hold up his arms.

In another instance, which seems to duplicate the image magic of Jacob, he is taught by God to counteract the poison of the divinely sent fiery serpents by placing a brass serpent upon a pole charged with the healing power of *vehayah*:

> And the Lord said unto Moses, Make thee a fiery serpent, and set it upon a pole: and it shall come to pass [VHYH], that every one that is bitten, when he looketh upon it, shall live. And Moses made a serpent of brass, and put it on a pole, and it came to pass [VHYH], that if a serpent had bitten any man, when he beheld the serpent of brass, he lived. (Num. 21:8–9)

In both the divine instructions and the Mosaic product, it would be better to eliminate the punctuation between pole and *vehayah* and understand the two words as coordinates, as the "Pole *Vehayah*" or the "*Vehayah* Pole." In making such a *vehayah* pole, Moses would have to have personally charged it with this power.

This is the first instance we have encountered of the use of *vehayah* for healing, but there will be others, for this is one of the highest powers of the master. Thus David seems to have been a practitioner of *vehayah* therapeutic harping:

> Let our lord now command thy servants, which are before thee, to seek out a man, who is a cunning player on an harp: and it shall come to pass [VHYH], when the evil spirit from God is upon thee, that he shall play with his hand, and thou shalt be well. . . . And it came to pass [VHYH], when the evil spirit from God was upon Saul, that David took a harp, and played with his hand: so Saul was refreshed, and was well, and the evil spirit departed from him. (I Sam. 16:16, 23)

Whether the harp is tuned to the *vehayah* vibration or played to its sounded chanting, there seems to have been a well-established tradition of healing mental illness through spiritual music.

Music seems to provide a direct conduit to a yet higher power of *vehayah*, the power of prophecy, as when Elisha calls for a minstrel to aid his prophetic powers: "But now bring me a minstrel. And it came to pass [VHYH], when the minstrel played, that the hand of the Lord came upon him. And he said, Thus saith the Lord" (II Kings 3:15–16). Elisha seems to be inspired when the minstrel "plays" *vehayah* and somehow incorporates either its sound or its power into his performance. But Elisha's greatest act of healing, the restoration to life of the Shunammite woman's dead son (II Kings 4:32–35), seems to have been the indirect product of the knowing use of *vehayah* by this "great woman" (II Kings 4:8). It is she who prepares lodgings for Elisha with the words: "And it shall be [VHYH], when he cometh to us, that he shall turn in thither" (II Kings 4:10). In gratitude, this "holy man of God" (II Kings 4:9) prophesies that she shall bare a son, though her husband is old, and then, when the child dies, restores him to life. Through the power of *vehayah* she has been able to draw Elisha into her own sphere of interest and direct his surpassing holiness to her own benefit.

To return now to Moses, there are two further uses to which Moses puts the power of *vehayah*. As with Eliezer, he uses it to set up a scenario within which God is to manifest His will. To quell the rebellion of Korah, he takes it upon himself to direct both the rebels and God:

> This do; Take you censers, Korah, and all his company; And put fire therein, and put incense in them before the Lord tomorrow: and it shall be [VHYH] that the man whom the Lord doth choose, he shall be holy: ye take too much upon you, ye sons of Levi. (Num. 16:6–7)

And just on cue, "the glory of the Lord appeared unto all the congregation" (Num. 16:19) to proclaim His support of Moses and purposed destruction of the rebels.

A final example of this use of *vehayah* to structure a scene in which God is called upon to act a specific part may be seen in Elijah's great contest with the four hundred and fifty prophets of Baal. In this test of the true God, Elijah and the prophets of Baal are both to prepare a sacrifice without putting fire under it, the challenge being: "Call ye on the name of your gods, and I will call on the name of the Lord: and the God that answereth by fire, let him be [VHYH] God" (I Kings 18:24).

Again we see the phrase "the name of YHVH" in close proximity to what can be considered the divine name VHYH. And with this invocation of the manifesting aspect of God, "the fire of the Lord fell, and consumed the burnt sacrifice. . . . And when all the people saw it . . . they said, The Lord, he is the God; the Lord, he is the God" (I Kings 18:38–39). Thus the two greatest prophets of the historical books, Moses and Elijah, are able to use *vehayah* spectacularly to stage powerful manifestations of divine power.

There is one other area in which *vehayah* power is used most spectacularly, and that is in war. Moses' use of this power in the battle with Amalek was but a prelude to his introduction of its power into his concept of holy war:

> And it shall be [VHYH], when ye are come nigh unto the battle, that the priest shall approach and speak unto the people, And shall say unto them, Hear, O Israel, ye approach this day unto battle against your enemies: let not your hearts faint, fear not, and do not tremble,

neither be ye terrified because of them; For the Lord your God is he that goeth with you, to fight for you against your enemies, to save you. (Deut. 20:2–4)

Moses' great student Joshua puts it more succinctly: "Be strong and of a good courage; be not afraid, neither be thou dismayed: for the Lord thy God is with thee whithersoever thou goest" (Jos. 1:9).

The Hebraic concept of holy war is in marked contrast with the Hellenic concept of honorable war, of war as an arena in which free individuals may win personal glory. This concept is epitomized in Pericles' Funeral Oration, quoted in the superb Zimmern translation:

Counting the quest to avenge her [Athen's] honour as the most glorious of all ventures, and leaving Hope, the uncertain goddess, to send them what she would, they faced the foe as they drew near him in the strength of their own manhood; and when the shock of battle came, they chose rather to suffer the uttermost than to win life by weakness. So their memory has escaped the reproaches of men's lips, but they bore instead on their bodies the marks of men's hands, and in a moment of time, at the climax of their lives, were rapt away from a world filled, for their dying eyes, not with terror but with glory.[7]

The eternal fame the Greek warrior seeks is purchased precisely with the cost of his life because he chooses not "to win life by weakness" and relies entirely on the strength of his "own manhood." He is willing to give up his only life for a moment of glory that paradoxically transcends his earthly limitations through the heroic act of choosing death.

The Hebraic warrior is just as courageous in battle but for an exactly opposite reason. He does not face death for honor but rather believes he faces no such threat. He believes that, however much death seems to lurk on the battlefield, he need not fear, for God is with him and has given him the victory. He relies not on his own strength but on the surpassing power of God, and so his victory confers no glory upon him but only upon God. His courage, however, is no more easily come by than that of the Greek hero; it involves as much daring as the facing of possible death. It is the courage of belief, of the faith that despite all the signs of immanent death one need not fear as long as one depends on God and chooses that life which is God: "For he is thy life and the end of thy days" (Deut. 30:19). The Mosaic concept of holy war not only informs all of the battles in the Bible but also the later battles of Islam and of the Christian Crusades against the Muslims, and it continues to the present day in the pre-battle prayers for victory made on both sides of the battlefield. This is the battle plan that Joshua carries out in conquering the Promised Land.

We can see that Joshua was not only a brilliant general but a great *vehayah* master because of his remarkable feat at the Jordan River, whose waters he is able to part with the use of *vehayah*:

> And it shall come to pass [VHYH], as soon as the soles of the feet of the priests that bear the ark of the Lord, the Lord of all the earth, shall rest in the waters of Jordan, that the waters of Jordan shall be cut off from the waters that come down from above; and they shall stand upon an heap. (Jos. 3:13)

He displays his brilliant generalship in his plan for the ambush of Ai, a plan whose success he ensures through the double use of *vehayah* (Jos. 8:5–8). But his greatest military use of *vehayah* is to be found in the battle for which he is most famous, Jericho:

> And it shall come to pass [VHYH], that when they make a long blast with the ram's horn, and when ye hear the sound of the trumpet, all the people shall shout with a great shout; and the wall of the city shall fall down flat, and the people shall ascend up every man straight before him. (Jos. 6:5)

It is not the Shofar or the trumpet or the people's shouting alone which flattens the walls of Jericho but the fact that all of this sound is a carrier for the manifesting sound of *vehayah*.

This association of the sound of *vehayah* and battle victory is also found in another battle demonstrating the power of God, the battle of Gideon against the Midianites. Before the battle, Gideon charges his followers with the *vehayah* power that will lift them up to the might of divine warriors in the image of Gideon:

> And he said unto them, Look on me, and do likewise: and, behold,
> when I come to the outside of the camp, it shall be [VHYH] that, as I
> do, so shall ye do. When I blow with a trumpet, I and all that are
> with me, then blow ye the trumpets also on every side of all the
> camp, and say, The sword of the Lord, and of Gideon. . . . and they
> blew the trumpets, and brake the pitchers that were in their hands
> . . . and all the host ran, and cried, and fled. (Jud. 7:17–18, 19, 21)

Before coming to the actual battle, these divine warriors engage in
symbolic action, as instructed by Gideon. They blow trumpets and
then break pitchers. The first action symbolically causes the second
and the two together symbolize the destruction of the enemy's power
through the greater power of divinely directed sound. These symbolic
enactments prove effective in transmitting spiritual power according
to the precise will of a master: the enemy host flees before a single
sword has been lifted. When chosen by a master such as Gideon, a
symbol becomes empowered to transform potential force into actual
force. It can do so both because of its coherence with the laws governing such transformation and the power directly imparted to it by such
a master. Thus the sound of the trumpets serves not simply as a sign of
divine power but also as its carrier, and the power that it carries seems
to be the power of *vehayah*.

A final instance of the use of *vehayah* to bring success to the weak
in battle against the strong can be seen in the victory of David over
the giant Goliath. He first uses it to explain the force that enabled
him to slay both a lion and bear and that he will again employ in his
proposed battle with Goliath:

> Thy servant slew both the lion and the bear: and this uncircum-
> cised Philistine shall be [VHYH] as one of them, seeing he hath de-
> fied the armies of the living God. And David said moreover, The
> Lord that delivered me out of the paw of the lion, and out of the
> paw of the bear, he will deliver me out of the hand of this Philis-
> tine. (I. Sam. 17:36–37)

David claims that since Goliath has come against the armies of God,
Goliath is one of those whom he can slay with the power of *vehayah*.
David is also quick to acknowledge that it is the power of the living

God that he has thus been directing in his previous testing of *vehayah* power with the lion and the bear and that he knows he must rely upon in his coming encounter. As he comes before the giant, armed only with his sling and bag of stones, he explains the full nature of holy war to the assembled armies: victory is not given to the mighty of this world but is the Lord's and is given by Him to those who trust in and glorify only God. It is a test not of might but of faith and of the knowing use of spiritual power:

> Then said David to the Philistine, Thou comest to me with a sword, and with a spear, and with a shield: but I come to thee in the name of the Lord of hosts, the God of the armies of Israel . . . for the battle is the Lord's, and he will give you into our hands. And it came to pass [VHYH], when the Philistine arose, and came and drew nigh to meet David, that David hasted, and ran toward the army to meet the Philistine. . . . So David prevailed. (I Sam. 17:45–50)

David not only comes to fight Goliath in the name of the Lord but *with* it. He hastens to meet him with the power of *vehayah* in his heart and probably upon his tongue, possibly in the form of a musical chant whose rhythm kept pace with his footsteps and which built to a crescendo as, reaching into his bag, he "took thence a stone, and slang it" (I Sam. 17:49) to the final sound: *Yah!*

In our discussion of the *vehayah* master, we have seen that the highest levels of all such master powers were first exemplified by the most exalted of biblical figures, Moses. In putting down the rebellion of Korah, Moses lifted to new heights the power of manifesting the signs of God's presence in synchronicity with his own will. And in the battle with Amalek, he was able to influence directly the course of human events by giving a shaping direction to the chaos of innumerable conflicts so that the composite outcome would be transformed into the image of his will. These are the only cases in which Moses uses *vehayah* to influence events independently of instructions from God, but they are enough to show his consummate mastery of the second and third levels of spiritual power—those of the Master of Synchronicity and the Master of Transformation. Though he clearly has full command of the power of *vehayah*, both with and without the use of his own hands, he normally chooses to use it only through his rod and at the direct command of God.

In contrast to his sparing use of *vehayah* for magical purposes, Moses makes repeated use of the very highest level of *vehayah*, its power to determine the future prophetically and to direct as well the divine power of blessing and cursing. Though this use may be seen throughout Deuteronomy, it is most marked at the beginning and end of this book, in Deuteronomy 6:10, 7:12, 8:19, and 11:13, and in 28:1, 15, 63, 30:1, and 31:7, 21, 26. Perhaps most noteworthy are the two instances in which he empowers his prophecies and commandments to stand as his perpetual witnesses to the future behavior of Israel, rendering rewards and punishments according to his word and through the power of *vehayah*:

> And it shall be [VHYH], if thou do at all forget the Lord thy God, and walk after other gods, and serve them, and worship them, I testify against you this day that ye shall surely perish. (Deut: 8:19)

> Take this book of the law, and put it in the side of the ark of the covenant of the Lord your God, that it may be [VHYH] there for a witness against thee. (Deut. 31:26)

In his prophetic command of time Moses reveals his mastery of the fourth and highest level of master power. We may call him a Master of Creation.

We have already seen the prophetic power of *vehayah* in the blessings of Isaac and Jacob, and *vehayah* continues to be connected with prophecy in many later instances. It is associated with Joshua (Jos. 22:18, 23:15), with Saul (I Sam. 10:7, 9), with Nathan (I Chron. 17:11), with Solomon (I Kings 2:37, 8:61), and with Ahijay (I Kings 11:38). It also appears in many of God's prophetic statements to individuals, such as Solomon (I Kings 9:7) and Elijah (I Kings 17:4, 19:18). And, of course, it appears throughout the books of the prophets. What distinguishes all these master prophets from mere fortune-tellers is not simply the basic test of whether the prophecy is true, but the power of such prophecies to determine the future.

There is a sense in which all prophecies are self-fulfilling, that they set up a resonance that is able to channel the myriad lines of potentiality arising from any event or encounter so that one of them will be strengthened and resonate to the structure that has been articulated. The Talmud says that all dreams follow the mouth, that future events will conform themselves to the interpretation given to a dream, whatever that interpretation may be.[8] In the same way, it would seem that prophecy, which is a form of interpreting the future implications of the disorderly appearances of the present, has a power to give direction to that disorder and influence the outcome. Once a thought is formed and articulated, it develops a power of influence that may go far beyond the expectations or intentions of its originating mind. It can give a meaningful organization to what before had resisted the conceptualization that might render it useful. The master prophet is one who recognizes that all prophecies are *causal* and who uses this law of spiritual causality with such a deliberate concentration of consciousness as to propel its positive energy into the future with the added power of his personal will. Into the confusion of the moment, he inserts a new cause that can attract to itself all those potencies that had lain dormant for lack of an expressive outlet. He becomes a creator of causes. It is this power to determine the future prophetically, not simply to foretell the will of God but to channel it, that lifts the prophet to the highest level of mastery. Such a master was Moses and he has filled the Jewish heritage with his power.

Conclusion

"And a river went out of Eden to water the garden; and from thence it was parted, and became into four heads." In its written and oral forms, the Jewish heritage has been filled with the four heads of power we have been surveying, the power of prayer, of covenant, of sacrifice, and of spiritual mastery. What seems to have been lost since the completion of the biblical canon, at a time close to the destruction of the Second Temple and the second exile from Israel, is the knowledge of the term that subsumed and could control these four heads of its power, the reversed form of the Tetragrammaton whose letters would appear to be the manifesting Name of God, *vehayah*. The word, of course, was there to be read all through the Holy Book, but its meaning became obscured by time. What this study has shown, however, is that there was once a tradition in which the power of *vehayah* was understood and used. This tradition persisted during the long period in which the texts of the Bible were being composed and assembled. Whatever one's view of the process of biblical composition, this study has demonstrated that there was a remarkable homogeneity throughout the historical books in the use of the word *vehayah*. It is never used simply to denote the future but is always a signifier of special meaning. It is impossible in such a short study to analyze all of its biblical occurrences, but each of its twenty-five appearances in Genesis *was* studied precisely to demonstrate that its use is always significant, and more than half of the remaining instances have been discussed. The implication is that the magical and spiritual uses of *vehayah* were not an esoteric secret during the period of biblical composition and that its meaning was clear to its writers, first readers, and final editors.

But it is also true that this meaning was either lost or suppressed during the period of the Diaspora with the different problems it posed for Jewish survival. That such a loss of meaning should have accidentally befallen this word is startling in view of the letters of which it is composed—*vav, hey, yod, hey*—the very letters of the Tetragrammaton in a most suggestively transposed form. It seems more likely, therefore, that knowledge of its use was suppressed, along with such other occult practices as mediumship and astrology, because of fear of its ungoverned usage, especially in the communities being fused through the leadership of the new rabbinical authorities. This is not surprising since we have seen its biblical use by all sorts of unlikely individuals, from harlots to perjurers. Some may even have thought that it bore the mark of its first user, Cain. From its suppression as a tool of sorcery it is likely that its true meaning eventually became lost, even to the kabbalistic tradition.

But there is one exception. The only scholar of whom I am aware who has given attention to the always special usage of *vehayah* in the Bible is Thorleif Boman, in his masterful comparison of Hebrew and Greek thought. As will be seen, my understanding of *vehayah* is consistent with his grammatical analysis.

There are a great number of instances in which *hayah* stands in the protasis in order to strengthen and emphasize another verb in the apodosis, somewhat on this order: And it shall come to pass that the rod of the man whom I choose shall send forth shoots (Num. 17.5; other examples include Gen. 15.7a; 24.14, 43; Num. 10.32; 21.8, etc.). *Hayah* has the same function when the succeeding verb is in the infinitive: (and it came to pass) when the sun went down, a deep sleep fell upon Abram (Gen. 15.12; also 35.16; Ex. 30.4, 16; Num. 7.5; 8.11, etc.). It could be contested whether in these cases *hayah* has a peculiar *meaning*, but in such cases *hayah* has incontestably the important verbal *function* of preparing for a verb that is coming and drawing attention to it. Predominantly in such cases *hayah* introduces complete sentences which contain the entry of a future event (Ex. 1.10), lays stress thereon (Gen. 27.40), or represents the preceding event as surprising, sudden or miraculous (Gen. 38.39a [*sic*, should be Gen. 38.27?]; I Sam. 13.10; Gen. 19.29). For the purposes of our investigation we need not enter into these cases in any greater detail since the *dynamic* character of *hayah* is generally clear.[9]

Boman's question of whether "*hayah* has a peculiar *meaning*" in the cases of *vehayah* and *vayehi*,[10] examples of which he discusses together, supports my own conclusion that *vehayah* is not simply a grammatical indicator of the future tense but rather has a *function* with respect to what follows. We differ only in our understanding of the nature of this function. He argues that it serves to "strengthen" what follows in terms largely of emphasis while I believe its strengthening is intended to effect not just our attention to a following event but the event, itself, that all its effects are meant to be "miraculous." But what he has shown about its verbal functioning certainly allows for the interpretation I have given of its special linguistic usage as a power word.

In conclusion, I hope that this study will contribute to a new appreciation of the meaning of *vehayah* in the biblical text and of its power for personal growth. As the former should lead to more knowing translations so should the latter lead to the incorporation of *vehayah* in prayer and meditation. Before disappearing utterly from memory it was used by the most inspired patriarchs, prophets, priests, and kings of Israel, and the time may now be propitious for the rediscovery of this long buried but most potent tool of spiritual mastery. I also hope that future translators and students of the Bible will, in general, be more inclined to treat the spiritual content of the Bible as the sacred history it is—a history of the operations of spirit in the whole of creation and in certain charismatic individuals revealing the nature of divine Law. For these operations embody a power to transmit holiness to the practitioner, and the biblical texts reveal a profound knowledge of esoteric spiritual principles and techniques consistent with the later development of this tradition in the Kabbalah. It is time that the Bible be studied not simply as a historical document or as an unquestioned foundation for faith but as a work both detailing the precise interactions of the human and the divine and one also capable of direct transmissions of spiritual power through the understanding reading of its divine names and acts. It is a Holy Book just because it is capable of transmitting the very spiritual power of which it everywhere speaks, to give both instruction and support in the redemptive process of spiritual growth whose chronicles we can join. "There were giants in the earth in those days" (Gen. 6:4), says the Bible, and, stirred by the power of *vehayah*, may they once again walk on a transfigured Earth.

Notes

Chapter 1

1. When referring to Hebrew words or phrases, my practice will be to italicize only those which either are given to clarify their English translations or are used infrequently. But words that involve important, frequently cited kabbalistic concepts or have come into popular Jewish usage will be distinguished only by capitalizing their initial letters.
2. Unless otherwise indicated, all biblical quotations will be from the King James Version because of its greater literalness.
3. See Aryeh Kaplan, *Meditation and the Bible* (New York: Samuel Weiser, 1978) and my quotations from this book in chapter 3.
4. Samuel Taylor Coleridge, *Biographia Literaria*, chapter 4. All references to classical works of literature, as here, will not be to any specific edition.
5. One noted exception to this is Erwin R. Goodenough who provides a masterful treatment of the later ramifications of the Akedah both in talmudic and kabbalistic literature, as also in Hellenistic Jewish monuments, in *Jewish Symbols in the Greco-Roman Period*, Abridged Edition, ed. Jacob Neusner, Bollingen Series (Princeton: Princeton University Press, 1988), pp. 81–115.
6. Here and throughout this section the word "Shofar" has been inserted in brackets in biblical passages wherever the Hebrew text specifies it.
7. For a full development of this understanding of the priestly ritual of animal sacrifice, see my forthcoming book *The Secret Doctrine of the Kabbalah* (Rochester, Vt.: Inner Traditions, 1999).
8. The first example is given literary expression in Euripides' *Iphigenia at Aulis* and the second example at the beginning of Homer's *Iliad*.

9. Ernst Cassirer, *Language and Myth*, trans. Suzanne K. Langer (New York: Dover, 1953), p. 8.
10. See Gershom Scholem, *Origins of the Kabbalah*, trans. Allan Arkush, ed. R. J. Zwi Werblowsky (N. C.: Jewish Publication Society and Princeton University Press, 1987; orig. German pub. 1962) for his revised dating of the *Sefer ha-Temunah* from the thirteenth to the fourteenth century, based on the research of his students Moshe Idel and Ephraim Gottlieb (pp. 460–61n). See also Werblowsky's editorial report of the revised dating to "after 1300" (p. xiv).
11. Gershom Scholem, *Kabbalah* (New York: New Amsterdam Library, 1974), p. 121.
12. Robert Gordis, "Authority in Jewish Law," in *Conservative Judaism and Jewish Law*, ed. Seymour Siegel (New York: The Rabbinical Assembly, 1977), p. 53.
13. Gordis, p. 53.
14. H. Hertz, *The Pentateuch and Haftorahs* (London: Soncino Press, 1972), p. 33n.
15. Aryeh Kaplan, *The Living Torah: A New Translation Based on Traditional Jewish Sources* (New York: Maznaim, 1981), p. 351n. See also Hertz, p. 503n.
16. See Kaplan, *The Living Torah*, p. 554n.
17. Kaplan, *The Living Torah*, p. 340n.

Chapter 2

1. Chaim Vital, *Etz Chayyim* (Tel Aviv: Kitve Rabbeinu ha–Ari, 1959), ch. 4; vol. 1, p. 8. All translations from the *Etz Chayyim* are my own.
2. See of my forthcoming book *The Secret Doctrine of the Kabbalah* for comprehensive treatment of this doctrine.
3. Chaim Vital, *Sha'ar Ruach ha-Kodesh*, in Kaplan, *Meditation and Kabbalah* (York Beach, Maine: Samuel Weiser, 1982), pp. 255, 257.
4. *Zohar*, 2:216a–b, in Kaplan, *Kabbalah*, pp. 33–34.
5. See Kaplan, *Kabbalah*, p. 93.
6. Abraham Abulafia, *Chayyei ha-Olam ha-Ba*, in Kaplan, *Kabbalah*, pp. 96–97.
7. *Berakhot*, 55b. I am indebted for this interpretation to the oral teachings of Rabbi Meir Fund.
8. Azriel of Gerona, *Sha'ar ha-Kavanah*, in Kaplan, *Kabbalah*, pp. 119–20.
9. Azriel, pp. 121–22.
10. Azriel, p. 122.
11. Abulafia, *Otzar Eden ha-Ganuz*, in Kaplan, *Kabbalah*, p. 84.
12. Azriel, p. 122.
13. The Hebrew word *vehayah*, normally translated "And it shall come to pass," can also be used as a manifesting power word. It will be employed in this way in the kabbalistic meditation to be developed shortly. The appendix to this volume will provide comprehensive treatment of its widespread biblical usage.
14. Dov Baer, *Maggid Devarav le-Ya'akov*, in Kaplan, *Kabbalah*, p. 301.
15. Dov Baer, *Imrey Tzadikim*, in Kaplan, *Kabbalah*, pp. 301–2.
16. Baer, *Maggid*, p. 301.

17. As quoted in Ben Zion Bokser, *The Jewish Mystical Tradition* (New York: Pilgrim Press, 1981), p. 104.

18. See Joseph Tractenberg, *Jewish Magic and Superstition* (New York: Atheneum, 1984), p. 95.

19. For my fuller analysis of this construction of the "double heart" as signifying the unification of the Sefirot of Tiferet and Netzach, which includes the placement of these Sefirot in the human body, see my forthcoming book *The Secret Doctrine of the Kabbalah*. See also my interpretation of the four Tetragrammaton expansions in that book, an analysis that similarly relates the expansion whose Gematria is seventy-two and is known by the Name of Ab with the same Sefirot of Chokhmah and Binah, an identification there shown to have earlier been made by Chaim Vital.

20. This interpretation of the phrases "when thou sittest in thine house," and "when thou walkest by the way" rests on the following considerations. The term used for "sitting," a form of *shevet,* has most interesting associations, particularly with *shabbat,* which has the same Hebrew letters—shin, bet/vet, and *tav*—with the implication that both words originally connoted forms of holy rest. Another suggestive cognate *shevut*—shin, vet, the vowel-letter *vav,* and *tav*—which means "return," also implies that this three-letter root associated the act of sitting with a meditative return to a condition of primordial rest. Particularly in talmudic usage, the word *shevet* had the connotation of "to sit still," a meaning that clearly has associations with meditative practice, most notably with the Zen Buddhist practice of Zazen, or "sitting." If "sitting" may thus be associated with the form of meditative concentration that Aryeh Kaplan has associated with the term *hagah,* "walking" may similarly be associated with the form of mediation he has shown to be correlated with the terms *suach* and *siyach,* a form of floating meditation. For further references, see his *Meditation and the Bible* pp. 100–118, and my quotations from it in the next chapter. Significantly, it was in connection with walking that the word *suach* is used for the only time in the Bible: "And Isaac went out to meditate in the field at eventide" (Gen. 24:63). The concept of walking also appears in the most important commandment God gave to Abraham: "Walk before me, and be thou perfect" (Gen. 17:1). If sitting in one's house may be considered to involve a state of turning inward to the transcendent, walking "by the way" implies a state of attunement to the flow of the immanent aspect of divinity in the world, to the Way of God, the *Derekh ha-Shem.* Since *shevet* and *shabbat* are linguistic cognates, it may be possible to go further and associate the sitting form of meditation with the Sabbath and the form of walking "by the way" (*derekh)* with such an outward turning of weekday consciousness as is informed by the Way, by *suach* consciousness. Such Sabbath and weekday consciousness would fulfill the original test of the Manna, six days of gathering and one day of rest, to "prove them, whether they will walk in my law or no" (Ex. 16:4). Deuteronomy 6:7 commands us to say the Sh'ma when lying down and when rising up and, in this interpretation, on the Sabbath and the weekdays and with the appropriate modes

of meditative consciousness.

21. See my book *The Secret Doctrine of the Kabbalah* for a full discussion of such vowel resonances, which includes another spiritual practice involving the intoning of the harmonics in concert with a stretching exercise.

22. The distinction between the six breaths for the first line and the five breaths for the second line may be related through number mysticism to the content of these lines. The first line defining the nature of the divine can be related to the number six, called perfect because it is the sum of its factors, and the second line defining man's proper relationship to the divine can similarly be related to the number five, in mystical numerology the number of perfected man because the "golden" proportions in terms of which the ideal human body can be analyzed are based on equations containing the square root of five.

23. See Aryeh Kaplan, *The Living Torah*, pp. 517, 528.

24. Kaplan, *The Living Torah*, p. 267.

25. Vital, *Etz Chayyim*, ch. 1; vol. 1, p. 2.

26. In addition to or in place of the Kavanah of Creation, I would like to suggest two further spiritual techniques by which the effectiveness of the fourteen-breath cycle can be greatly enhanced and that can also add important health benefits to this practice. The first of these is the yogic practice of alternate nostril breathing. Rather than alternating the hands used in counting, only the left hand need be used for counting and the right hand can close one nostril and then the other so that the four-part breath cycle is completed through only one nostril at a time, the left hand counting only seven double cycles and each cycle beginning with an exhalation of the breath. Practice of alternate nostril breathing is recommended for balancing the left and right sides of the brain and is particularly effective at dawn and dusk.

The second technique derives from Taoism and will be more fully detailed. This is the Chinese Chi Kung meditative practice of breath circulation through the Microcosmic Orbit, which seems a direct analogue to the practice I have decoded in the *Sefer Yetzirah* and can be profitably synthesized with it. The Microcosmic Orbit is a circuit joining the two most important of the acupuncture meridians, the Governing Vessel going up the spine and the Conception or Functional Vessel going, in this practice, down the front of the torso. The purpose is to arouse and circulate the chi, the vital-spiritual force that seems identifiable with the Ruach (spirit-breath). In this practice, one begins at the Hara or navel area and slowly breathes in. As one does this, one should also mentally direct the flow of chi down through the sexual center to the perineum and up the spine, with special attention to the sacrum, back of the waist, midback, top of the spine, base of the skull and crown, ending at the third-eye point behind the forehead. Here it is necessary to lift the tongue to the roof of the mouth, preferably behind the hard palate, to turn the Functional Vessel from the upward to a downward direction of flow that can complete the Microcosmic Orbit. The breath is now slowly exhaled with concentration at the throat, heart, solar plexus, and navel.

Combining this with the *Sefer Yetzirah* breath cycle and beginning with an inhalation to the head and a holding of the breath to the words *Ruach Elohim Chayyim*, one would now lift the tongue and slowly exhale, drawing the Ruach energy first to the throat and then to the heart to the words *Ruach me-Ruach*, concentrating on the throat for the first Ruach and on drawing the energy into the heart to the words *me-Ruach*. The further descent to the solar plexus and navel would correlate the word *Mayyim* with the solar plexus and the words *me-Ruach* with the Hara. One would now start the slow inhalation to the words *Esh mi-Mayyim*, which can carry the energy around through the rest of the circuit to the crown, taking small sips of breath at each of the stations of the upward path to aid the mental elevation of the energy. Then the breath should be held as one draws the current to the crown with the words *Ruach Elohim Chayyim*, also opening the crown to receive the higher energy and directing it into the third-eye area while lifting the tongue in preparation for the descent of the energy through the front centers with the next exhalation of the breath and the repetition of the orbit. It is also advisable to rotate the torso slowly during this practice. Unlike the yogic concern simply to lift the spiritual energy through the chakras from the base of the spine to the crown, the Taoist concern is to balance such aroused energy through its inner circulation. Its precise spiritual technology can contribute to the suggestions of a similar practice of energy circulation encoded in the *Sefer Yetzirah* that can lay the foundation for a new revival of kabbalistic meditation. For those interested, I would recommend the following book specifically on the Microcosmic Orbit: Mantak Chia, *Awaken Healing Energy Through the Tao: The Taoist Secret of Circulating Internal Power* (Santa Fe: Aurora Press, 1983).

27. All references in this section are to the "Short Version" in the edition of the *Sefer Yetzirah* translated with commentary by Aryeh Kaplan (York Beach, Maine: Samuel Weiser, 1990), pp. 264–65.

28. Kaplan, *Sefer Yetzirah*, 5:1, p. 265.

29. See my book *The Secret Doctrine of the Kabbalah*, one chapter of which is devoted to the *Sefer Yetzirah* and further develops both the meditative practice I have decoded in this text and my solution of its geometric enigma, as well as the use of this *Sefer Yetzirah* Diagram to model the Lurianic Partzufim.

Chapter 3

1. Mircea Eliade, *The Sacred and the Profane: The Nature of Religion*, trans. Willard R. Trask (New York: Harcourt, Brace and World, 1959), pp. 68–70.

2. Eliade, pp. 72, 110.

3. Kaplan, *The Living Torah*. All references to this translation are indicated by the initials AK.

4. Ralph Waldo Emerson, "Fate," concluding paragraph.

5. Robert Frost, "Two Tramps in Mud Time," concluding lines.

6. T. S. Eliot, "Burnt Norton," 1. 3.

7. Henry David Thoreau, *Walden*, from ch. 2.
8. *Code of Jewish Law (Kitzur Shulhan Aruh)*, compiled by Rabbi Solomon Ganzfried, trans. Hyman E. Goldin, rev. ed. (New York: Hebrew Publ. Co., 1927), 150:1 (vol. IV, p. 15).
9. Ganzfried, 150:1 (vol. IV, p. 13).
10. Kaplan, *Meditation and Kabbalah*, p. 270.
11. Vital, *Etz Chayyim*, ch. 1; vol. 1, p. 3.
12. Vital, ch. 5; vol. 1, p. 11.
13. Ganzfried, 17:1 (vol. I, pp. 52, 53).
14. Kaplan, *Meditation and the Bible*, pp. 112, 114, 116.
15. Abraham J. Heschel, "Toward an Understanding of Halachah," in *Conservative Judaism and Jewish Law*, ed. Seymour Siegel (New York: The Rabbinical Assembly, 1977), p. 137.
16. Kaplan, *Meditation and the Bible*, pp. 108, 110.
17. William Wordsworth, opening lines of a sonnet referred to by its first line.
18. Bruce Brown, "The Shining: The Mysterious Power of the Northern Lights," *New York Times Magazine* (Dec. 12, 1982), pp. 46, 60, 62.
19. See Robert O. Becker and Andrew A. Marino, *Electromagnetism and Life* (Albany: State University of New York Press, 1982), pp. 22, 55, 56, 61.
20. See Becker and Marino, pp. 60, 66–67, 69, 71–72, 167, 205.
21. Becker and Marino, p. xi.
22. Becker and Marino, p. 107.
23. Becker and Marino, p. 205.
24. William Wordsworth, "Tintern Abbey," 11.93–102.
25. Abraham Heschel, *The Sabbath: Its Meaning for Modern Man* (New York: Farrar, Straus and Giroux, 1951), pp. 8, 59, 60, 75.

Chapter 4

1. In addition to Christianity, there is the Sufi tradition of Islam, for which see Mir Valiuddin, *Love of God: A Sufic Approach* (Farnam, Surrey, Eng.: Sufi Publishing Co., 1972). For possible Sufi influence on early Kabbalists, see R. J. Zwi Werblowsky, *Joseph Karo: Lawyer and Mystic* (Philadelphia: Jewish Publication Society of America, 1980), pp. 57–61; and Lawrence Fine, trans. and intro., *Safed Spirituality* (New York: Paulist Press, 1984), p. 170.
2. *The Torah, A new translation . . . according to the Masoretic text* (Philadelphia: Jewish Publication Society of America, 1962), p. 338. All other references to the Bible are to the King James Version.
3. Joseph B. Soloveitchik, *On Repentance*, intro. by Pinchas H. Peli (New York: Paulist Press, 1984), pp. 72, 73.
4. Soloveitchik, p. 306.
5. Soloveitchik, pp. 49, 302.
6. The translation is from the Siddur of the Lubavitch movement, which I would

recommend to all who may be interested in a kabbalistically oriented prayer book, the *Siddur Tehillat Hashem*, according to the text of Shneur Zalman of Liadi, trans. Nissen Mangel (Brooklyn, N.Y.: Merkos L'Inyonei Chinuch, 1978), p. 68.

7. Pierre Teilhard de Chardin, *The Phenomenon of Man*, trans. Bernard Wall, intro. Julian Huxley (New York: Harper and Row, 1975), pp. 267, 269, 292–93.

8. See the list of such works in Fine's Introduction to *Reshit Chokhmah*, by Elijah de Vidas, in *Safed Spirituality*, p. 84, as well as examples from this work by de Vidas on pp. 144–48.

9. Franz Rosenzweig, *The Star of Redemption*, trans. William W. Hallo (Boston: Beacon Press, 1971), p. 327.

10. Rosenzweig, pp. 162, 169, 170.

11. Rosenzweig, p. 168.

12. Rosenzweig, p. 164.

13. Rosenzweig, p. 169.

14. Abraham Isaac Kook, *The Lights of Penitence. . .*, trans. and intro. Ben Zion Bokser (New York: Paulist Press, 1978), p. 62.

15. Kook, p. 136.

16. Kook, pp. 64–65.

17. De Vidas, p. 143. See also the statements by Eliezer Azikri—"the principal dwelling place of the *Shekhinah* is in the heart of the Jew" and "God exists in the hearts of His lovers"—as quoted in Werblowsky, p. 59.

18. De Vidas, pp. 142, 148.

19. De Vidas, p. 143.

20. De Vidas, pp. 138, 141.

21. De Vidas, p. 141.

22. Kook, p. 139.

23. Soloveitchik, pp. 166, 174–75, 318.

24. De Vidas, p. 141.

25. Rosenzweig, p. 206.

26. Chaim Vital, *Etz Chayyim* (Tel Aviv: Kitve Rabaynu ha-Ari), ch. 1, vol. 1, pp. 2–3. 1:34, 36, 45, 47. My translation.

27. Martin Buber, *The Legend of the Baal-Shem*, trans. Maurice Friedman (New York: Schocken Books, 1969), pp. 27, 32.

28. Buber, *Legend*, p. 17.

29. Buber, *Legend*, p. 24.

30. Buber, *Legend*, pp. 33, 38.

31. As quoted in Aryeh Kaplan, *The Light Beyond: Adventures in Hassidic Thought* (New York: Maznaim, 1981), pp. 215, 216, 217. All translations in this work are by Kaplan.

32. As quoted in Kaplan, *Light Beyond*, p. 211.

33. As quoted in Kaplan, *Light Beyond*, p. 212.

34. As quoted in Kaplan, *Light Beyond*, pp. 213–14.

35. Buber, *Legend*, p. 18.
36. As quoted in Louis Jacobs, *Hasidic Prayer* (New York: Schocken Books, 1978), p. 44.
37. As quoted in Buber, *Legend*, p. 28.
38. See Aryeh Kaplan, *Meditation and Kabbalah* (York Beach, Maine: Samuel Weiser, 1982), p. 122 and my discussion with quotations of this subject in chapter 2.
39. See Aryeh Kaplan, *Meditation and the Bible* (New York: Samuel Weiser, 1978), pp. 100–116, for an analysis of the directed Hagah mode of meditation and the undirected Siyach mode. See also my discussions of these terms with quotations in chapters 2 and 3.
40. Jacobs, pp. 88, 89, 95.
41. As quoted in Jacobs, p. 65.
42. The Hebrew letter *nun* has been kabbalistically associated with the feminine creative force, most particularly with the Shekhinah and the Sefirah Malkhut with which she is associated. In a work attributed to the first known Kabbalist, Isaac the Blind, there are references to "Diadem, which is the nun" and "the final H is a sign for Diadem," the final *hey* of the Tetragrammaton, here referred to, also being identified with Malkhut. In his anthology containing this work, the editor Joseph Dan comments: "The letter *nun*, in both its regular and final forms, is linked in classical Kabbalah with the tenth and lowest *sefirah*, Kingdom. For a summary of the kabbalistic associations, see R. Moses Cordovero, *Pardes Rimmonim* (Munkacs, 1906), 26:17." All quotations are from *The Early Kabbalah*, ed. Joseph Dan, trans. Ronald C. Kiener (New York: Paulist Press, 1986), pp. 82, 84, 86. In addition to the historical evidence for an association between the letter *nun* and Malkhut (Kingdom), a logical case may be made for its association with the upper feminine Sefirah of Binah (Understanding) since the Gematria equivalent of the letter *nun* is the number fifty, and fifty is a number associated with Binah in the standard kabbalistic reference to the "Fifty Gates of Understanding." It is also from Binah or Imma, the Partzuf form of this Sefirah, that the sea of creation is thought to flow in seven streams to the seven lower Sefirot. Because of the numerical correspondence between the letter *nun* and Binah, I would suggest that this was the original basis for the association of this letter with a feminine Sefirah and that it was later transferred to the tenth Sefirah identified with the more central feminine personality of the Shekhinah.

    An interesting cross-cultural correspondence can be seen with regards to the Egyptian *nun*, as discussed by R. A. Schwaller de Lubicz, in *Sacred Science: The King of Pharaonic Theocracy*, trans. André and Goldian VandenBroeck (New York: Inner Traditions International, 1982), p. 17: "Pharaonic theology speaks of the origin through the Heliopolitan mystery: There is *Nun*, the primordial ocean; within *Nun* there is a fire which acts and produces *Tum*, the first earth or hillock which emerges from *Nun*. This fire is *Nun* itself." There would thus seem to be an association between the Egyptian *nun* and the Hebrew letter-number *nun*=50 which involves the feminine elements in the creation myths of these countries.

43. *Siddur Tehillat Hashem*, trans. Rabbi Nissen Mangel (Brooklyn:Merkos L'Inyonei Chinuch, 1982), p. 33.

44. For a fuller analysis of these vowel resonances, see chapter 5 of my book *The Secret Doctrine of the Kabbalah*.

45. See the Lurianic discussion as quoted by Kaplan in *Meditation and Kabbalah*, pp. 258–59, and Fine's note in *Safed Spirituality*, p. 184.

46. *The Zohar*, trans. Harry Sperling and Maurice Simon (London: Soncino Press, 1934), vol. 1, p. 3.

47. For a fuller development of my concept of the "double heart," see chapters 4 and 5 of my book *The Secret Doctrine of the Kabbalah*.

48. Aryeh Kaplan, ed. and trans., *Sefer Yetzirah: The Book of Creation in Theory and Practice* (York Beach, Maine: Samuel Weiser, 1990), pp. 170, 172–73.

49. Hugo Odeberg, ed. and trans., *3 Enoch or The Hebrew Book of Enoch* (New York: Ktav Publ., 1973, orig. pub. 1928), p. 186.

50. See Ismar Elbogen, *Jewish Liturgy: A Comprehensive History*, trans. Raymond P. Scheindlin (Philadelphia and New York: Jewish Publication Society and Jewish Theological Seminary of America, 1993, orig. pub. 1913), p. 18. Unlike the context of creation for the first appearance of the Kedushah in the first benediction before the Sh'ma, in the remaining two appearances the contexts are those of redemption. In the Amidah it comes right after the six references to resurrection, as part of the next blessing of a holiness which can bring the one praying to an otherworldly condition like that of the heavenly angels singing the Kedushah, and the final context is directly of redemption.

51. *Siddur Tehillat Hashem*, p. 133.

52. *Siddur Tehillat Hashem*, p. 85. The words of the line inserted after the first verse of the Sh'ma were originally the response of the people on Yom Kippur to the High Priest's once-yearly pronunciation of the Tetragrammaton. But my suggestion that their later insertion into the liturgy right after this verse was intended as a marker not only of reverence for the Tetragrammaton but also of hidden meaning is further supported by the fact that these words also appear right after Ana Beknoach, which does not contain the Tetragrammaton but does contain the multiplication of six by seven, earlier shown to signify just such a generative unification of the finite and infinite.

53. A major thesis of my book *The Secret Doctrine of the Kabbalah* is that the Kabbalah was derived from the secret teachings of the Temple priesthood, a process I suggest that developed with the deprofessionalism of this priesthood after the destruction of the Temple, when mystical priests are likely to have passed on these teachings to small cabals. Such mystical priests, who broke with the Temple services after the traditional Zadokite line had been replaced by the Hashmonians, are now thought to have earlier founded the Qumram community which produced the Dead Sea Scrolls, for which see Lawrence H. Schiffman, *Reclaiming the Dead Sea Scrolls* (Philadelphia: Jewish Publication Society, 1994), p. 83f. But here we see that the priesthood, during the Second Temple period, was also responsible for the development of the liturgy from the biblical core of

the Sh'ma and may well have invested it with the meaning I have just ascribed to it, an interpretation further developed in of my forthcoming book. The present analysis of the priestly liturgy should give added support to my larger thesis of the role of the ancient Hebraic priesthood in formulating the mystical secret doctrines of Judaism.

54. Elbogen,p. 189.

55. *The Mishnah*, trans. Herbert Danby (London: Oxford University Press, 1933), pp. 586–87.

56. A word may be said about the priestly inclusion of the Ten Commandments in the daily liturgy and its later exclusion. The talmudic reason given for this (BT Ber. 21a) is that it supported heretical views in limiting the covenant just to the Ten Commandments, and this has often been understood to refer to the Christians. But a close reading of related talmudic texts suggests that it rather represented the understanding of the Sinai Covenant held by the Sadducees, the priestly party, and attacked by the Pharisees, the rabbinical party that triumphed over the Sadducees in the post-Temple period to establish the final form of the liturgy, such a view of the Sinai Covenant as I have also espoused in this work. In support of this view I cite Elbogen, who shows that the term used for heresy, *minot*, "embraces the views of the Sadducees, Samaritans, Christians, and Gnostics" (p. 31). And in *The Babylonian Talmud: Seder Zera'im*, trans. Rabbi I. Epstein (London: Soncino Press, 1948), we are told (Ber. 12a) concerning the recitation of the Ten Commandments in the daily morning service that "they were stopped on account of the insinuations of the *Minim*," (p. 66), the translator leaving the term untranslated. Elsewhere (Ber. 10a, 28b, 58a) where the term *Min* appears, Rabbi Epstein notes that an earlier editor of the text had substituted the term Sadducee in these places for *Min* as a "censor's correction" (p. 175), apparently not wishing to brand it with the charge of heresy (see also pp. 51 and 361).

57. Elbogen, p. 18.

58. *Siddur Tehillat Hashem*, p. 45.

59. In fact, the historical problem raised by the talmudic references to the Great Assembly, which span the period from the priest Ezra in the fifth century B.C.E. to the priest Simon the Just in the second century B.C.E., the problem that there are no other historical accounts of such an allegedly long enduring institution, can be resolved by understanding the Great Assembly not to be an early assembly of rabbinical sages, as generally believed, but an adjunct of the Second Temple consisting largely of priests concerned with the formulation of a liturgy for the prayer services that the Mishnah tells us were held in the Temple.

60. Aryeh Kaplan, *Jewish Meditation: A Practical Guide* (New York: Schocken Books, 1985), pp. 136, 138.

61. Jacobs, p. 65.

62. Arthur Green and Barry W. Holtz, eds. and trans., Introduction. In *Your Word is Fire: The Hasidic Masters on Contemplative Prayer* (New York: Paulist Press, 1977), pp. 11, 12, 13.

63. Gershom Scholem, *Kabbalah* (New York: New American Library, 1978), p. 130.
64. Scholem, p. 130.
65. Scholem, p. 130.
66. Scholem, pp. 132, 133.
67. For a fuller analysis of the concept of the Tzimtzum in relation to quantum cosmology, see my book *The Secret Doctrine of the Kabbalah.*
68. For a comprehensive analysis of this "secret doctrine," see my book *The Secret Doctrine of the Kabbalah.*
69. As quoted in Werblowsky, pp. 67, 70, 76, 78.
70. Teilhard de Chardin, p. 260.
71. Teilhard de Chardin, pp. 260, 261, 262, 290.
72. Introduction. In *The Phenomenon of Man*, p. 19.
73. As quoted in Kaplan, *Light Beyond*, p. 193.
74. Kook, p. 220.
75. Kook, pp. 87, 117, 221.
76. Rosenzweig, pp. 162, 238, 410–11, 423.
77. Abraham Abulafia, *The Rose of Mysteries [Shoshan Sodot]*, trans Aryeh Kaplan. In *Meditation and Kabbalah* (York Beach, Maine: Samuel Weiser, 1982), pp. 109–10.
78. Martin Buber, *I and Thou*, trans. Ronald Gregor Smith (Edinburgh: T and T Clark and New York: Charles Scribner's Sons, 1953), pp. 82, 83.
79. Buber, *I and Thou*, pp. 109, 110, 111, 117, 118.
80. Buber, *I and Thou*, p. 115.
81. As quoted in Kaplan, *Light Beyond*, pp. 138, 139.
82. Kaplan, *Jewish Meditation*, pp. 150–51.
83. In *An Anthology of Jewish Mysticism*, trans. Raphael Ben Zion (New York: Judaica Press, 1981), pp. 166, 167.
84. *Sefer ha-Temunah* (Lemberg: Isak Eckhaus, 1892; photocopy Tel Aviv: Zion, 1972), p. 69a. See also another version in the text: "And all of them are called Elohim . . . they are the one supernal will because each one, according to his nature and according to his function, is my will. . . . Therefore, "Elohei Avraham, Elohei Yitzchak, Velohei Ya'akov" is used in the plural" (p. 69b). My translation.
85. As quoted in Green and Holtz, p. 47.
86. Jacobs, pp. 76, 102.
87. *Siddur Tehillat Hashem*, p. 84.
88. *Siddur Tehillat Hashem*, p. 171. From the Sabbath morning prayer.
89. This quotation is taken from the version of the *Shi'ur Komah* translated by The Work of The Chariot and appearing in *The Secret Garden*, ed. David Meltzer (New York: Seabury Press, 1976), p. 32, and is more useful for our purposes than the more recent scholarly edition of Martin Samuel Cohen, *The Shi'ur Qomah: Liturgy and Theurgy in Pre-Kabbalistic Jewish Mysticism* (Lanham, Md.: University Press of America, 1983), because it contains the literal rendering of the Hebrew word *ben*, meaning "son." I am grateful to Dr. Cohen for confirming to me in private correspondence that "the Hebrew word *ben* in the expres-

sion *ben ha'olam haba'* . . . does appear in virtually all of the manuscripts of the
Shiur Komah known to me."
90. Buber, *I and Thou*, pp. 115, 116.
91. Buber, *Legend*, pp. 41, 42–43, 49–50.
92. Kook, pp. 226, 227.
93. Rosenzweig, pp. 214, 234–35, 293.
94. *Siddur Tehillat Hashem*, p. 84.
95. As quoted in *Safed Spirituality*, p. 149.
96. Rosenzweig, p. 184.
97. *Siddur Tehillat Hashem*, p. 60.

Appendix

1. See Frances A. Yates, *Giordano Bruno and the Hermetic Tradition* (Chicago: Chicago University Press, 1964), p. 21, fns. 2 and 3.
2. As quoted in Yates, p. 37.
3. See Gershom Scholem, *Kabbalah* (New York: New American Library, 1974), pp. 351–52.
4. Christopher Marlowe, *The Tragical History of Doctor Faustus*, I, iii, pp. 8–9, 14–5.
5. All biblical references are to the King James Version because its greater literalness makes it easier to pinpoint use of the Hebrew word *vehayah*.
6. For his original definition of the term synchronicity, see C. G. Jung, "Foreword," *The I Ching*, trans. Richard Wilhelm and Cary F. Baynes, Bollingen Series XIX (Princeton: Princeton University Press, 1978), p. xxiv.
7. Pericles, "Funeral Oration," trans. Sir Alfred Zimmern, in Thucydides, *The History of the Peloponnesian War*, ed. in trans. by Sir R. W. Livingstone, The World's Classics series (London: Oxford University Press, 1951), p. 115.
8. *Berakhot*, 55b.
9. Thorleif Boman, *Hebrew Thought Compared with Greek* (Philadelphia: Westminster Press, 1960), pp. 44–45. James Barr has attacked Boman's rich analysis, though not specifically his treatment of *vehayah*, in *The Semantics of Biblical Language* (London: Oxford University Press, 1962), because it is the foremost representative of the philosophy of "biblical theology" that he criticizes, the belief that the peculiar quality of a people, and particularly of the Hebrew people, is reflected in its language: "He has gone farther in the investigation of this matter, and in drawing conclusions from it, than any of the writers with whom I am acquainted from the biblical theology standpoint" (p. 46). Barr's opposition to the philosophy of language derived from W. von Humboldt, which Boman has adopted, stems primarily from its spiritual nature: "Humboldt's conception of language has certain strong characteristics of the idealism of his time. . . . In these circumstances to see language 'genetically' is to see it teleologically, as a spiritual work" (p. 48). But Barr's ideologically motivated destructive effort can put nothing in its place: "I shall make no attempt to suggest

a better philosophy of language" (p. 2). Given the antispiritual bias of such criticism, one can understand the support Boman's work has received: "I think that most of the theologians engaged in the movement we are criticizing would be disposed to sympathize with Boman's attitude" (p. 22n), and so do I.

10. His similar treatment of *vayehi* has also caused me to give new consideration to this cognate form. A reference in the Zohar—trans. Harry Sperling and Maurice Simon (London: Soncino Press, 1978), I, 120 (Mantua: 31b)—which may well reflect a traditional understanding, indicates that it, too, has a significance beyond the grammatical: "Anything to which the term *vayehi* ('and there was') is applied is found in this world and the next world." Whether or not all biblical references to *vayehi* can be interpreted in conformity to this Zoharic dictum, it seems likely that a study similar to the one I have here given to *vehayah* could be made for *vayehi* and with similarly illuminating results. See also my treatment of Gematria relationships of *vehayah* and *vayehi* in my book *The Secret Doctrine of the Kabbalah*.

Bibliography

Babylonian Talmud, The: Seder Zera'im. Trans. Rabbi I. Epstein. London: Soncino Press, 1948.

Barr, James. *The Semantics of Biblical Language*. London: Oxford University Press, 1962.

Buber, Martin. *The Legend of the Baal-Shem*. Trans. Maurice Friedman. New York: Schocken Books, 1969.

———. *I and Thou*. Trans. Ronald Gregor Smith. Edinburgh and New York: T and T Clark and Charles Scribner's Sons, 1953.

Becker, Robert O. and Andrew A. Marino. *Electromagnetism and Life*. Albany: State University of New York Press, 1982.

Boman, Thorleif. *Hebrew Thought Compared with Greek*. Philadelphia: Westminster Press, l960.

Bokser, Ben Zion. *The Jewish Mystical Tradition*. New York: Pilgrim Press, 1981.

Brown, Bruce. "The Mysterious Power of the Northern Lights," *The New York Times Magazine*. Dec. 12, 1982.

Cassirer, Ernst. *Language and Myth*. Trans. Suzanne K. Langer. New York: Dover, 1953.

Chia, Mantak. *Awaken Healing Energy Through the Tao*. Sante Fe: Aurora Press, 1983.

Code of Jewish Law (Kitzur Shulhan Aruh). Compiled by Rabbi Solomon Ganzfried, trans. Hyman E. Goldin. Rev. ed. New York: Hebrew Publ. Co., 1927.

Cohen, Martin Samuel, ed. and trans. *The Shi'ur Qomah: Liturgy and Theurgy in Pre-Kabbalistic Jewish Mysticism*. Lanham, Md.: University Press of America, 1983.

Dan, Joseph, ed. *The Early Kabbalah*. New York: Paulist Press, 1986.

Elbogen, Ismar. *Jewish Liturgy: A Comprehensive History*. Trans. Raymond P. Scheindlin. Philadelphia and New York: Jewish Publication Society and Jewish Theological Seminary of America, 1993, orig. pub. 1913.

Eliade, Mircea. *The Sacred and the Profane: The Nature of Religion*. Trans. Willard R. Trask. New York: Harcourt, Brace and World, 1959.

Fine, Lawrence, trans. and intros. *Safed Spirituality*. New York: Paulist Press, 1984.

Goodenough, Erwin R. *Jewish Symbolism in the Greco-Roman Period*. Abridged Edition, ed. Jacob Neusner, Bollingen Series. Princeton: Princeton University Press, 1988.

Gordis, Robert. "Authority in Jewish Law." In *Conservative Judaism and Jewish Law*. Ed.Seymour Siegel. New York: The Rabbinical Assembly, 1977.

Green, Arthur and Barry W. Holtz, ed. and trans. *Your Word is Fire: The Hasidic Masters on Contemplative Prayer*. New York Paulist Press, 1977.

Hertz, H., ed. and trans. *The Pentateuch and Haftorahs*. London: Soncino Press, 1972.

Heschel, Abraham Joshua. *The Sabbath: Its Meaning for Modern Man*. New York: Farrar, Straus and Giroux, 1951.

———. "Toward and Understanding of Halachah." In *Conservative Judaism and Jewish Law*. Ed. Seymour Siegel. New York: The Rabbinical Assembly, 1977.

Jacobs, Louis. *Hasidic Prayer*. New York: Schocken Books, 1978.

Jung, C. G. "Forward." *The I Ching*. Trans. Richard Wilhelm and Cary F. Baynes. Bollingen Series XIX. Princeton: Princeton University Press, 1978.

Kaplan, Aryeh. *Jewish Meditation: A Practical Guide*. New York: Schocken Books, 1985.

———. *Meditation and the Bible*. York Beach, Maine: Samuel Weiser, 1978.

———. *Meditation and Kabbalah*. York Beach, Maine: Samuel Weiser, 1982.

———, ed. and trans. *Sefer Yetzirah: The Book of Creation in Theory and Practice*. York Beach, Maine: Samuel Weiser, 1990.

———, ed. and trans. *The Light Beyond: Adventures in Hassidic Thought*. New York: Maznaim, 1981.

———, ed. and trans. *The Living Torah: A New Translation Based on Traditional Jewish Sources*. New York: Maznaim, 1981.

Kook, Abraham Isaac. *The Lights of Penitence . . .* Trans. and intro. Ben Zion Bokser. New York: Paulist Press, 1978.

Leet, Leonora. *The Secret Doctrine of the Kabbalah: Recovering the Key to Hebraic Sacred Science*. Rochester, VT: Inner Traditions, 1999.

Meltzer, David, ed. and trans. *The Secret Garden*. New York: Seabury Press, 1976.

Mishnah, The. Trans. Herbert Danby. London: Oxford University Press, 1933.

Odeberg, Hugo, ed. and trans. *3 Enoch or The Hebrew Book of Enoch*. New York: Ktav Publ., 1973, orig. pub. 1928.

Pericles. "Funeral Oration." Trans. Sir Alfred Zimmern. In Thucydides. *The History of the Peloponnesian War*. Ed. in trans. by Sir R. W. Livingstone. The World's Classics series. London: Oxford University Press, 1962.

Rosenzweig, Franz. *The Star of Redemption*. Trans. William W. Hallo (Boston: Beacon Press, 1971.

Schiffman, Lawrence H. *Reclaiming the Dead Sea Scrolls*. Philadelphia: Jewish Publication Society, 1994.

Scholem, Gershom. *Kabbalah*. New York: New Amsterdam Library, 1974.

———. *Origins of the Kabbalah*. Trans. Allan Arkush, ed. R.J. Zwi Werblowsky. N.C.: Jewish Publication Society and Princeton University Press, 1987, orig. pub. 1962.

Schwaller de Lubicz, R. A. *Sacred Science: The King of Pharaonic Theocracy*. Trans. Andre and Goldian VandenBroeck. New York: Inner Traditions, 1982.

Sefer ha-Temunah. Lemberg: Isak Eckhaus, 1892; photocopy Tel Aviv: Zoion, 1972.

Siddur Tehillat Hashem. Trans. Rabbi Nissen Mangel. Brooklyn: Merkos L'Inyonei Chinuch, 1982.

Soloveitchik, Joseph B. *On Repentance*. Intro. by Pinchas H. Peli. New York: Paulist Press, 1984.

Torah, The: A New Translation . . . according to the Masoretic text. Philadelphia: Jewish Publication Society, 1962.

Teilhard de Chardin, Pierre. *The Phenomenon of Man*. Trans. Bernard Wall, intro. Julian Huxley. New York: Harper and Row, 1975.

Tractenberg, Joseph. *Jewish Magic and Superstition*. New York: Pilgrim Press, 1981.

Valiuddin, Mir. *Love of God: A Sufic Approach*. Farnam, Surrey, Eng.: Sufi Publishing Co., 1972.

Vidas, Elijah de. *Reshit Chokhmah*. In *Safed Spirituality*. Trans. Lawrence Fine. New York: Paulist Press, 1984.

Vital, Chaim. *Etz Chayyim (Tree of Life)*. Tel Aviv: Kitve Rabaynu ha-Ari, 1959.

Werblowsky, R. J. Zwi. *Joseph Karo: Lawyer and Mystic*. Philadelphia: Jewish Publication Society,1980.

Yates, Frances A. *Giordano Bruno and the Hermetic Tradition*. Chicago: Chicago University Press, 1964.

Zion, Raphael Ben, ed and trans. *An Anthology of Jewish Mysticsm*. New York: Judaica Press, 1981.

Zohar, The. Trans. Harry Sperling and Maurice Simon. 5 vols. London: Soncino Press, 1934–1978.

Index